THE
INVASION
THAT NEVER WAS

SURVIVAL OF THE PEOPLE OF
EAST KENT ON THE FRONTLINE
1914-1945

DOUGLAS WELBY

DEDICATION

This book is dedicated to the memory of the men and women who served in the armed forces, and to the countless number of civilians in civil defence roles engaged on the 'Frontline' to defend and ultimately defeat the enemy.

Cover design by Mark Welby

ISBN 978-0-906124-32-1

© Copyright Douglas Welby 2012

Published in 2012 by D. Welby (Crabwell Publications)
September Lea, 35 Boystown Place, Eastry, Sandwich, Kent CT13 0DS

Printed in England by George J. Harris, The Press on the Lake, Stonar, Sandwich, Kent CT13 9ND

Foreword

This book records the struggle for survival and the constant fear of an enemy invasion as experienced by the ordinary folk in the towns and villages of East Kent over the period 1914-1945. It includes first hand stories and official documents and is profusely illustrated. It is designed to evoke memories amongst the older generation and to inform the younger age groups what their parents and grandparents had to endure to overcome a tyrannical enemy bent on destroying this great country.

The wartime years were grim but having what was referred to as the 'Wartime Spirit' engendered by the notion that we were right, enabled the people of this country to 'Keep Smiling Through' (one of the rallying songs of the time) and win through even against overwhelming odds.

Douglas Welby
Eastry 2012

Introduction

The First World War: It is very unlikely that any of the participants in the First World War considered that they were embarking on a four year war which would produce millions of casualties, and had this been the case it is questionable whether the war would ever have been started.

On the battlefield the German's superior army forced the French and the British Expeditionary Forces to fall back in line, and by the winter of 1914 almost all of Belgium and a large slice of France were in German hands. Thus began the protracted miseries of trench warfare on a line from the borders of Switzerland to the English Channel.

A stalemate situation arose with no possibility of a compromise since the Anglo-French armies failed to drive the Germans back to recover lost territory, and with the Germans unable to advance and unwilling to surrender what they had won. A major turning point in the later stages of the war was the German submarine warfare against enemy and neutral shipping which was an important factor in bringing the United Sates of America on to the Allies side.

When armistice was declared on 11 November 1918, the Germans still occupied large areas which they had captured, so their surrender was unexpected. Earlier that year the President of the United States issued a statement outlining various promises which were greeted by war-weary nations as a great idea with peace being attributed equally to both sides. The plan was to set up a League of Nations with its main objective of preventing war, achieve disarmament and the liberation of all Europe's oppressed minorities.

In time it became evident that the French fostered understandable bitterness towards the Germans. They were confused by treaties with impractical conditions and the

British with their policy of appeasement. Germany was deprived of all her colonies; disarmed; forbidden to unite with the new Austrian republic and not allowed to negotiate with the Allies. They were merely to accept the treaty of Versailles.

The build-up to the Second World War: In 1930 an international conference on disarmament took place at which Germany was allowed some measure of rearmament to give her some equality with other powers. After Hitler came to power in 1932, he withdrew Germany from the Disarmament Conference and from the League of Nations, and embarked on a policy of rearmament, often with the help and co-operation of Russia.

Attention was diverted from Germany to Italy during 1935-36. Italy under Mussolini was transformed from being an ally of France and Britain to a potential enemy likely to assist Hitler's Germany. This caused Britain to oppose Italy when they invaded Abyssinia, and were responsible for the League of Nations to impose sanctions on the aggressor. Hitler made the most of the confusion amongst his enemies denouncing the treaty of Versailles and announcing the start of conscription in Germany. Encouraged by the result of his actions Hitler marched his troops into the Rhineland in 1936, at the same time cleverly offering non-aggression pacts with various nations. The same year when the Spanish Civil War broke out, the British and French governments organized an international non-intervention agreement but Mussolini continued to supply troops and weapons to General Franco's rebels. This was followed in 1938 by Hitler invading and annexing Austria.

The British Prime Minister, Neville Chamberlain, spent the summer months trying to find a pro-German solution that would not involve the use of force, and to find an answer to the problems of Sudeten Germans living in Czechoslovakia but Hitler demanded 'self-determination'. The Czechs were told that the Sudeten parts of their country would be given to the Germans and if they resisted they would be on their own. Chamberlain got Hitler to sign a piece of paper promising that any Anglo-German differences would be settled peacefully, hence his famous statement 'it is peace for our time'. How wrong that would turn out to be.

Hitler threatened Poland after they refused to concede to German demands and on 1 September 1939 they invaded Poland forcing the British Prime Minister to declare war on Germany two days later.

The Second World War: For a period of time a 'phoney war' existed. When real war came it was activated by German troops entering Copenhagen and Oslo on 14 and 17 May 1940 respectively, and by 14 June they arrived in Paris. Hitler's Blitzkrieg had succeeded and France was defeated in weeks. The only British troops left on the Continent were prisoners of war.

Hitler did not experience any serious opposition and after a triumphal ride down the Champs Elysees in Paris perhaps he fancied such a parade through London. Whether or not he planned to invade or had intended 'Sea lion' as an elaborate bluff to bring this country to the negotiating table as some historians suggest is unclear. In this book the author has ignored the 'bluff' argument and concentrated on the belief that Hitler's ambition was to take this country. One thing is certain, along with the British Government and the millions of citizens of this country and the Commonwealth we could not risk taking a chance, particularly as we witnessed what was happening to our European neighbours no more than twenty miles across the Dover Strait.

Immediately following Dunkirk, the Prime Minister and his War Cabinet thought the Germans might attempt an invasion on this country. They formed the opinion that the German Luftwaffe would use their well tried 'Blitzkrieg' method of attack of smashing the enemy's resistance, and preparing the way for an attack by their army which had been so effective in the Polish campaign and in the attacks on Norway and the Low Countries. Aerodromes had been put out of action and ports and communications destroyed paralyzing any serious resistance. Their success in achieving these aims would mean the erosion of civilian morale, leading to internal disruption and finally surrender.

By the 8 August 1940, the enemy was ready to begin the opening phase of 'Sea lion'. However before the German Army could attempt a landing it was necessary for the Luftwaffe to seize and exploit full mastery of the air. The first phase was to destroy our coastal convoys, sink or immobilize such units of the Royal Navy as would hinder their passage, and above all destroy the Royal Air Force both on the ground and in the air. But by 31 October, the Allied air forces victory in the air decided the destiny of this country and the course of the war resulting in the German invasion plan being delayed and finally not achievable.

Had Hitler won the Battle of Britain and invaded this country, it could have been the 'Battle of Sussex and Kent' that decided the war and Britain's future. Fortunately we were not put to this test and resulting horror.

The aim of this book is to describe and illustrate, where possible, how the south-east corner of Britain built up defences in the face of the constant threat of invasion. It describes how communities and individuals prepared and coped with the day-to-day anxieties which beset them during those years of uncertainty. An overview is taken of life on the FRONT LINE during conflicts which threatened an area of east Kent, roughly contained within the old Eastry and Thanet Rural Districts, the Dover and Sandwich Boroughs and adjacent coastal towns, posed by the Germans in the First World War 1914-1918 and Second World War 1939-1945.

'Great Britain has produced a race of heroes who, in moments of danger and terror, have stood as firm as the rocks of their native shores.'

From *Soldier's Experience* by Thomas Gowing 1896

Contents

		Page
Chapter 1	The First World War	7
Chapter 2	Between the Wars	31
Chapter 3	The Second World War	43
Chapter 4	The Home Guard	135
Chapter 5	The British Resistance Organisation	155
Chapter 6	Dig for Victory	171
	Bibliography / Acknowledgements	185
	Index	187

Chapter 1

The First World War

1914 Until that summer a sensible, law-abiding citizen in this part of Kent could pass through life and hardly notice the existence of the State except for the post office or the village policeman. He carried no official number or identity card; could travel abroad without permission; and could change money without limit or restriction. All this was about to change. Rumours of war had been spreading for some time but very few civilians had any concept of the developing hostilities. The notion that the Germans would ever consider taking on the combined might of the great British Empire did not arise. When this possibility became apparent it must have come as a great shock and the fear of an invasion concentrated the minds of the people.

The town of Dover being a front line town, was declared a special military area and declared out of bounds except for military personnel and a few civilians with passes on active duty. All roads were made as secure as possible with those leading into the town having guard posts. All adults had to show a permit to enter and leave the town. Even the trams were stopped and a guard would examine each passenger's documents before the tram was allowed to proceed.

No.4 Guard Post positioned at London Road, River.

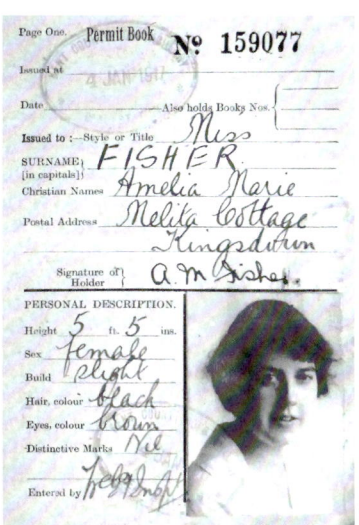

Dover was not only an army garrison town but also a base for the Royal Navy, and armed guards were quickly placed on the gates of the Admiralty Harbour and at the entrance to the piers.

Notices were posted warning people not to approach the defences and all foreigners ordered to report and register.

New field defences were dug by civilian labour under military guidance on either side of the town to protect the anchorage. Anti-aircraft guns were positioned at Citadel Battery, Frith Farm, Fan Bay (Langdon Bay), Bottom Wood at River, and West Hougham.

As an addition to the defence of the town and harbour, a flight of allied aeroplanes flew into the Dover area on the evening of 3 August. The authorities directed this flight to a landing field on Swingate Downs which had been built on the town's racecourse.

On the 4 August 1914 war was declared with Germany. People residing in Dover recalled it was just like any summer's day with hundreds of visitors flocking to this lovely Victorian coastal town, attracted to the quality hotels and guest houses, and taking in the sea breezes. To visitors standing on the famous white cliffs viewing the ships full of passengers sailing to and from the recently constructed grand harbour, war must have been the least of their worries. Two days after Britain had entered the war the Prime Minister Herbert Asquith addressed Parliament. The following is a short extract from his speech:

> 'With the utmost reluctance and with infinite regret, His Majesty's Government have been compelled to put this country in a state of war with what for many years and indeed generations past has been a friendly Power'.

In Deal, the banks which had closed for the Bank Holiday remained shut for several days. The reason soon became apparent when it was announced that it was to avoid a run on gold.

It was quickly followed by a message in the *Dover Express* by the Mayor. It requested the inhabitants of the area to show strict observance to the following points :

1. Paper and silver money is to be used as far as possible – not gold.
2. Provisions should not be purchased in greater quantities than usual.
3. Panic and alarm is unnecessary as Dover is unlikely to be attacked while there is a British fleet at sea.

Controls soon began to affect the citizens of the town as food became in short supply and freedom of movement controlled. Newspapers were censured and even beer became scarce. There are accounts of it being watered down to make it go further.

The illustration indicates the sentiment that existed towards the Belgian people in their defiance against aggressive Germany.

An indication of the misery about to engulf Europe came to Folkestone on the 20 August, when fishing boats and other craft crammed with Belgian nationals began arriving at the harbour. The town's elders quickly set up an organization called 'The Belgian Committee for Refugees' to provide food and shelter for these poor people. It was estimated around 64,000 landed at Folkestone of whom 15,000 settled locally. Unable to accommodate all the refugees, Deal came to Folkestone's assistance and was able to find places for about 1500 in the community.

This influx of refugees was caused by the German army marching into Belgium and Luxembourg on the 3 August, violating the 1839 Treaty of London which guaranteed

Belgium neutrality, and bringing this country into the war allowing fleeing Belgians a safe haven.

At the time Britain entered into the war the army was entirely voluntary and made up of three forms of recruitment:
(1) As a professional soldier of the regular army.
(2) As a part-time member of the Territorial Force.
(3) As a part-time soldier of the Special Reserve.

Shortly after war was declared, an image of the new Secretary of State for War appeared on every hoarding with a pointing finger declaring **Your Country Needs You.** Lord Kitchener issued a call for volunteers to rapidly increase the size of the army.

In a circular issued to the Lord Lieutenant of Counties and to Territorial Force Associations, Kitchener wrote:

'*In the present grave emergency the War Office looks with the utmost confidence to you for a continuance of the invaluable help which you have given in the past*'

The new recruits were assigned to units of the 'New Army' or 'Kitcheners', and once trained they were posted to replace the casualties in the regular army units.

In the autumn of 1914 a national newspaper promoted a contest to find Britain's Bravest Village. Of the 400 villages that entered, the tiny hamlet of Knowlton near Eastry was pronounced the winner with 31% of its inhabitants enlisting. It is also astonishing and comforting to note that all the volunteers returned home safely.

In December, four Battalions of Kitcheners were formed in Dover and billeted in temporary camps or with civilians in the town.

Volunteers usually had a choice over which regiment and unit they wished to join. They were often attracted to a regiment by its reputation or a local one where they had relatives or friends which made the choice much more appealing.

The public's response was at first overwhelming but soon the recruitment numbers declined and further steps had to be considered to encourage more enlistment.

In the early stages of the war nearly every village or town was requested to appoint and enrol Special Constables. They were sworn in before the local Justice of the Peace. The following was the form of oath taken by the constables:

I ....do solemnly sincerely and truly declare that I will and truly serve our sovereign Lord the King without favour or affection malice or ill will, and that I will to the best of my power cause the peace to be kept and preserved and prevent all offences against the persons and properties of His Majesty's subjects, and that while I continue to hold the said office I will to the best of my skill and knowledge discharge all the duties thereof faithfully according to law.

Approved and declared before one of His Majesty's Justices of the Peace in and for the said County this ….. Day of .... in the year 19……..

Fred Miles (seated on the right) and his friends from Ash pose for their photograph shortly after volunteering.

In the village of Eastry the parish was divided into eleven areas with three Special Constables, each with a number of responsibilities. For instance they had to see that men over 18 years of age registered for military service. They worked long hours and in poor weather conditions and were often underestimated. They had to be on alert to see that no lights were shown from private houses after dark, and it was not easy to issue warnings to their friends and neighbours for allowing a gleam of light to shine through a curtain or blind. Largely as a result of their efforts in keeping the village blackout the residents were fortunate to escape the horrors of air raids. They were ready to deal with any field fires started by enemy action, and to see that people who were out and about were promptly found cover as this area was in range of German aircraft based on the continent, as well as airships. They had to use their discretion in reporting the approach of the enemy. Maroons were not allowed to be used as a warning of air raids as this was the method used to call out the fire brigade. The Eastry Fire Brigade engine was at this time horse drawn, the horses being

Eastry's horse drawn appliance ready for action. This steam pump had been gifted to the brigade by Lord Northbourne in 1901.

supplied by Mr. Joe Luck who ran a horse drawn bus service to Sandwich during daylight hours. On occasion when all his horses were out on service it was known for the fire engine to be drawn by volunteer firemen.

As during the wars with France in the previous century, there was always the possibility of an invasion of this part of the coast. As a consequence the military authorities prepared new plans for the civilian population to leave the district and proceed westwards. Similarly as in times of earlier threats, a full inventory was taken of every cart, wagon and van in the village and surrounding area, together with the numbers of horses and livestock, and preparations made for a sudden exit at any time of the day or night should the need arise.

PREPARATIONS FOR INVASION IN 1801.

The following orders as to the methods to be employed in the event of the invasion of England by the enemy were issued in 1801 by the then Commander-in-Chief, the Duke of York. They are of special relevance and importance at the present time, when the Germans are loudly proclaiming their intention of attempting an invasion of this country.

Information and Instructions
FOR
COMMANDING GENERALS
AND OTHERS.

A newspaper cutting warning the General Public to be vigilant should the Germans attempt an invasion.

In October 1914 the Home Office drew up regulations to be followed should an evacuation of the civilian population be necessary.
The following is an abridged set of instructions:

KENT DEFENCE
LOCAL EMERGENCY COMMITTEE
WINGHAM DIVISION

The Government, through the Vice-Lieutenant of the County, appointed an Emergency Committee for the purpose in case of invasion –

(1) Preventing supplies of all kinds falling into the hands of the enemy.
(2) Assisting our own military forces.
(3) Schemes for the guidance of the civil population and of their removal further inland.

The Committee has prepared the following scheme which will be put into effect under the direction of the Police should the necessity arise. An invasion is not anticipated but the steps shown are by way of precaution and in the event of an enemy raid the safety of the population will chiefly depend upon willing assistance being given, and the carrying out of the arrangements which have been planned.

The following instructions are to be noted:
1. No clearance of any kind is to be made unless and until a state of emergency is declared in the district.
2. It is considered advisable that the Civil Population should move in the case of a state of emergency being declared, but they are not obliged to move. It is absolutely necessary that those who elect to move shall follow the routes laid down for them.
3. It is probable that a state of emergency will only be declared in this Division in the event of a hostile landing on the east or north east coasts of Kent.

If the landing should be made on the south coast of Kent, this Division would not be called on to move; and it may happen that only a part of the Division may be moved.

AREA AND ORGANISATION

This Committee's control consists of 37 of the parishes of the Wingham Petty Sessional Division; the remainder are included in 'Dover Fortress'. The Committee have made 11 groups of parishes and the names of members of the Committee in charge of each group:

No. 1 – ICKHAM, WICKHAMBREAUX, LITTLEBOURNE & STODMARSH
Mr. J.D. Maxted

No. 2 – BISHOPSBOURNE, KINGSTON & BARHAM
Mr. R. Tanner

No. 3 – DENTON, WOOTTON & SWINGFIELD
Mr. F.P. King

No. 4 – GOODNESTONE, CHILLENDEN, KNOWLTON & ADISHAM
Messrs. H. Fitzwalter Plumptre & C.S. Ratcliffe

No. 5 – WINGHAM, PRESTON, ELMSTONE & STOURMOUTH
Captain J.W. Robinson

No. 6 – ASH & STAPLE
Messrs. T.F. Spanton & G.C. Solley

No. 7 – EASTRY, WOODNESBOROUGH & WORTH
Admiral Sir R.H. Henderson, G.C.B., Messrs. G. Buley, J.J. Caspell & G. Goodson.

No. 8 – BETTESHANGER, HAM & NORTHBOURNE
Lord Northbourne, Messrs. A.C. Birch & T.P. Goodson

No. 9 – SHOLDEN, GREAT & LITTLE MONGEHAM
Mr. J.C. Burgess

No. 10 – WALDERSHARE, TILMANSTONE, COLDRED, EYTHORNE & SHEPHERDSWELL
Admiral Sir E. Rice, KCB., Messrs. H.E.H. Rice & M.F. Ramsay

No. 11 – NONINGTON, BARFRESTONE & WOMENSWOLD
Messrs. H.W. Plumptre & Egerton Hammond

The General Plan is to move all livestock to the West side of Stone Street Road and, if necessary, continue westwards to the Stour Valley.

The Civil Population will move in the same directions as the livestock, but may be required to continue their movement into the district lying west of Cranbrook, ie., an area of which the corners are roughly marked by Cranbrook, Etchingham, Uckfield and Tunbridge Wells.

---

1. The Committee has instructed each parish to allot vehicles and horses for the **removal of the old and infirm people** and young children, and they estimate that they have a sufficient supply of vehicles for this purpose. Sufficient food and necessaries for at least two days should be taken for all persons moving and for horses, also waggon-sails and tarpaulins.
2. **Livestock** is to be driven by owners' own stockmen; and their wives and families will travel with the stock in wagons allotted to them.
3. There are no large **stores of foodstuffs** or **petrol** in this Division. No destruction of property is to be carried out without express Military orders; but vehicles left behind and not required by Military Authorities are to be disabled by removal of wheels or otherwise.
4. **Boats** on the river will be dealt with by number 6 (below)
5. **Saddlehorses** are few in number and will be used by Special Constables in the performance of their duties.
6. The destruction of **signposts** will be arranged for by the Surveyors of the Local Authorities.
7. The Military Authorities require **trenching tools** and men to use them. It is doubtful if many men will be left behind or if they will be properly organised for work unless Special Constables are ordered to return to their parishes.

The following are the principal duties to be carried out by the **Police and Special Constables**:-

1. To see that the livestock is collected and driven off by the proper routes, also control its movement along the routes and see that the stock is kept out of the way of military.
2. To supervise the removal in conveyances of aged and infirm people and young children.

To see that they have the proper necessaries with them and supervise the loading up of suitable foodstuffs. Each parish should take at least one water-cart; and waggon-sails and tarpaulins should be taken with the wagons.
  To see that they take the proper routes, and to control the movement of all vehicles and foot passengers along the routes.
3. To control all crossings on main roads – especially on Canterbury-Sandwich main road; the traffic at the crossings at Littlebourne, Wingham, and Ash must be strictly controlled.
4. **Upon receiving instructions from Military Authorities** to see that -
    (a) All vehicles left behind are disabled.
    (b) All petrol not wanted is run to waste.
    (c) Livestock not removed is destroyed. (NOTE: If animals are to be destroyed, they should be shot, left unbled, and the entrails not removed).
    (d) Any machinery likely to be of value to the enemy is put out of action.
5. To generally assist the military authorities.

The Committee direct the attention of all the Police, County and Specials, to the great responsibility resting on them in case of invasion. The safe withdrawal of the inhabitants will need strict carrying out of the scheme of the Committee and the utmost devotion of every member of the Police.

Fortunately, all these preparations were never needed to be put into practice. Thanks to the bravery and skill of our armed services and the vigilant efforts of our navy, the great evacuation did not need to take place.

The first bomb to be dropped by an aircraft was considered a great piece of publicity by the Germans to the extent that a prize was offered for the first airman to bomb Dover. This was achieved on Christmas Eve in 1914 when Lieut Von Prondzynski, the pilot of a lone Taube aircraft dropped a bomb aimed at the castle. In fact it missed its target exploding in a garden in Leyburne Road. The explosion broke a few windows and a gardener, who was cutting holly out of a tree, fell down slightly injuring himself. Miss Violet Townend writing of her childhood in the area, remembered the first air raid, '*My mother came into the room in the middle of the night and said we must all dress and come downstairs, she remembers shaking with fright as she dressed.*'
In Dover people were advised to take shelter, not to stand about in crowds and not to touch unexploded bombs.

1915 With Britain's entry into the war, patriotic citizens throughout the country established unofficial armed groups often organized around local rifle clubs, called Volunteer Training Corps (VTC). Many of these men were veterans; others had full-time occupations. All felt the need to help guard the country against invasion.
However, at a time when the army relied on voluntary enlistment, the War Office became worried that they would have to compete for recruits. On 15 August 1914 an announcement was made in the press stating that this form of volunteer corps were considered undesirable by the authorities. By November they were granted some limited recognition provided they accepted certain conditions. Chiefly, that men of military age could not be enrolled and the VTC had to provide their own arms, clothing and to be financially self-sufficient.

Early on in the war His Majesty's Stationery Office distributed public warning notices and posters depicting airships and aircraft. One notice gave the following advice:

By March 1915 there were approximately 50 units in the county with Lord Harris as the head of the Kent regiment. This was made up of a series of battalions each containing 4 to 6 companies, and each company broken down into 4 platoons under the title Kent Volunteer Fencibles (KVF). One of the battalions was 1st (Cinque Ports) East Kent Volunteer Fencibles whose companies were formed from Dover, Folkestone, Hythe and the Deal area. Local platoons were part of the 'A' Company (Sandwich & District) of the EKVF. The local paper recorded *'there was a good muster'* at Cooper's Meadow in Eastry on Sunday 22 August, where about 150 rank and file uniformed volunteers took place. The Company consisted of: Platoon 1 – Eastry and Ash, Platoon 2 – Northbourne and Platoons 3 & 4 – Sandwich.

In reality the enthusiastic volunteers had the opportunity to learn military drill and musketry but could be very useful to regular troops in providing local knowledge and acting as guides. The military also considered the Corps as being useful in guarding prisoners, as signallers, transporting ammunition and digging trenches.

Another rather unusual mechanised volunteer army formed before the war, was called the Army Cyclist Corps. Local men joined The Kent Cyclist Battalion. This was made up of various local Companies, these being 'G' Company (Sandwich, Ramsgate & Margate) and 'H' Company (Dover, Folkestone & Hythe).

When war was declared on 4 August, 1914, the Battalion was in camp at Broadstairs and immediately mobilised to patrol our coast against a possible invasion. Later during the war they became a non-cycling infantry battalion. In December a Special Service Section of cyclists from 5th Battalion of (Cinque Ports) Royal Sussex Regiment (TA) was stationed in Dover. It comprised of 3 officers and 42 other ranks. Their cycles were designed to enable the rider to travel as a self-contained, one-man fighting unit. The equipment needed from his rifle to cape and ground sheet could be stowed away on the cycle. A small kitbag was attached behind the seat holding rations and personal items together with a toolkit hung from the crossbar.

Whilst most Kent volunteers trained as infantry, medical and signallers, some were mechanised such as the National Motor Volunteers. This unit enrolled men with motor cars and motor bikes. Other companies were mounted on horseback and known as the East Kent Mounted Scouts having a connection with the fox-hunting fraternity and the East Kent Hunt.

At the beginning of the war it was decided to mount guns on the breakwaters which made up Dover Harbour as the existing forts and batteries had become obsolete and their weapons museum pieces. They were manned by Nos. 40 and 46 Companies Royal Garrison Artillery and one Company Kent Royal Garrison Artillery (TF). In 1915, the end of the Eastern Arm was equipped with two 12 pounder guns in an anti-motor torpedo boat role. The Southern Breakwater Battery built on the centre mole was armed with two 6 inch guns. The Pier Turret Battery was mounted on top of the existing 81 tonners on Admiralty Pier, and equipped with two 6 inch guns. In

addition two 12 pounder guns were installed on the pier. The Citadel and Langdon Batteries on the cliffs above had five 9.2 inch guns. These represented the total weaponry available for the defence of the port.

The skating rink on the seafront at the harbour was converted into a hanger to house a flight of Royal Naval Air Service seaplanes and some small flying boats. Aircraft would be wheeled across the promenade, down a slipway into the water, then skim across the harbour before taking off.

During the war the Germans sent fleets of U-boats into the English Channel in an attempt to stop the flow of British and American reinforcements to the Front Line in France. To counter this menace the Dover Patrol was established with fishermen joining with the Navy to crew lightly armed fishing vessels to form a protective force between the Kent and French coasts. As a result of the bravery and dedication of the men of the Dover Patrol vast numbers of troops, ammunition and equipment, along with hundreds of repatriated wounded servicemen were transported across the Strait.

Around this time the Admiralty began losing many merchant ships to German submarines, and urgently required a means of spotting them and preventing the ships from being torpedoed. It was realised that airships would fit the bill, thus prompting the First Sea Lord to order a fleet of small airships for reconnaissance work.

On 7 May 1915 the authorities planned the opening of a new naval airship base at Capel le Ferne near Folkestone. It was decided to dispatch an airship from the Royal Naval Airship station at Kingsnorth on the mouth of the River Medway to arrive at the opening ceremony but as it approached downwind at some speed the ground crew were unable to grab the trailing ropes to secure it. The unrestrained airship tangled with a telephone line which gave off a shower of sparks and within seconds the hydrogen filled ship was ablaze before collapsing in a mass of flames. Fortunately the crew managed to jump clear and escaped injury.

The role of airships was to escort troop-carrying ships across to France and to monitor the Channel for enemy shipping. Capel le Ferne had an airship mooring-out station in heavily wooded terrain at Godmersham Park.

In the autumn of 1916 work began in earnest and the illustration shows the Haig Camp nearing completion. A system using standard size cast concrete blocks which were produced quickly in huge numbers using the 'Winget System'. There were over 500 buildings constructed, including a church, a hospital, loco sheds and much else besides.

Tugs and cargo barges shown moored alongside the new wharf.

Railway trucks were ferried across to Calais and Dunkirk. Each vessel carried up to 54 ten ton trucks and could be unloaded in about 20 minutes to begin another crossing.

King George V on a tour of inspection on 5 June 1917.

An 'Ac' 1000 ton towing cargo barge being launched. Some of these vessels were of steel construction but in this case this was made from concrete which was a popular material to use at the time.

In all over 220 airships were constructed during the war, many being positioned at airship stations around the coast. In addition to airships, observation balloons were also based at Capel le Ferne. These balloons were used to carry observers to a height from which enemy movements could be seen both on land and at sea.

Late in 1915 a party of Royal Marine officers came and viewed Port Richborough at Sandwich, and under the *Defence of the Realm, Acquisition of Land Act, 1916,* the port was acquired. The land totalled over 2,000 acres and the War Department set about extending the port facilities. This, together with other installations constructed at Stonar, had a tremendous impact on the small town of Sandwich and the surrounding area. Adjacent to the port installations a permanently built transit camp was constructed for the troops being built on marshland on either side of the river. The facilities were initially set up to ferry large numbers of men together with huge quantities of equipment and munitions across the English Channel.

A large wharf, just north of the Stonar Cut, was constructed. It took about seven months to build and when completed was about 700 metres in length. From here over 20,000 cross-channel barge crossings were made.

A railway line was extended from the main line to the quays for the train ferries to transport trains loaded with equipment, ammunition and thousands of troops assembled at the camps or billeted in the town and surrounding area, across to the French battlefields. In addition Richborough was a very large engineering site where a total of 153 barges, 34 seaplane towing lighters, 600 railway wagons and 715 cranes were constructed.

Large natural sand and gravel deposits existed on site providing supplies of aggregate for the concrete block casting works, already in operation under the Royal Engineers. It is therefore fitting that the production of field pillboxes to the design by Sir Ernest Moir were to be produced on the site. The pillbox had a six foot interior diameter concrete block wall supporting a steel dome from which was suspended a revolving steel bullet-proof ring and a machine gun. A total of 1,500 pillboxes were produced. Each kit of parts required four lorries for transportation. The majority of Moir pillboxes were sent to various sectors on the Western Front.

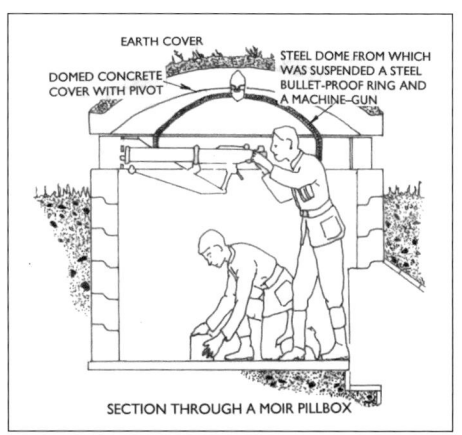
SECTION THROUGH A MOIR PILLBOX

During the war years Port Richborough developed into a major manufacturing site. At the end of hostilities, after having played a significant part in the war effort, it was closed.

The war had a profound impact on many villages and other communities with their young men going to war possibly never to return. With lists of fatalities appearing in the local papers each week, the people of this country were constantly reminded of the horrors happening to our menfolk across the Channel. The following printed in the *Dover Express* dated 4 June 1915, illustrates the pain and the worry that existed awaiting information of loved ones.

> *This letter was sent to Mrs. Jones from her son Private William Everard Jones, one of three sons serving in the army in France. William was in the 2nd Oxford and Bucks Light Infantry and had been wounded and was writing from a military hospital -'On the night of 15th May we made a night attack on the German trenches. Before we got half way, I received a bullet in the right shoulder. I stopped and examined the wound as best I could but found it was not bleeding much so raced on, and got nearly up to the German trench when I received another hit in the left wrist. I then sat in a 'Jack Johnson'hole, and whilst bandaging my wrist (fortunately the bullet had not gone through), I got a smack in the right ear with a lump of shrapnel, and had to fetch out another bandage (luckily I had plenty with me). By this time our chaps were in the German trench, so I went in to help finish them off.*
> *I shall never forget that attack; they had big guns, rifles and machine guns on us from the start, and it is a marvel that one of us lived through it. We captured two lines of trenches. You should have heard the cheer when we took the first trench.' I stayed with the boys until Sunday night, and then went back to get my wounds dressed. I am anxiously waiting to see the casualty list, for I do not know who we lost and who is safe'.*

Unfortunately William Jones aged 28 was later killed in action on 9 August 1916 and was buried in Potijze Burial Ground Cemetery, Ypres.

An article appeared in the *Dover Express* on 11 June 1915, reading *'Eastry Invaded by soldiers of the West Lancs Corps Royal Field Artillery'*. There were some complaints about their behaviour but it was generally overlooked on account of the money they spent in the village shops!

A troop of Royal Artillery soldiers at Eastry. It is probable that they were in transit waiting to be sent to France. They billeted under canvas on Cricket Meadow now The Gun Park.

The area was swamped with troops coming and going as the main embarkation point for the continent was at Port Richborough. The Royal Garrison Artillery took over Cricket Meadow (now Gun Park). They mounted a battery of guns with their sights trained on the coast near Deal in the event of an invasion. In addition other mobile weapons and ammunition tenders were housed there alongside the hundreds of horses required to move them.

One elderly resident of the village recalled when he was about 10 years of age he saw the army using the meadow. Also on another occasion an incident of a wagon with two horses which bolted into the High Street and down Lower Street. The wagon eventually stopped on the up-slope of Dover Hill as the horses tired. Another recollection was that permission was given to dig trenches on the village's cricket ground, and for the erection of poles from which sacks were hung for the purpose of bayonet practice.

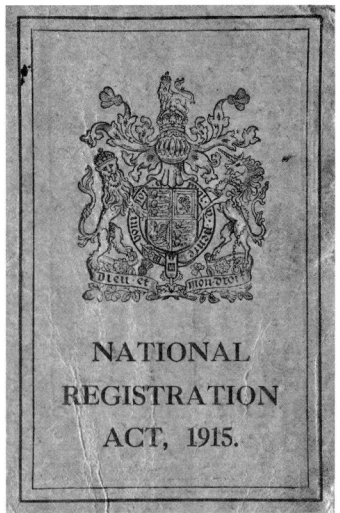

By the spring of 1915 it had become clear to the Government that previous recruitment policies had failed to provide the numbers of men required. On the 15 July the National Registration Act was passed to discover how many men there were between the ages of 15 and 65, and what trades they were engaged in. The results of this Act, which had been completed by mid September, provided the Government with all the information they required. By November they were able to proceed in sending out letters to all households in the country from the Headquarters of the Parliamentary Recruiting Committee.

Dear Sir or Madam,   *19th November*

We desire to draw your attention to the enclosed form, in which you are asked to state the names of those of your household who are willing to enlist for the War. By filling in and posting the Householders Return without delay, you will render material assistance to the War Office. The names returned will be entered in a Register, and the nearest Recruiting Officer will arrange to attest those registered as their services are required.

There has been a generous response to the appeal for men for the New Armies, but the numbers of recruits, though large, does not nearly meet the Nation's needs. In order to maintain and reinforce our troops abroad and to complete the new Armies which we hope within a few months to throw into the field, we need all the best the Nation can give us of its youth and strength. If we are to repair as far as humanly possible the innumerable wrongs inflicted on our Allies, if we are to avoid for ourselves the ills which they have suffered, if we are to maintain for our children all that we hold dear – honour, freedom, our very life as a Nation – we must fight with courage and endurance which won for us the struggle of the past.

Every man, therefore, who is eligible, will ask his own conscience whether, in this emergency, it is not his duty to hold himself ready to enlist in the forces of the Crown.

The difficulties and dangers which confront us have never been so great ; we await the issue with confidence, relying on the spirit and self-sacrifice of our fellow countrymen to prevail.

We are, Your obedient Servants,

H. H. Asquith, A. Bonar Law and Arthur Henderson – Presidents.

Lord Derby's scheme encouraged men to enlist as volunteers on the understanding that they would be recruited into the regular army if and when required, and was considered as a halfway system to conscription. Local Councils throughout the country set up committees to carry out canvassing and to promote recruitment under this scheme.

1916 It soon became evident that recruitment under Lord Derby's scheme had failed. As a result of this the Government introduced a new Act in January 1916 bringing voluntary enlistment to an end. The Military Service Act introduced a system by which all British males were enlisted. Furthermore conscripted men between the ages of 18 to 41 were no longer given a choice of which service, regiment or unit they wished to join.

In the early months of the year more and more troops arrived in Folkestone, many staying for a few days before embarkation. In an attempt to accommodate and cater for this great influx of men transit rest camps were hurriedly constructed at the western end of the town. At their peak the camps were seeing in excess of ten thousand troops passing through each day.

Royal Engineers pose for a photograph after completing a bridge building exercise on the banks of the River Stour.

As Deal was considered a prime landing site for an invasion, a Royal Marine Emergency Force was formed from serving ranks at the Depot. An operational order was issued at 6pm on the 24 February 1916, stating that a hostile landing might be attempted that night or over the following few days, and the Emergency Force manned the trenches from the Coast Guard Station at Kingsdown to Sandown Castle.

A system of appeal tribunals was established to hear cases of men who believed they were eligible for exemption on grounds of ill health, occupation or conscientious objection. There were very real problems in locally established small family businesses and farms at the prospect of the menfolk being conscripted.

A report appeared in the *Dover Express* in April 1916 on the findings of the Eastry Rural District Tribunal which sat at Eastry Workhouse. In one case the tribunal examined a request by Henry Tritton of Eastry: Mr. Tritton applied for an exemption of his 34 year old married son Henry W.T. Tritton, a plumber and fitter, from being called up on the grounds of a demand for this trade in the district. The tribunal granted a six months' exemption.

In the towns and villages around the coast residents were encouraged to construct shelters called 'dug-outs'. These were built to a basic concept but varied to suit the surroundings. Generally people were instructed to dig two parallel tunnels into a bank and a shelter at right angles to join them together. This idea was to prevent any direct blast reaching the occupants of the dugouts should an explosion occur directly outside, and to provide a second exit should one be blocked.

In Dover the enormous caves behind the Oil Mill Barracks in Snargate Street became a public shelter, providing cover for up to 10,000 persons. It was basic with just seating arrangements and some electric lighting. In the *Dover Express* dated 27 November it was reported that trenches had been dug around the parish of Worth by order of the Military.

Families shelter from the bombing in the vaults of the Phoenix Brewery in Dolphin Lane, Dover.

Later the same paper reported on the monthly meeting of the Pleasure Grounds Committee in Dover. The paper stated that the committee had received a request from the Cinque Ports Fortress Engineers to use Crabble Athletic Ground for a football match, but at the same meeting permission was given for the erection of poles for the military to engage in bayonet practice. From this we can see that all aspects of preparation were well in hand.

Volunteer Aid Detachments (VAD) in Kent was first formed in 1910 following a War Office publication the year before. In all over 80 Volunteer Aid Detachment Hospitals or emergency hospitals were set up in villages in church halls, schools, cottage hospitals and large houses in the County. Many had been busy making preparations to receive casualties since the beginning of the war. However no one could have anticipated how soon these facilities would be full of wounded soldiers needing care, but they were ready for such an eventuality.

It was not long before the residents of Eastry witnessed the horrors of war. With the outbreak of the war the cottages of the Children's Home were offered to the military. The *Dover Express* carried a story in November 1914 of wounded Belgian soldiers being looked after in the village. It was said that the Children's Home provided over

20 beds and used by permission of the Board of Guardians as a Red Cross Hospital supported by the Volunteer Aid Detachment Committee. The management of the institution, however, was superintended by Nurse Long. The newspaper states that '*21 patients are receiving attention at present and some are recovering rapidly and will soon be fit enough to return to the front.*'

The Cottage Hospital built in 1879 by Lord Northbourne contained 2 wards each with 7 beds and was also a Volunteer Aid Detachment Hospital. During the period of the war this small hospital was affiliated to Shorncliffe Military Hospital and used to accommodate military patients. During this time it was known as Eastry New Hospital having 24 occupied beds. In Deal Volunteer Aid Detachments of the Red Cross Society were set up in various houses in the town and at Sholden Lodge, and turned into emergency hospitals. At Ash a public meeting was held on 8 August 1914, at which the Village Hall was offered as a 20 bed emergency hospital, and volunteers offered money, beds and furniture. By the following May the building had been rearranged to accommodate another six beds, and was full of wounded soldiers from the front in Belgium and France. Funds were nearly always short and requests for cash were made in the parish magazine to support the hospital and to pay for a trained sister.

In the Thanet area there were nine VAD hospitals all taking their patients directly from the hospital ships docking in Dover Harbour. They would be transferred onto trains and taken to Ramsgate Town Station, and then quickly taken by a fleet of converted cars and ambulances to the various hospitals, the most urgent cases being taken to Nethercourt VAD Hospital in Ramsgate.

In Hazel Basford's excellent booklet '*Quex at War*', she tells the story of how the Powell-Cotton family converted the beautiful Quex House into an auxiliary military hospital staffed and run by the Birchington Voluntary Aid Detachment for over four years. During this time over 1,600 wounded and sick men were cared for at Quex. The hospital received a maintenance grant of three shillings a day per patient from the War Office towards the cost of running the detachment but members of staff gave their time voluntarily. They were comprised of local women who underwent training in first aid and home nursing. This included Mrs. Hannah Powell-Cotton who was Commandant of the Hospital. This family in their lovely surroundings contributed a most worthy effort to the needs of the injured.

In Folkestone various convalescent homes were converted into makeshift hospitals. On Sandgate seafront one was taken over by a VAD contingent and converted into a comfortable building called Bevan Hospital. By the end of the war over twelve thousand patients had passed through its wards.

The Metropole Hotel on the Leas at Folkestone became the headquarters for the Women's Army Auxiliary Corps (WAAC). These female auxiliaries were trained as cooks and clerks, and, surprisingly for the times, as vehicle mechanics and drivers before setting off for duties overseas. Posters at the time proclaimed '*that every fit woman can release a fit man*' for service.

The press and letters from the front were censored in an attempt to conceal the horrors of the war. Information eventually filtered through as some of the soldiers came home on leave but it was only after the cessation of fighting that the real horror was revealed to the public. Due to the high casualties on the Western Front and a falling number of recruits, two Military Service Acts were passed in January and May 1916, forcing those who had registered earlier to report for duty. To emphasize the gravity of the situation a message to the nation was issued by King George V which appeared in the press.

RETAILER'S SUGAR TICKET.

This Ticket is issued under the authority of the Food Controller by:—

(Retailer's Name and Address, written or rubber-stamped.)

Henry Love.
Lyminge.

In respect of the person named in Part A on the back, being a member of the household of:—

(Householder's Name) Alfred George Beer

and must be produced to the Retailer upon every purchase of sugar in respect of that person.

NOTE.—The space above for the householder's name and Part A on the back must be filled up immediately upon the issue of this Ticket, and in any case before it is produced to the Retailer.

TRANSFER ON REMOVAL, Etc.

If the person named on the back removes altogether or ceases to be a member of the above-mentioned household, Part B on the back should be filled up and the Ticket should then be taken to a Post Office.

59752) Wt. 4615. 10/17. John Corah & Son. (E2033.) F.22.

MINISTRY OF FOOD.

No. K 710137

SUGAR REGISTRATION CARD.

This part to be kept by the Householder.

C. Name Alfred Beer

Address

Retailer with whom the Householder has registered:—

D. Signature of Retailer H. Love.

Address

No. of persons Two Initials

District Elham.

S. 2.

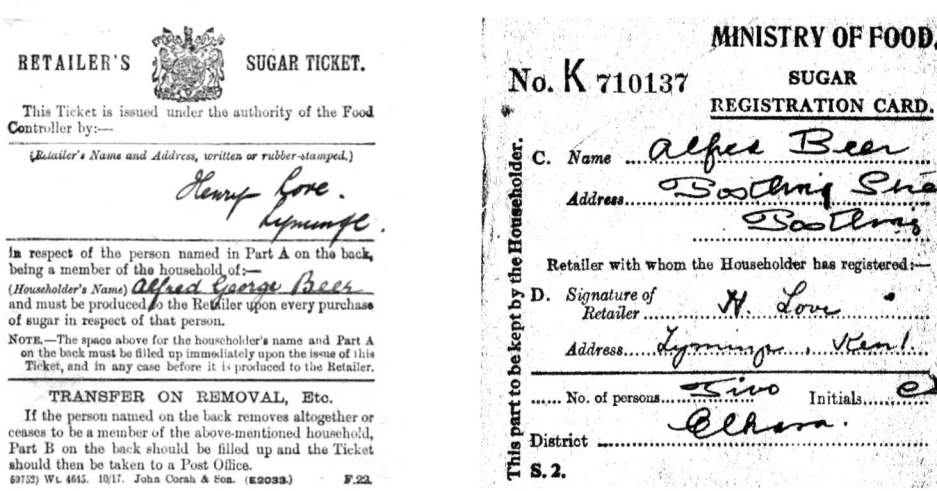

Government legislation was strictly enforced with controls on food, lighting, the press and even pub opening times. As sugar, milk, butter and meat became difficult to buy coupons were issued to combat profiteering. As food rationing began to bite municipal soup kitchens began to be set up in poorer communities. They also encouraged the people to grow their own vegetables and many new allotments were started. In some communities they even distributed seed potatoes at cost to encourage people to start producing.

To combat food shortages a system of food rationing was introduced and the Women's Land Army was formed. A further social change to take place at this time was the new role for women from working as nurses at the front to production work in munitions factories, in addition to many other occupations previously excluded to them. There was a tremendous demand not only for manpower but for munitions, animals, shipping and food. In a further attempt to increase productivity the Government introduced '*summer time*' in May 1916 lengthening the hours of daylight.

In Dover the town's defences against enemy air attack were woefully inadequate at the beginning of the war considering the large naval presence, and Dover being a military garrison. The farsighted Mayor of Dover realized the deficiency and helped form a group of volunteers called the Dover Anti-Aircraft Corps. They were trained in the use of searchlights and were successful in illuminating the large airships sent by the Germans to bomb the town and the harbour. The volunteers worked in small teams on a shift basis, operating the lights at the Drop Redoubt, Dover Castle and from Langdon Battery. After several years the enemy switched from airships to much faster aircraft to bomb the town. In consequence in 1916 the anti-aircraft defences manned by 3rd Kent Royal Garrison Artillery were reorganized and supplied with better equipment. Each searchlight unit was linked by telephone to the headquarters in the basement of the Town Hall and with Fire Command at Dover Castle. In August the searchlights were put under the control of the Royal Engineers and the Volunteer Corps was disbanded. To warn the inhabitants of the town of an impending daylight air raid a black ball was hoisted on a flag pole on the castle keep and a siren sounded.

However, from early November 1916 to the end of the war the old Archcliffe Fort in Dover was manned daily by 'D' Company 1st Volunteer Battalion, which was part of East Kent Regiment (EKR) also known as the 'The Buffs', consisting of two NCOs and nine privates. It had been considered unnecessary to upgrade the obsolete heavy weapons at the beginning of the war because of its low position, and was only equipped with small calibre, quick firing guns to ward off possible landing of enemy forces on the beach below. Other units guarded the railway lines and the searchlights.

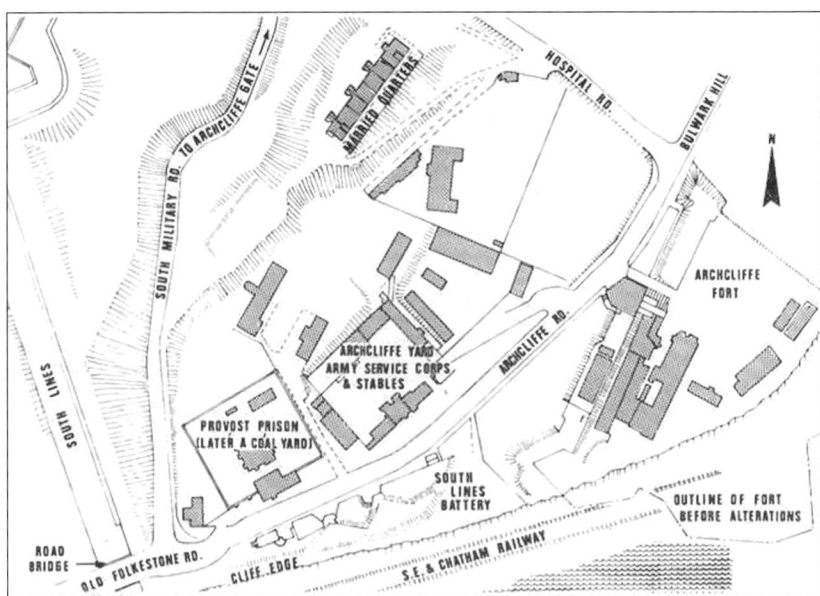

Map showing Archcliffe Fort, Archcliffe yard and South Front Battery

In the spring of 1918, the Kent Volunteer Regiment was again reorganized when the Government appealed for men for special service companies. One of the Kent companies was attached to the Kent Cyclist Battalion working on defences at Lydd.

Initially airfields in Kent were set up to combat the air raids by Zeppelin airships and Gotha aircraft, and the defence of the country was entrusted to the Royal Flying Corp and the Royal Naval Air Service with no collective organization as such. When enemy aircraft were spotted every available plane took off and chased the Germans. For the first time enemy airships and aeroplanes attacked the ordinary British civilian, and although these attacks were only occasional, there was great alarm when they occurred over both towns and countryside. An old lady writing about her childhood in the Dover area remembers seeing and hearing the huge Zeppelins passing overhead to bomb London, returning later over the town to jettison any remaining bombs before making their way back home.

In Dover, in common with the other coastal towns, a total blackout was observed except for a few lights in the main street which were controlled by a switch from the power station. Here a telegraph line was connected from Dover Castle enabling a signal to be sent as soon as enemy airships or aircraft were spotted. This signal notified that lights were to be extinguished and 'mournful Lizzie' (nickname for the air raid siren) sounded.

Zeppelins continued attacks on the town and harbour during 1915. They were driven off by anti-aircraft guns although generally without being hit. However a raid by airship L12 on 10 August resulted in it being illuminated by the town's searchlight corps and brought down by the anti-aircraft guns at Langdon Battery. The large airship came down in the sea and was last seen being towed back to Ostend by enemy tugs. On another occasion in October five of the enemy craft were seen crossing the Channel as it got dark en route to bomb London. However, one of them turned towards Folkestone with the purpose of attacking the military camps at Lympne and Westenhanger, and at a camp in Lympne 15 servicemen were killed and 21 injured along with a number of horses. People in outlying country districts were advised to immediately telephone the police should they see a hostile aircraft. They were required to specify the time, the direction of the flight and whether it was an airship or aeroplane.

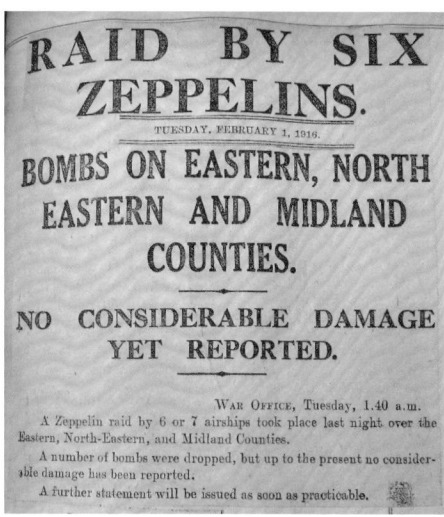

Newspaper headlines.

By 1916 the Zeppelin attacks by night increased, and the Royal Flying Corp was ordered to pull back some of its squadrons from the battlefields of France to help defend this country. At Guilton Aerodrome at Ash a field was laid out as an emergency landing ground for aeroplanes based at Bekesbourne for intercepting raiding Zeppelins. Although the raids by enemy aircraft and huge airships were nothing like the blanket bombing that was to follow in the Second World War, these German raids caused a great deal of damage in the coastal towns. Later in the war when the enemy was becoming desperate, moonlight airship raids on London happened regularly.

Dover was subjected to an air raid by a lone FF33b bomber on 23 January 1916, when eight high explosive bombs and incendiaries were dropped, leaving one dead and seven injured together with a trail of damage in the town. The malt house of the Phoenix Brewery in Castle Street was wrecked and the gas office in Russell Street, Red Lion Inn in St. James's Street, and houses in Waterloo Crescent, Cambridge Terrace and at Victoria Park were damaged. The following day two enemy aircraft dropped five bombs on the airship station at Capel but without causing much damage.

On 20 February a single FF33 aircraft aimed six bombs at the Royal Marine Barracks at Walmer, three of which fell into the sea. One of the others landed killing a young boy and injuring his friend.

Six enemy seaplanes raided Ramsgate and Dover on Sunday 19 March leaving a trail of damage and carnage (14 dead and 26 wounded). In Dover one bomb burst in the garden of a house on the corner of Woolcomber Street and Trevanion Street, and pieces penetrated the roof of Old St. James' Church doing a great deal of damage.
Deal was targeted on 3 May by a single seaplane which dropped nine bombs on the town. Six fell close to the railway station, and another fell on the Admiral Keppel public house in Upper Deal but without exploding. On 20 May three planes came in over Sandwich targeting the area around Deal and Dover. Nine bombs were dropped on Sholden, ten more on the fields around Ringwould before flying on to Dover. In all fifteen bombs were dropped, one damaging the Ordnance Inn in Snargate Street and another close to the Shaft Barracks killing a soldier. Otherwise very little damage was done in the town.

The German naval airship L32, one of the new 'super Zeppelins'.

In the autumn the final offensive began against the coastal towns and London by 'super Zeppelins'. These airships were much larger and more streamlined than their predecessors which gave them extra speed and able to carry a larger bomb load but unbeknown to the Germans their opponents were equipping their aircraft with machine guns firing incendiary ammunition, which could easily turn their hydrogen-filled airships into a blazing inferno.

1917 Then the following year on 17 March, Zeppelins returned during the night dropping four high explosive bombs on Swingfield and some incendiaries at Hougham. On the evening of the 25 May, German Gotha aircraft caused a great deal of damage and carnage at Folkestone. In all 78 civilians and 18 military personnel were killed, 61 from one bomb dropped on Tontine Street. The same aircraft attempted to attack Dover but were met with a barrage of anti-aircraft fire and veered off without dropping further bombs.

On 23 June, a bomb destroyed the roof of the Red Lion Inn in St. James Street, Dover. After these heavy air raids the caves in Trevanion Street area were opened up and used for shelters.
Then on 22 August ten enemy aircraft were spotted resulting in allied machines taking off from Royal Naval Air Service stations at Manston, East Church, Walmer and

Dover to intercept. Two Gothas were shot down near Margate. The surviving aircraft managed to drop a number of bombs on Ramsgate before turning south toward Dover where they were met with anti-aircraft fire from the batteries around the town. The Gothas managed to unload a number of bombs on the town and on the harbour before the allied fighters were reinforced by Royal Flying Corps machines from Detling and Lympne, who assisted in driving off the raiders.

As the enemy was losing aircraft in daylight raids they began night-time bombing instead. These attacks were limited having to be carried out on clear moonlight nights due to lack of proper navigational aids but nevertheless were successful. The port and town of Dover was bombed six times on 3 September and a raid by 4 Gotha bombers on Chatham Naval Barracks left 130 dead.

1918 During the war there were great advances in British military aviation. At first the aircraft were used in reconnaissance but were soon adapted to engage enemy aircraft and to harass ground forces. At the outbreak of hostilities in 1914 the combined resources of the Royal Flying Corps and the Royal Naval Air Service totalled 260 aircraft and 7 airships. By the time the two services were amalgamated in April 1918 there were more than 2000 aircraft and 100 airships.

In Richard Higgs' book 'Our Village and the Great War' he recalls and describes daylight air raids over his village of Shepherdswell, near Dover:

> *'Many an alarm was given, and on one occasion a fight between aeroplanes in the air was seen at some distance away, and provided a thrilling spectacle for many of us. The biggest display of bursting shells seen during an air raid was experienced in our village at Whitsuntide, 1918, when the German aeroplanes were surrounded by a terrific barrage of shells from our own guns, ...The first Zeppelin to be brought down in flames was seen from our village, although it occurred over 80 miles away – at Cuffley'.*

Note: The Zeppelin quoted above was the military airship SL11 which was shot down on 2 September 1916 at Cuffley, Essex. All 16 on board were killed.

Many towns and villages in the area were bombed and shelled during this war. One such community was at St. Margaret's which, in the event, escaped with little damage or casualties. It is also recorded that in May an enemy aircraft released the last bomb to fall on this country and was on this particular village.

On the 11 November 1918, the Prime Minister, Lloyd George made the following announcement:

'The Armistice was signed at 5 am. this morning and hostilities are to cease on all fronts at 11 am. today.'

There was great relief and rejoicing in the country when an Armistice was announced, and the world held its breath in anticipation hoping that peace would be permanently secured. In Deal and in Dover the news quickly spread and was greeted by the sounding of ships' and air raid sirens and church bells. Peace Celebrations to celebrate the end of war and the signing of a Peace Treaty with Germany followed.

1919 In Dover the municipal 'Peace Treat' was a large affair held in Connaught Park. In addition many street parties were arranged in the town with much feasting. Each street was decorated with lots of red, white and blue bunting and Union Jacks.

To celebrate the end of hostilities several 'victory treats' were arranged in the villages of River and Kearsney near Dover. A social evening with music and refreshments was arranged by the Reception Committee of St. Peter's Church, River, on 4 March 1919 at which the armed service personnel were given a hearty welcome home. Each serviceman was sent an invitation card (sounding like an order) thanking them for services '*you have rendered your Country during the Great War*'… '*Your presence with One Friend is requested*'!

On 19 July, the Peace Day Celebrations at Shepherdswell began with a united service at St. Andrew's Church at 11 am. In the afternoon sports and maypole dancing commenced in the field next to Sibertswold Place at 2.30 pm., continuing until tea time, the children having their meal in the meadow and the adults in the Church Hall. At 11 pm. a bonfire was lit on Moon Hill.

River residents enjoying the festivities.

In Eastry the festivities were organized by a group of ladies from the village with some help from the Parish Council. A fancy dress procession was held starting from Lauriston House (now Boystown Place) and going through the village to Cooper's Meadow at the bottom of Lower Street. At the meadow a sports event took place with sideshows, everybody enjoying the sandwiches and cakes provided. Some time later it was decided that a special Victory Dinner for all returning soldiers was to be held on 31 December.

In an announcement made by the Government the responsibility of the port at Sandwich was to be transferred from the War Office to the Ministry of Munitions on 4 December 1919, and put up for sale by the Disposals Board as a single going concern.

The peace settlement was eventually concluded and at last the great horror was over and everyone put out flags and rejoiced to think that our time of trial was past. Or was it? Men staggered back from the trenches many injured, shell-shocked, gassed or blinded to a life that would never be the same again. Of the eight million mobilized it was estimated that some 850,000 military personnel had been killed and two million wounded.

Grief hung over all sections of society with families broken up and communities destroyed. Wives had lost their husbands, young girls their boy friends and personal relationships irretrievably affected. Those fortunate enough to survive the trauma of war had to rehabilitate into civilian life. This was another battle to win.

Chapter 2

Between the Wars

1920-1939 A state of prosperity proved elusive. Quite the opposite as in some sections of British industry chronic unemployment caused by depressed markets resulted in thousands of employees being laid off. Furthermore the fear of a second world conflict was present for some time, and stated clearly in an address made by the Archbishop of Canterbury, Cosmo Gordon Lang, at Dover on 6 December 1931 of which the following is a short extract:

> 'And now there comes upon us in the history of our country, this time when great demands are made on the patience, courage, and fortitude of our people to realize, and bring us through a critical time of which we have not seen the end, perhaps not even the period of our greatest stress. This time is so grave, the danger so real, the call so urgent, that it can only be met by a real strengthening and deepening of the character of our people.'

As stated by the Archbishop in his address, the fear of a conflict was ever present, and some planning amongst the various authorities was evident from as early as the spring of 1935 when the Mayors of East Kent towns were summoned to London to be warned of the possibility of enemy attack. A year later with a shortage of trained aircrew, civilians were being trained as pilots and navigators at Manston aerodrome. Other defences and barracks with air raid shelters were constructed as the tension in Europe increased. By the time war was declared, therefore, the RAF had arrived and Manston became one of Britain's frontline fighter stations.

By now the Eastry Fire Brigade had successfully mounted their old steam pump onto a lorry chassis. This remained in service until 1937 when it was replaced by a second-hand chain-pump purchased from Margate.

In May 1936, the Air Raid Precautions Committee of Deal Town Council reported that checks would be carried out to ensure that 'efficient and adequate sirens were available to reach all parts of the neighbourhood in case of air raids'. In many villages close by, parish councils received a request from the Central Government early in 1937 to form an Air Raid Precautions Committee. At Guston, near Dover, the Dover Fire Brigade advised the Parish Council that they could no longer cover country parishes. This prompted the council to consider purchasing their own hose pipe. Negotiations with the fire brigade produced a compromise whereby they were to be paid a sum of £30 to attend fires in the parish. This also prompted the Parish Council to consider requisitioning houses with cellars to be used as air raid shelters.

In the village of Eastry the Air Raid Precaution order was not taken lightly. In order to move such a contentious undertaking forward quickly the whole council agreed to become members of this committee. A public meeting was called on 5 February to hear about the ARP scheme from a Major Godfrey of Ash who was Chairman of Eastry Rural District Council's Committee. About 100 people attended the meeting with Councillor R. Hopper in the chair, with the task of allocating various duties such as Air Raid (Street) Wardens and First Aid Parties. Tradesmen's vans were to be commandeered to serve as ambulances should the need arise; gas masks would be stored locally; and air raid warnings would be given by means of a hooter.

Until 1938 the ARP Services were made up of First Aid and Medical Services; Rescue and Demolition Services; Air Raid Wardens and Gas Detection Officers.

The Eastry Fire Brigade, which took on the duties of Fire Wardens, put in a request for more equipment and protective clothing. It was also proposed that the caves at Beckets could be used in the event of a gas attack and as an air raid shelter. Major Unwin from Great Walton took over the position of Head Warden. In May 1938, Major Unwin presided at a meeting to appoint wardens for the village and the surrounding area. Those appointed were:

Col. Godfrey, Messrs. F. C. Hopper, A. M. Pittock, H. P. Hoile, E. Williams, H. P. Clark, W. M. Stupples, H. L. Ford, F. Uden, J. Smallman, S. Strond, H. Humphreys, R. J. Hopper, T. E. Austen, A. Briscall, A. G. Rolfe, C. T. Miller and F. Holyer.

Shortly afterwards the Home Office issued a booklet to every household in the country entitled.

THE PROTECTION OF YOUR HOME AGAINST AIR RAIDS

It warned that if you were told that war threatens do these things at once –
1. Prepare and equip your refuge room.
2. Make all preparations for darkening the house at night, all windows must be completely obscured.
3. Clear the loft, attic, top floor of inflammable stuff to lessen the risk of fire from an incendiary bomb that might penetrate the roof.
    Assemble appliances to fight fires.

This was quickly followed by an information poster issued by the Ministry of Information of things to have in a refuge room. The following is a condensed list of what was recommended:

1. A roll call list of all who should be present, books, writing materials, toys.
2. Table, chairs, blankets, rugs, washstand and basin, wireless set or gramophone.

3. Screen for privacy, soap, towel, sponge, disinfectant, a first aid box.
4. **Water** for drinking, washing & damping blankets to be used to extinguish incendiary bombs.
5. **Food chest** - tinned food and tin opener, plates, cups, knives and forks.
6. **Tools** - hammer, nails, string, needle & cotton, scissors, torch, buckets or pots of sand, shovel or fire extinguisher.
7. **Protection** - mattress or bag of straw to protect windows, spare blankets for sealing windows, pot of paste to paste paper over cracks, sheets of brown paper, adhesive tape, cellophane, tins and jars with airtight lids, dark lens glasses, turn gas off at the mains.

In the towns and villages around Dover the consensus of opinion was that they would be in real danger of air attacks should the hostilities develop. So in the village of River a parish meeting was held and it was decided to combine with close neighbours Temple Ewell for all ARP purposes. A further urgent meeting was arranged so that volunteers for various duties could enrol, and a course of lectures on anti-gas protection was held at Temple Ewell parish hall.

Much of the pre-war training for the ARP was undertaken at the Civil Defence Training School at Betteshanger Park where up to 200 volunteers were processed every two weeks.

In Europe the prevailing situation was reaching crisis point in late September 1938

Sandwich and Deal St. John Ambulance ready to go into action.

when Czechoslovakia fell to the invading German army. Suddenly by the end of the year thousands of refugees from Germany, Austria and Czechoslovakia, driven out by Nazi persecution, arrived in Sandwich. Their numbers were made up of Jews, Christians and political refugees. The only place in which they could be housed was at the old Richborough Camp, Sandwich, which had been empty for about twenty years and had fallen into a state of disrepair and decay. The authorities were overwhelmed and considered the facilities only as a transit camp until it was possible to arrange for dispersal overseas, and the refugees were not to be integrated with the population of this country let alone the town.

During the nine months up to the outbreak of the war with Germany the camp's population increased to approximately 5000 persons. Amongst the new arrivals there were many skilled craftsmen who quickly sorted out the run down living accommodation, fixed the plumbing and managed to get the electricity supply working at the camp.

Aerial view of Kitchener and Haig Camps.

There were two camps alongside the Ramsgate Road; on the west side the Kitchener Camp and on the east side the Haig Camp. The huts on the west side consisted of dormitories and dining rooms; the east side buildings were used for education and entertainment. Many of the newcomers had expected to be transferred to Palestine (now Israel), United States of America, Canada or Australia, but in the camp they were encouraged to take up courses in agricultural and technical subjects to help with their settlement. All men had daily 2 hour lessons in learning English, and those wanting to emigrate to Palestine could learn Hebrew. The refugees were completely free to move where they wished and to organize themselves as a community. They even had their own police force. There were many talented musicians, actors and other entertainers in the camp, and they arranged to perform dramas and concerts for the inmates as well as the citizens of Sandwich and neighbouring villages. Some worked as agricultural labourers in the neighbourhood, some earned money from making toys and many of the women in the camp were engaged by local families as domestic servants but all the money earned went into a common pool. Each person received one shilling (5p) a week pocket money, or if travel money was required, the fare was allocated. With the outbreak of war transporting those who wanted to move on to the country of their destination came to an abrupt end. Immediately a large number of men in the camp were eager to volunteer for service in the British

Forces. They were at first employed in defence works on the coast but integration into the military was not so simple. The War Office was concerned about enlisting men who were enemy aliens and who might be enemy agents. As a precautionary step each individual was examined in the camp by a tribunal. Each was questioned separately and their papers checked. Ultimately only two men failed to satisfy the authorities. The men accepted were allowed to become members of the 'Auxiliary Military Pioneering Corps', which was a non-combatant force doing construction tasks behind the Front. Men who had not volunteered for military service were largely engaged in the service to those who had: cooking, tailoring, cobbling etc.

It must not be overlooked the important specialized service of 24 hour monitoring and recording of broadcasts from all German radio stations rendered by a section of German speaking inmates. This important work contributed to our intelligence gathering capability at the outbreak of war.

In the early months of 1940 six companies of volunteers were formed of which five went to France, mainly to Brittany, to be attached to the British Army. With the French collapse in May, many were evacuated from St. Malo just in time and returned to this country but not to Sandwich. This was due to the fact that whilst they were away, the Alien Companies Depot and Headquarters had been transferred to the West Country. In their place battalions of British infantry engaged in Home Defence had arrived. Then later in 1942 the camp was a posting for Marines.

The consensus of opinion in this part of Kent was that we would be in real danger of air attacks should hostilities develop. On the national front Sir John Anderson was brought into the war cabinet, and in November 1938 put in charge of air raid precautions. A policy was put in place to evacuate school children and mothers with children under the age of five, and provision made for special trains to be allocated for this task along with the provision of food for the journey.

The Government announced in the press that shelters were to be provided free but the catch was that it would be the responsibility of the recipient to have it erected. Furthermore this was restricted to householders compulsorily insured under the National Health Insurance Act or dependent on earnings not exceeding £250 per annum plus £50 per child under the school age. Some local companies were quick off the mark offering easy-to-assemble kits of parts made from heavy gauge galvanized iron which could be erected by the purchaser.

Plans were drawn up in Dover during December 1938 for the construction of Air Raid protection tunnels in the town and in the immediate area. The plan was to link the village of River by a system of tunnels stretching from the caves on the seafront in Snargate Street, up through Charlton and Buckland to River, terminating close to St. Peter's Church. These tunnels were to be more or less continuous similar to colliery tunnels, approximately 2 metres wide and a similar dimension in height, constructed at a depth of 20 metres. The entrances were to be fitted with air filters, especially selected to be gas-proof. Generators would supply the necessary electricity for lighting. For some reason, however, the project was never completed.

In Dover the local authorities undertook some work on existing tunnels close to the seafront in Snargate Street with the strengthening of the entrances and boring of connecting tunnels for the use of air raid shelters. The main part some 300 metres in length, connected Snargate Street with Durham Hill and was known as Cowgate Tunnel. As the town was riddled with caves many were opened up and reused as air raid shelters. In other cases new tunnels were excavated some linking old cave systems particularly along the High Street. The Noah's Ark Tunnel was slightly different. Starting from an existing service tunnel this was extended at the beginning of the war to provide shelter for over 800 people in Tower Hamlets and Coombe Valley area of Dover. It was over 300 metres long joining Noah's Ark Road to Union Road. This shelter was concrete lined with electric lighting and flush toilets.

The Borough Surveyor at Dover proposed that 'splinter proof trenches' for 266 persons should be constructed on River Recreation Ground. Soon the football clubs who used the ground started complaining about the trenches being dug close to their pitches, and the fixture secretaries of local cricket clubs weighed in by saying that they were reluctant to make fixtures for the coming season for the same reason!

The caves provided excellent shelter for the villagers. Some of the passages were extended for Home Guard rifle practice.

In the village of Eastry the Air Raid Precautions Committee proposed that Beckets Caves in the centre of the community would be used in the event of a gas attack as a deep air raid shelter. One of the Wardens who ran the local grocery business was made responsible for stocking up and maintaining an emergency food supply in the tunnels. But after a flurry of activity a year earlier it was not until the beginning of 1939 that any special lectures and training for Street Wardens and First Aid workers began. The Street Wardens' duties were to be enforcing the blackout, directing people to shelters and detecting unexploded bombs etc.

At Ramsgate caves again provided natural air raid shelters. The local authorities had started to enlarge an existing tunnel in the spring of 1939 which was completed soon after the outbreak of the war. After completion this was one of the most extensive networks of deep air raid shelters anywhere in the country. Later the first network of tunnels was linked to an additional 3 miles (4.8km) of new tunnels at a depth of over 15 metres with many entrances skirting the town. The first section to be opened had its own generators to provide electricity but the extension relied on the town's supply which was erratic so hundreds of hurricane lamps were supplied as a back up.

There was space for 60,000 people, well in excess of Ramsgate's needs. The labyrinthine tunnels were well signposted to prevent people getting lost and as a back up, a public address system and radio were installed.

With well over one hundred Local Authority and Volunteer brigades in the County, their duty under the Fire Brigade Act and the Air Raid Precautions Act was to provide fire cover in peacetime but also to make provision in the event of war.

Following the Air Raid Protection Act each local authority set up an Auxiliary Fire Service (AFS) for Air Raid Protection. It was formed in 1938 and mobilized on 1 September 1939. Until mobilization all personnel were employed on a part-time basis and only required to complete 60 hours training.

Initially there were problems between the AFS and the Regular Fire Service. The main reason for this was that until that time the fire brigades had been seen as a man's world, and now on the arrival of women in fire stations this caused a mixed reaction of amusement and horror.

Under the new provisions of this Act the responsibility of fire protection in the village of Eastry was passed from the Eastry Parish Council to the Eastry Rural District Council thus becoming a rate borne charge. This undoubtedly was a major change in many communities from the old volunteer fire brigade which had served them for many years.

Preparing the population for what might be happening in the near future, cigarette manufacturers W.D. & H.O. Wills issued a series of cigarette cards depicting the things that the Government and Local Authorities needed the general public to be aware of, as well as of the things that could be done by the individual in time of emergency. Promoting these cards the Home Secretary stated *'they are based on commonsense suggestions and the essential things recommended, cost very little and demand ingenuity and improvisation rather than expenditure'*.

The following are a few examples and captions:

Incendiary bomb and its effect – The 2 lb (910gm) magnesium bomb does not explode, its only object being to start a fire. It will probably penetrate no further than the attic or an upper floor. Vast numbers of these can be carried by a single aircraft, and many fires started than could be dealt with by fire brigades. Householders with little training and equipment can deal with these bombs and so protect their homes.

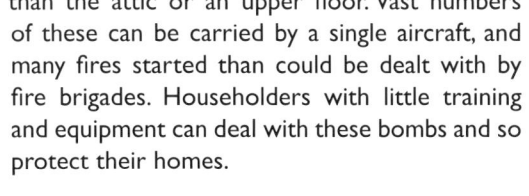

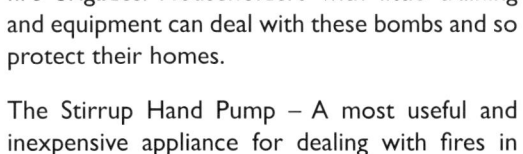

The Stirrup Hand Pump – A most useful and inexpensive appliance for dealing with fires in their early stages. It can be worked from any available water supply. This hand pump is useful for other household purposes such as washing down a car, cleaning windows or watering the garden.

The Balloon Barrage – This forms an important part of the co-ordinated scheme – consisting of guns, searchlights, fighter aircraft and balloons. In time of war, the balloons are attached by a steel cable to a winch on the ground by which it can be let up or hauled down to the required height. The cables form a 'death trap' to any enemy aircraft colliding with them. The balloons are organized in flights and squadrons, the squadrons being on an auxiliary basis manned by volunteers with a nucleus of fully trained regular personnel.

Anti-Aircraft Searchlight Units – They are to find and illuminate enemy aircraft so that they can be attacked by our own fighter machines or fired at by anti-aircraft guns. The searchlight has a glass paraboloid reflector approximately one metre in diameter and an electric arc lamp which gives a light of many millions of candle power. In fine weather has a range of over 8 km. The complete searchlight detachment consists of ten men who work the searchlight, a sound locator and a generating plant which provides power for the arc lamp.

The Illustrated London News carried a propaganda article on 4 February 1939 on the growth of the British Aircraft Industry. This acclaimed the arrival of 'The eight gun, single seater Vickers Supermarine *Spitfire*. Probably the World's Fastest Standard Fighter'.

The article stated that the first deliveries of this 350 mph aircraft to RAF squadrons had been made the previous year. The special features of this aircraft were the Rolls Royce *Merlin* engine and the eight Browning machine guns mounted in the wings. The mass production of this advanced aircraft is achieved by the fuselage being completely assembled sections before being joined together in the final assembly area. The method also facilitates the interchangeability of all components. Sir Kingsley Wood the Secretary of State for Air is quoted as saying, *'that between 5000 and 6000 of these machines were on order or would be ordered'.*

At the beginning of 1939, the Parish Council in Eastry was informed that accommodation was required to be ready in the village in the event of an evacuation of children from the Medway Towns. The Clerk carried out a survey of all the houses in the village taking notes of the accommodation available in each house and how many evacuees, particularly children, could be allocated.

It was suggested that the Infants Schools should be returned to the Church Street School so that the Village Hall could be used as an Accident and Emergency Centre should the need arise but this idea was turned down.

During the summer months the Government introduced the conscription of young men into the reserve units. Within weeks there was a further announcement that women would also be conscripted but would not be put in the firing line. Women would be allotted tasks such as driving trucks and working on farms or in factories.

Compared with the First World War, women were expected to play a fuller part in defending this country.

More than one million women joined the Women's Voluntary Service (WVS) and became transport drivers and air raid wardens, staffed reception centres for refugees, and set up mobile canteens for both soldiers and civilians. They also provided general assistance for wartime homemaking by circulating information on rationing, Make Do and Mend, and Dig for Victory amongst countless other tasks.

The Royal British Legion Women's Section was formed in 1931, initially to improve the lives of widows and families of ex-service men and women. But during this war and the austere postwar years the women's section helped many whose lives had been disrupted with the distribution of large quantities of clothing, particularly to families whose properties had been destroyed, along with shoes, cigarettes and food parcels.

The Women's Auxiliary Air Force was formed in June 1939, and by September 1940, 15,000 had enrolled. At first they were recruited for administrational duties, cooking etc., but gradually the women were being trained for servicing and maintenance of aircraft, medical and transport duties. Another large group was employed in signals, radar and in operations rooms.

The Sandwich Radar Station situated near the White Mill, comprised of a large rectangular aerial and a series of low flat-roofed brick buildings. For 24 hours a day WAAFs manned the big plotting table and others gazed at twelve inch radar screens in darkened cubicles. When an enemy aircraft was detected on the screen a Fighter Direction Officer would take over by notifying the appropriate authorities, and the WAAFs job was then to track the echoes on the screen and mark their progress on the plotting table. WAAFs with flying experience joined the Air Transport Auxiliary which was responsible for delivering aircraft from the factories to Air Force stations.

In August the Home Office announced the formation of a Women's Auxiliary Police Corps (WAPC), with the plan to replace men in certain clerical, driving and catering jobs. Some would be employed on a full-time basis and others part-time.

The Mechanized Transport Corps (MTC) was formed as a uniformed voluntary transport organization for women. The aim was to enable women, unable to join the Services due to existing commitments, to do part-time driving duties. Members drove various types of vehicles for organizations under the control of the Ministry of Transport.

Questions began being asked in the press regarding the upper age limit for various national home defence units. The following ages were taken from the National Service Handbook:

A.A. and Coast Defence Units	50 years for home service.
National Defence Companies	55 years.
Balloon Squadrons	50 years.
Observer Corps	No upper age limit.
RAF Volunteer Reserve	Men between 38 and 50 years.
RN (Volunteer) Wireless Reserve	Up to 45 years.
Royal Marine Police G.R.	Up to 55 years.

During August Vice Admiral Bertram Ramsay was appointed Vice Admiral Dover. He was charged with denying the Dover Strait to German naval forces, and securing the safety of allied cross channel shipping. He and his naval staff moved into the Admiralty casemate beneath the castle. This was partitioned into a number of offices, the largest of which was the Operations Room. It was from here Ramsay directed the planning of 'Operation Dynamo'- the evacuation of 400,000 soldiers from the French beaches beginning on 26 May 1940.

Winston Churchill writing a paper for the Air Defence Research Committee on 10 August stated: *'It is not child's play to come and attack England'*
In this Churchill expressed an opinion that mass air raids would gradually decline as enemy losses took effect, and finally daylight bombing would come to an end to be replaced with random night bombing of our cities and manufacturing centres.

As the Summer was drawing to a close Southern Railway was still offering *'cheap trips to the Continent from both Folkestone and Dover : Boulogne from 10 shillings (50p) : Passports not required by British subjects'.*

People knew that war was inevitable but didn't talk about it much. One person writing in the Eastry Parish Newsletter recalled seeing a Tiger Moth aircraft pulling a drogue (a device towed behind an aircraft for target practice) along the shoreline at Sandgate whilst gunners on Shorncliffe Camp aimed at it. The same person remembers sitting on the hills above Folkestone watching the lights go out all along the coast (a practice run).

Then, on 25 August it was announced in the *Dover Express* that it might be necessary to blackout the area between midnight and 4am at short notice. There would be no more rehearsals in sounding the siren and any siren in future would be a warning of an expected air raid. The newspaper also recommended that all households should obtain and store non-perishable foods, and establish where cover could be found in the event of an attack. The Mayor of Dover appealed to everybody to remain calm as the Council had everything well in hand and was prepared for any emergency.

In the rush to provide air raid protection, trenches that had been dug in Pencester Gardens in the centre of the town were having to be filled in owing to the fact that proximity to the river resulted in them filling up with water. Should have asked the locals first!

'Operation Pied Piper' the mass evacuation, particularly of children, from areas considered as danger zones began on the evening of the last night in August. In the Sandwich area the first evacuees arrived from Gillingham. An evacuation of children was started from the Medway Towns which the Government thought to be at the greatest risk of enemy air attacks. In all about 4,000 were moved into the Eastry Rural District by special trains contracted from Southern Railways arriving at Sandwich Station. They were then taken to Sandwich Central School by bus where they were given emergency rations and allocated to homes in the various villages. The adults who accompanied the children were often in a very agitated state, particularly expectant mothers, even asking if the war had started yet? Gradually matters were sorted out and the evacuees settled in.

When the schools in Eastry opened for the autumn term the infants attended full-time at the Village Hall. At the school in Church Street, children attended in the mornings and the Gillingham children in the afternoon. Senior children attended part-time at Sandwich where they soon found out that a series of trenches had been dug across the school's playing fields to provide shelter in the event of an air raid which was hardly a satisfactory arrangement, more of a compromise. Later, however, when the threat of attack was directed more to this area the evacuees were returned home. During the time the children were in this area their educational needs were provided by the local schools, the staff coping under extremely difficult conditions.

Around the country the population was on tenterhooks, glued to their radios and their newspapers as the politicians grappled with the disaster which was unfolding in Europe. Newspapers were full of photographs of barrage balloons going up and reports of army manoeuvres and other preparations for war. A day before Mr. Chamberlain announced we were at war, the Ministry of Health issued the following statement on the BBC:

'34 hospitals in the London area have been allowed as clearing stations for air raid casualties – and removing thousands of patients by Ambulance Trains 50 miles from the capital.'

This confirmed the Government's grave concern knowing we had little protection against what was then the finest air force in the world. Civic air raid shelters had already been constructed in many areas. Householders with gardens had been encouraged to build their own shelters

Commercial companies were quick to respond to the shortage of adequate protection. The advert provides an unique answer for the more affluent customer.

from plans provided by the local councils. Families who did not have this facility could buy a metal table under which they could huddle in the event of an air raid. Such was the panic and short-sightedness existing in the emergence of this terrible threat.

Life goes on! Children continue to play but now on top of their garden shelter in Gore Road, Eastry, in 1939.

Chapter 3

The Second World War

1939 On 3 September the Prime Minister, Neville Chamberlain, announced in a radio broadcast to the nation that from 11 am Great Britain was at war with Germany. In Parliament Winston Churchill was speaking and stating:

> 'Outside the storms of war may blow and the land may be lashed with the fury of its gale, but in our own hearts this Sunday morning there is peace. Our hands may be active, but our consciences are at rest. Let us not mistake the gravity of the task which lies before us; the severity of the ordeal to which we shall not be found unequal.'

The following is an extract from the King's rallying call to the Empire the same evening.

> 'We are called with our Allies to meet the challenge of a principle which if it were to prevail would be fatal to any civilized order in the world..........The peoples of the world would be kept in the bondage of fear and all hopes of settled peace and the security of justice and liberty among nations would be ended....... It is this high purpose that I now call my people at home and my peoples across the Sea, who will make our cause their own. I ask them to stand calm, firm and united in this time of trial.'

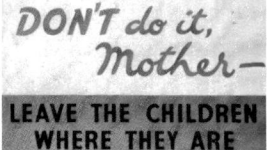

This government poster attempted to persuade mothers to leave their evacuated children in safe areas.

A national paper reported on 3 September that by tonight it is expected that three million children, mothers, blind persons, expectant mothers and cripples will have been evacuated to the country or seaside, nearly half of them from Greater London. A further extract from the *Daily Mirror* carried a comforting message:

> 'If you are a mother whose little ones have been evacuated to a safety area, don't worry about them. Just think how kind you would be to another woman's child who was sent to you in the same circumstances.
>
> So don't spoil that courageous act now by worrying and fretting about them in their absence. Carry on your job as usual, or, if you are doing ARP work, throw yourself wholeheartedly into that'.

Warnings regarding the '**blackout**' appeared in the press, creating a rush to buy blackout material. Local shops even reported that they had run out of brown paper, drawing pins and torch batteries.

On 4 September, *The Daily Telegraph* carried a Government announcement entitled

War Orders to Civilians

The instructions included the procedure to be followed.

> *In the event of air raids, warnings will be given by sirens or hooters – take shelter.*

Do not leave your shelter until you hear the 'raiders passed' signal, which will be a continuously sounding siren or hooters for two minutes on the same note.

If poison gas has been used a warning is given by hand rattles. When it is clear to come out from the shelter, hand bells will be rang, and there is no longer any danger from poison gas. But carry a gas mask with you at all times.

All cinemas, theatres and other places for entertainment are to be closed immediately until further notice. Sports meetings whether outdoor or indoor, which involve large numbers congregating together are also prohibited. Churches and other places of public worship will not be closed.

All day schools in education in the United Kingdom will be closed for lessons for a week. The date of reopening will be decided by the school authorities.

The first air raid siren sounded in Sandwich almost before Mr. Chamberlain had finished his announcement and brought home the fact that this country was now at war. This was the first of over 4,500 alerts reported in the Mayor's daily record between 1939 and 1945. In the early days of the war the air raid warning system in Sandwich was a steam siren fitted at the Corporation Gas Works which was the only premises in the town that had a head of steam day and night. It was also necessary to man the telephone continuously and additional wages were paid to the workmen.

By the outbreak of hostilities the Auxiliary Fire Service (AFS) had about 96,000 men and women incorporated as full-time members of the fire service nationally. In Kent fire defence of the county was still inadequate and poorly organized. Members were still without proper uniforms, elementary equipment and housed in old or poorly constructed substations. But keen to get to work the auxiliaries became dispirited as the **'phoney war'** continued month after month. This was until the spring of the following year when they were to be in the thick of it! This was going to be a 'baptism by fire' that they could never have envisaged when they enrolled. Many were killed or injured as the enemy's bombs and incendiaries rained down on them.

In the village of River near Dover, some of the village school's classrooms had been set aside in readiness to become a first aid centre should the need arise. When the new term was due to start the school remained closed. Instead teachers went around the area visiting their pupils at home and setting them homework which was an example of the great 'war spirit' at work!

At the direct request of the Government, the British Red Cross and St. John Ambulance joined together as the Joint War Organization running nearly 250 auxiliary hospitals and convalescent homes for injured and recovering servicemen and women. They looked after foreign nationals injured whilst serving in the allied forces and injured Civil Defence workers. Although the Government gave them a grant the organization was responsible for the upkeep of these Homes. They were supplemented by Voluntary Aid Detachment (VAD) workers providing services in the various military hospitals and convalescent homes. In addition they drove ambulances, helped disabled service people, visited patients, wrote letters for the wounded, sent POW food parcels, and even arranged entertainment for patients. They had a hospital library service and a stores department which supplied all the equipment from beds

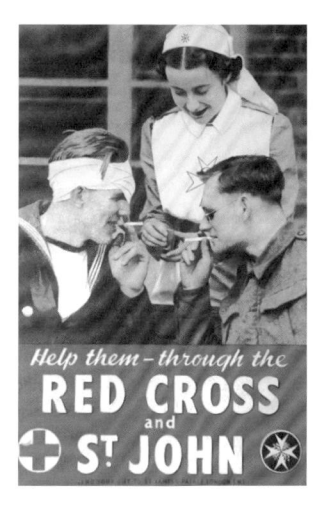

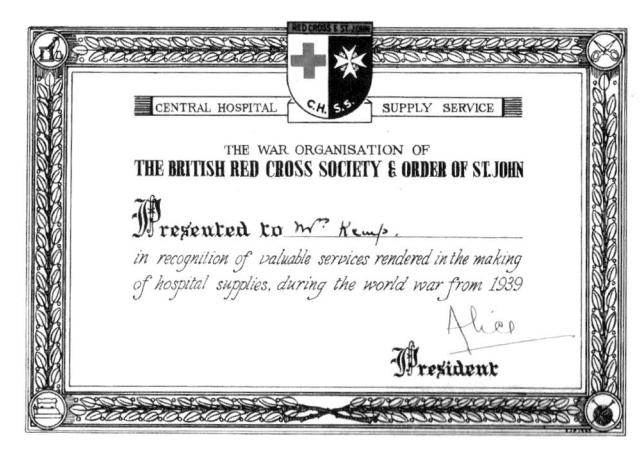

A certificate in recognition of service in the Central Hospital Supply Service.

and cookers to games, sports gear and handicraft materials for occupational therapy. Another department called the Central Hospital Supply Service (CHSS) provided 'soft goods' like pyjamas, towels, bandages and bed linen. Many first aid posts were located in adapted buildings such as schools (mentioned above in River) and church halls. Some posts were staffed entirely by the British Red Cross or St. John Ambulance or mixed staff. They often took part in practice exercises with Civil Defence workers, Home Guard and the police.

On 4 September the *Daily Mirror* carried the following advice to its readers.
> 'Be silent, be discreet, enemy ears are listening to you… Don't listen to Rumours – You will get all the news that matters – bad or good – in your newspapers. Disbelieve anything else you hear – particularly alarmist news. Next thing to remember don't broadcast information'.

Wartime Conditions began to make an impact: An article in *The Daily Telegraph,* under the headline *'Food Rationing Plan Ready'* pointed out that the Government's plans had been prepared for some time, and may be put into operation within a fortnight. It stated that there was no shortage and the scheme was mainly designed to secure orderly marketing. The rationing scheme should prevent waste and avoid temporary shortages, and by the end of the month a National Register was to be set up which would also be used for food rationing purposes.

On the 27 September people were stunned with the statement in the press that Income Tax would be increased to 7 /6d. (37½ p) in the pound or 37.5%. At the time the highest rate ever.

The *Dover Express* announced that all 'aliens and pigeon keepers' should report to their nearest police station for registration. Also the Meteorological Department of the Air Ministry reported that weather forecasts would no longer be issued so preventing vital information being given to the enemy.

National papers reported that road traffic accidents in Kent during September were 70% higher than the same month the previous year due to the blackout conditions. There was panic buying of sandbags causing the price to double to 6d. (2½ p).

With the government introducing petrol rationing on 22 September, there were long queues at the pumps. Branded petrol was replaced by a medium octane blend, and petrol for commercial vehicles was dyed red to prevent its illicit use by civilians.
Every motorist was entitled to a basic monthly ration of petrol. The quantity varied with the horse-power (hp) of the vehicle, 4 gallons (18.2 litres) for the smallest car to 10 gallons (45.5 litres) for cars of 20 horse-power and over. As one can imagine there was much petrol fiddling, some of which involved straining red petrol through a gas mask filter to remove the coloured dye, whilst other motorists bought their fuel on the black market.

Much to the surprise of everybody the Home Office announced that places of entertainment would reopen. Proprietors warned their customers that, *'If an air raid warning be received during the performance the audience will be informed …..Those desiring to leave may do so, but the performance will continue and members are advised in their own interests to remain in the building.'*

A barrage balloon ready to be raised.

The Daily Telegraph reported in December that after a period of only three months of war, the military authorities were convinced that the balloon barrage had been more successful than was foreseen. The article stated that as a weapon it had the ability of being mobile. Also when the order was given, every balloon was on its way to its pre-determined site within 24 hours, and that over 30,000 men were now engaged on balloon barrage duties.

Late in 1939 Eastry Parish Council sprang into action to aid the war effort. A National Savings Committee was set up involving the Women's Institute and the village school, and Mrs. Florence Stroud took on the responsibility of raising funds for the Red Cross. The scouts were responsible for collecting waste paper for the Ministry of Supply who controlled the purchase price at - *One penny for 3 lbs. (1.36kg) of newspaper; for 4 lbs. (1.81kg) of magazines; for 6 lbs. (2.72kg) of other waste & cardboard. All waste was to be separately bundled & securely tied.* A collection point for metal waste was set up in a meadow at the rear of the High Street cottages belonging to the butcher, and there is a record of over 8 tons of scrap iron being collected and dispatched. Throughout the war scrap metal was collected from every available place. On one occasion the iron fence surrounding the Recreation Ground in Church Street, Eastry, came to the attention of the authorities, and workmen arrived to remove it. Fortunately this was prevented when the vicar Rev. Cartman spotted what was happening and prevented the men from undertaking their mission.

A circular arrived reminding residents that owing to the pressing demands for copper, zinc and brass for war purposes, there was an urgent need for economy in the uses of these metals. Later the Minister of Aircraft Production, Lord Beaverbrook announced: *'Women of Britain, give us your aluminum. We will turn your pots and pans into Spitfires, Hurricanes, Blenheims and Wellingtons.'*

Those who had cash in their pockets soon became the subject of an intense campaign to help the war effort by buying National Savings Certificates. People were urged on by posters with the slogan, *'Lend to Defend the Fight to be Free'*. Other fund raising efforts included national Warship and Aircraft Weeks with plaques being presented to communities for their efforts. The 'Penny a Week Fund' was one of the most successful ways of obtaining money for the war effort. It was mainly achieved from wage earners voluntarily contributing 1d. per week from their pay packet, at the time when the average weekly wage was £10. The fund was also supplemented by door-to-door collections. The scheme was introduced in November and within six months the fund was receiving £8000 a week and by July the following year £14,000.

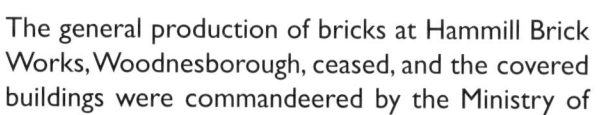

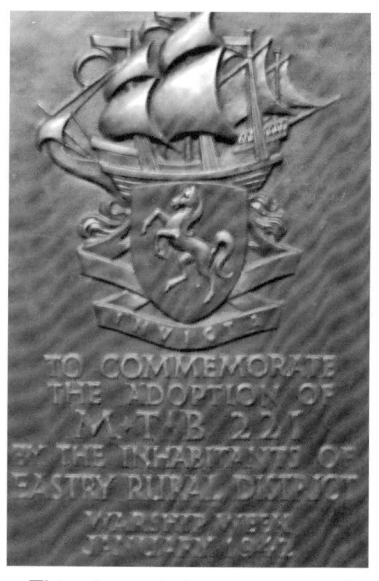

This plaque is in recognition of the local people who adopted a motor torpedo boat during Warship Week.

The general production of bricks at Hammill Brick Works, Woodnesborough, ceased, and the covered buildings were commandeered by the Ministry of Food for storage and drying of water damaged grain. Nevertheless the company continued to produce tons of dried ground clay for the production of insulating bricks, and engaged in installing grinding mills for farmers to produce animal feed. Another building on the site was set aside to be used as a central emergency mortuary. It was decided that bodies of German airmen falling in the district should be sent to this mortuary, and then taken to Aylesham Cemetery for burial.

By 1 October all householders in this part of Kent had to be registered for coal supplies, and a month later the *Dover Express* announced that 34,000 ration books had been delivered during the week. Ration books were supplied in three colours:
    Buff -   Most Adults
    Green - Pregnant women, nursing mothers and children under 5 years of age. They had first choice of fruit, a daily pint of milk and double supply of eggs.
    Blue -   Children between 5 and 16 years of age. These children should have fruit, the full meat ration and a half pint of milk a day.

Members of the public were reminded that they should now register with retailers of their choice for bacon, ham, butter and sugar. This was followed by an evil looking cartoon insect called the *'Squanderbug'* which became the symbol to warn people off buying unnecessary items and other extravagances. A further campaign quickly followed urging women to *'Make do and Mend'*, and was spearheaded by a variety of posters and booklets full of useful tips and advice.

During December gas masks arrived to be distributed by the local council. Adults had a standard black type which was carried over the shoulder in a cardboard box. Masks for the children were available in different sizes and some had 'Mickey Mouse' designs although it was some time before the special masks for babies up to 2 years were available.

By the end of the year the delivery of Anderson Shelters had been completed to all those householders entitled to them. They were made of six corrugated steel sheets bolted together at the top, with steel plates at either end measuring 6ft. 6ins x 4ft. 6ins (2m x 1.38m). The entrance was protected by a steel shield and an earthen blast wall. The entitlement at this time appears to be: those who were less well off received shelters free of charge, but men who earned more than £250 a year could buy one for £7. As part of a national campaign the Civil Defence issued a *'Clearance of Lofts Order'* as a precaution against incendiary bombs igniting in vacated properties. The *Dover Express* newspaper carried an advert for *'Bomb Scoops for incendiary bombs, complete with rake price 7/6d.'*(37½ p).

Fire Service personnel in their new uniforms.

Those men and women who were too old for active service volunteered to serve as air raid wardens, civil defence workers, part time firefighters and first aiders. The wardens were part of the Air Raid Precautions Service (ARP). They enforced the blackout, directed people into shelters, and kept people away from unexploded bombs. Some volunteers were trained as firefighters in the Auxiliary Fire Service (AFS), others were used as messengers, firewatchers and stretcher bearers. Others were employed in first aid posts and on ambulances. As time went on these home defence groups, which started with voluntary recruitment, were gradually 'frozen in' by 1940 with their members not being allowed to resign and getting additional staff by official recruitment.

In the village of Eastry the church room in Church Street was taken over by the military, and the Council Room on the Recreation Ground opposite was used for village societies and lectures on air raid precautions. Village life continued and shops opened more or less as usual. Mr. W. P. Clark as Deputy Head Warden (ARP) witnessed the war from start to finish. He ran a grocery

OFFICIAL INSTRUCTIONS ISSUED BY THE MINISTRY OF HOME SECURITY

GAS ATTACK

HOW TO PUT ON YOUR GAS MASK

Always keep your gas mask with you — day and night. Learn to put it on quickly. Practise wearing it.

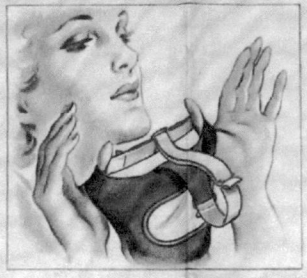

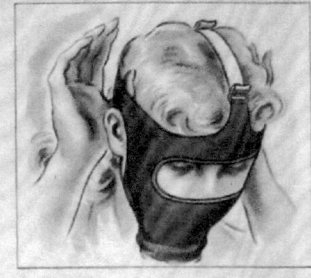

1. Hold your breath. 2. Hold mask in front of face, with thumbs inside straps.
3. Thrust chin well forward into mask, pull straps over head as far as they will go.
4. Run finger round face-piece taking care head-straps are not twisted.

IF THE GAS RATTLES SOUND

1. Hold your breath. Put on mask wherever you are. Close window.
2. If out of doors, take off hat, put on your mask. Turn up collar. 
3. Put on gloves or keep hands in pockets. Take cover in nearest building. 

IF YOU GET GASSED

BY VAPOUR GAS Keep your gas mask on even if you feel discomfort. If discomfort continues go to First Aid Post

BY LIQUID or BLISTER GAS

| 1 Dab, but *don't* rub the splash with handkerchief. Then destroy handkerchief. | 2 Rub No. 2 Ointment well into place. *(Buy a 6d. jar now from any chemist).* In emergency chemists supply Bleach Cream free. | 3 If you can't get Ointment or Cream within 5 minutes wash place with soap and warm water. | 4 Take off at once any garment splashed with gas. |

business and kept his tearooms (canteen) above the shop open for the military personnel to enjoy. He even installed a piano and a wind up gramophone to provide some entertainment. In addition to all his responsibilities he took care of stocking up and maintaining an emergency food supply in the tunnels at Beckets.

Another resident, Miss Waterfield, who lived in the large house called *The Aumbry*, placed her three cottages (now called *Aumbry Cottages*) in Church Street at the disposal of the authorities. She furnished No.1 as a First Aid Post; No.2 became the local HQ of the Home Guard and No.3 the ARP Wardens' Post. These had to be manned every night and also during the day when air raids took place. The Head Warden, Mr. F. Hopper, and Mr. Clark manned the post on alternate nights. Coded air raid warnings were given as follows:

Impending air raid -	*a fluctuating warbling signal*
Raiders passed -	*steady pitch continuous signal*
Poison gas -	*given by hand rattles*
Danger from gas has passed -	*ringing of hand bells.*

In some quarters the compulsory blackout regulations were getting out of hand. On 1 December, Churchill agreed they were vital and should continue but the prosecutions (not to my knowledge in Eastry) for minor violations should stop. He made reference to a man being prosecuted for smoking a cigarette too conspicuously and a woman turning the light on to tend her baby.

This first Christmas of the war had few restrictions as food rationing had not yet been implemented but the traditional sight of a lit-up Christmas tree in a window had disappeared, along with shop displays obscured by anti-blast tape on the windows. In many homes the family Christmas Day festivities had to be concluded early as father and granddad were on duty.

1940 On the 2 January, the third Royal Proclamation under the National Service (Armed Forces) Act was signed by the King, when nearly 2,000,000 men were affected. As a consequence all men who had reached the age of 19 but were not yet 28 were liable for service in the armed services. As the call up gained momentum there was a surge in the number of couples wanting to get married. It was reported that in some towns the Registrar's Office extended their opening hours to cope with the rush.

On 5 January, news broke that the famous female aviator Amy Johnson had died whilst serving with the Air Transport Auxiliary. Her aircraft crashed in the Thames Estuary whilst on a delivery flight. The crash was likely to have been due to bad weather conditions or just running out of fuel. Her body was never recovered.

At least the gaping hole in the pier assisted as an anti-invasion precaution.

During January a Dutch ship named *Nora* drifted into Deal Pier after being struck by a mine whilst at anchor. Reports indicated that all the crew were saved and there were only a few injuries.

Before the war began this country had imported many millions of tons of food a year from other countries. The supply of much of this food ceased due to the activity of enemy submarines sinking British ships, and there was a fear of food shortages. At this point the British Government introduced rationing. This rationing commenced on 8 January although the Government, with foresight, had been stockpiling ration cards for some time.

With the introduction of rationing people saw the disappearance from the shops of all but the necessities with each person being allowed a specific amount of basic foods. Butter, sugar, bacon and ham were the first commodities to go on ration followed by meat in March. Offal, fish, potatoes and bread were left untouched. However the quality of a loaf of bread declined, and in the end a new loaf called the *'National wheat meal loaf'* was introduced but was very unpopular.

At this time food became scarce and it was an offence to throw even a small amount of bread away even if it had become mouldy. To enforce this ruling The Ministry of Food prosecuted people who were caught so bread pudding became very popular.

Posters proclaiming *'We want your kitchen waste'* were displayed on notice boards, requesting any food waste to be used to feed pigs and to be collected by the District Council.

During January RAF Manston was upgraded from a Training Centre to being part of No.11 Group Fighter Command controlled from Hornchurch. A Territorial anti-aircraft unit which had been raised in Ashford arrived at the aerodrome on 10 May, being the most forward of the home fighter bases. The gun site was positioned in a field off the Acol Road and was armed with four vintage, 3 inch (76mm) anti-aircraft guns and Lewis guns, and surrounded by barbed wire. Due to a possible invasion the crew were supplied with three weeks' rations, and told they were to fight to the last man and no retreat. It was questionable how with only eight rifles and two Lewis guns the men were expected to hold off an attack for three weeks. Another site was located at Telegraph Hill, Minster. Later the old static anti-aircraft guns were replaced by 3.7 inch (94mm) mobile units which were connected to range finders and predictors.

Known first in 1938 as No. 1 Defence Group being raised to protect vulnerable points in East Kent and was recruited mainly from ex-servicemen. By May 1940 had become the 6th Home

WWII Home Defence Battalions

Defence Battalion (The Buffs) providing Officers and NCOs to train young soldiers for home defence duties such as aerodrome defence and to assist XII Corps who were now in Kent.

In the spring, as part of a decoy plan, the RAF requisitioned nearby Staple Railway Station for the delivery of material for constructing a dummy airfield on the Goldstone Marshes on the Ash Levels nearby in an attempt to fool the enemy aircraft away from the real airfield. This was a 'Q 50B' night decoy which displayed a sequence of lights to simulate an active airfield, and was used from August 1940 until August 1942.
Another 'spoof' diversion was constructed at Monkton Marshes, and residents of nearby Ash record seeing flashing lights and a truck being driven round at night as part of the deception. In another attempt to obstruct enemy aircraft and gliders attempting to land in the marshes, obstacles were placed in fields around the area.

On 4 February Sir H. Kingsley Wood, the Chancellor of the Exchequer announced that the cost of the war had soared from £7.5 million per day to £11 million per day. The Chancellor also announced to the House of Commons on the 5 March the issue of a £300,000,000 War Loan. The loan would carry interest at 3% and would be repayable in 15 to 19 years' time. The Bank of England issue of the loan permitted a minimum subscription of £100. However the Postmaster General and the banks issue accepted subscriptions as low as £10.

Later in April the standard rate of British income tax was raised by one shilling and sixpence (7½ p) to ten shillings (50p) in the pound, making it a rate of 50%, which was almost unthinkable.

Everything was about to change. On 9 April the Germans invaded Denmark and Norway. On 10 May they invaded Holland, Belgium and Luxembourg. Winston Churchill became Prime Minister. On the 14 May Holland surrendered, and that evening Anthony Eden, the Minister for War, announced the mustering of the Local Defence Volunteers (LDV). Eden's announcement meant that men aged between 17 and 65 years who were not eligible for military service, were to serve with the Local Defence Volunteers (later known as the Home Guard), and within a couple of days with their LDV arm bands the men were on patrol.

In a public announcement in the press, the Government invited members of the public to hand in any weapons they might have to their local police station to be used by the Local Defence Volunteer Corps. Almost a 'make do and mend' aspect to the call to arms!

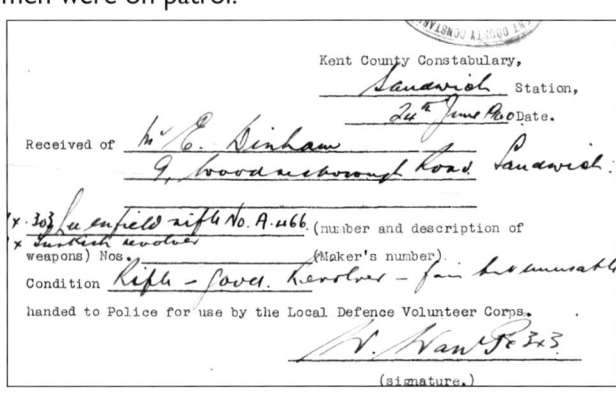

A receipt for a rifle and a revolver handed in to Sandwich Police Station.

On 24 April, a conference was held in Maidstone requesting Eastry Rural District Medical Officer of Health to attend regarding a circular from London entitled War Refugees. The document outlined the possible influx of refugees from Holland and Belgium.
1. The first group would sail direct from ports of these countries and be directed to ports on the West Coast. The ports selected were Mersey, Belfast and the Clyde.
2. The second group would cross into France where some would shelter but others would arrive in this country via the Channel Ports and be directed to London.
3. In addition there were to be scattered landings, and temporary shelter needs to be provided. Thereafter more permanent accommodation must be found, preferably in empty houses or in accommodation offered by householders who were willing to provide board and lodging in consideration of a billeting allowance.

A letter from the Town Clerk of Sandwich the day after the conference, stated:
'It is proposed to use the Market Hall, situated in the Cattle Market, for the purpose of temporary accommodation for Refugees who may land within the limits of this Borough.
I understand that there are about 100 blankets received under the Evacuation Scheme which would be available'.

In early May a letter arrived in Sandwich from Whitehall, stating:
*'If urgent action becomes necessary further instructions will take the form of a telegram in the terms, **Prepare for war refugees**. They are now our Allies and I am sure that I can rely on your co-operation and that of your district in this war work.'*

The telegram duly arrived on the 10th May.

On the 25 May, the Town Clerk received a letter from the Ministry of Health notifying him that arrangements had been made at the local banks whereby Belga or Guilder notes could be cashed by refugees up to a maximum of £10 a week on the production of their War Refugee Landing Card. Other letters followed from the Ministry outlining the town's responsibility:

Burial of refugees – *'should be carried out in a decent and seemly fashion, the responsibility for cost incurred will be accepted by H. M. Government.'*

Health services - *'The Minister is confident that your Council will be prepared to provide by way of its maternity and child welfare, infectious disease and mental health services. The Authority hopes that recovery of the cost of services rendered or part should be made from the refugee. If not the Council can claim reimbursement from the Exchequer.'*

Medical examination – *'The Minister regards it is very important that medical examinations of those arriving should be made immediately as a safeguard against the risk of infectious diseases, as there is considerable prevalence of such disease on the continent.'*

A circular dated 30 May to Sandwich Borough Council, entitled 'Transfer of Skilled Labour to the War Effort' read:
'The Minister of Health draws their attention to the vital need at this time of making available for the war effort every possible man, with the requisite skill, at present in their employment who can be spared. The present situation demands an immediate acceleration of armament production.
This can be best achieved by securing the maximum number of additional skilled workers who are at present employed on less essential work.'

At the Richborough Refugee Camp in Sandwich the large majority of the men were enthusiastic to volunteer for service in the British Forces, forming refugee Pioneer Companies.

After the German invasion and defeat of Poland, thousands of Polish servicemen made every attempt to get away and to reach France, but following the collapse of France thousands managed to escape to Britain. These included a great number of airmen giving the RAF considerable reinforcement. During May a platoon of Polish cadets was formed at Manston. It is estimated that in the Battle of Britain over 10% of the German aircraft destroyed was due to the action by Polish airmen. A fact that as a nation we should never forget!

Ministers in London were getting worried about **Home Land Security**. For instance a warning was issued from the Home Office that it was illegal to send messages by carrier pigeon.

In February, the Ministry of Information launched a campaign in an attempt to prevent information getting into the hands of the enemy with a poster showing a characterized head of Hitler with an oversized ear, with the slogan –

Careless talk costs lives. Mr. Hitler wants to know! But silence makes him simply **FUEHRIOUS**

This clever cartoon poster was part of the Government's 'Careless talk Costs Lives' campaign.

A circular addressed to the Clerk of Eastry Rural District Council requested a complete list of names and addresses of all aliens employed in public utility undertakings and any others deemed to have doubtful loyalty. This also applied to aliens employed in civil defence services, including the Auxiliary Fire Service. A plan was devised to suspend all aliens in these services only to be reinstated if such persons were found to be of no risk but should not be engaged in duties in a Report or Control Centre situation.

The Minister of Home Security also felt it advisable that an auxiliary fireman should be allocated for sentry duty at the Station entrance to prevent the entry of unauthorized persons. Questions arose whether the guard should be armed which contravened Fire Brigade rules as they were not a combatant force. This problem was resolved by employing a Local Defence Volunteer who was equipped with a weapon which at the time might have been a shotgun.

The Kent Messenger on 8 June carried a report with the headline *'Council Sacks Two Conchies'*. Both men worked for Gillingham Council, and it was stated they were conscientious objectors and been given a month's salary in lieu of notice.

In another report, headlined *'Unwise talk Charge'* a man was charged at Deal with using language likely to provoke a breach of the peace. A 21 year old man from Margate was fined £1 for writing a fascist slogan on a wall in the town, and a further £2 for causing damage. The irony is whilst awaiting his trial his call up papers arrived.

The *East Kent Mercury* reported on a London man who was visiting Ramsgate being fined £5 for asking 'indiscreet questions' regarding details of anti-aircraft defences. He apparently had visited the coastal town on several occasions and had slept in the tunnels. The same paper reported the story of a man from Herne Bay who was remanded in custody for making a remark in public that was likely to provoke a 'breach of the peace'. The alleged remark was that: *'Deal Pier will be rebuilt in 3 days by the Germans'*.

Elaborate precautions were soon in place with all German subjects in the country being interned. All railway station and road signs were removed or painted out. Newspapers had photographs of workmen removing signposts with captions similar to *'in order to add to the German parachutist's difficulties, should they land and get past the 'parashots' and police.'*

Air raids often took place during daylight hours and on one occasion at Eastry there was a running 'dogfight' between two aircraft almost at roof level. The enemy pilot rammed our defending fighter killing the pilot and pieces of the Spitfire fell into the field below Eastry Court. The dead pilot's body was laid in the oast house awaiting collection by the RAF. The German aircraft flew over The Brooks at Eastry landing in a field nearby and the crew captured.

On another occasion a single bomber came in releasing a landmine aimed at Snowdown Colliery but which landed in Nonington causing a lot of damage. An ambulance was dispatched to help take the injured to the makeshift Buckland Hospital in Waldershare Park Mansion

In June an enemy Heinkel HE11P bomber crashed on the beach at Sacketts Gap, Margate. One of the crew was killed but the rest were unhurt and duly arrested.

Victory at all costs
These were the words spoken by Winston Churchill on 13 May 1940. This call charted our nation's history for the next five years.

In May the Emergency Powers Act was passed giving the War Cabinet practically unrestricted powers over all British citizens and their property. Almost immediately the situation took a turn for the worst when in June the British Army retreated from France with the loss of many lives and most of its equipment. From this disaster was coined the phrase 'The Dunkirk Spirit', which was to be a rallying call for the war years.

On 8 June, *The Kent Messenger* carried the headlines -

A column of allied servicemen wading out to an evacuation vessel.

Miracle of Deliverance
'The British Expeditionary Force and French troops were trapped in the Port of Dunkirk. On 26/27 May, Boulogne and Calais were captured by the enemy. That evening Operation Dynamo started and the Dunkirk evacuation began.

> *Initially it was hoped that 45,000 troops might have been rescued from Dunkirk before it fell to the Germans. But the 'Little Ships', alongside the Royal Navy were key to bringing back over 338,000 troops from the French beaches. – The Dunkirk Spirit (a phrase still used today) represented triumph over adversity.'*

In the same paper Lord Baden-Powell, the Chief Scout, thanked all members of his organization for their contribution in this historic event:

> 'You have done grand work behind the scenes already, but as fighting has intensified more desperate calls are required for further effort from you.
> So with tails and sleeves up go to it in every way you can to help win the war.'

Back in Dover the defences on the Eastern, Western Arms and the Southern Breakwater of the harbour were manned by the Territorial Army Reserve with few weapons. The commanding officer was friendly with the skipper of a destroyer called *HMS Sabre*, which had been rescuing the troops off the beaches, and had asked him if he could lay hands on any abandoned equipment and ammunition, whatever was there. Colonel Arnold in his book 'Conflict across the Strait' said, 'in all he provided me with no less than nine Bren guns, and a number of boxes of ammunition. On his last trip, he even provided me with a Boys anti-tank rifle, but could only find seventeen rounds of ammunition for it. This was the final gift, and it was a miracle that he even survived this last journey. The ship's funnel looked like a pepper pot with the bridge and deck a mass of twisted metal'.

He continued, 'One final defence was given to the Eastern and Pier Extension, to operate in an emergency. These were three 21 inch (533mm) torpedo tubes, erected on fixed mountings, and sited across the harbour entrances. They were to be fired only at point blank range if the German troopships were entering the harbour............... We had come through a phase which had, in a short period, turned us from Saturday afternoon soldiers into what I hoped I could now consider an efficient fighting unit'.

Colonel Arnold felt he had the situation under control but did not realize that the German High Command had a plan too. One small part was to open up and secure Dover Harbour for the support of their invasion fleet to be achieved by the men of the No.4 Company of the Brandenburg Regiment who were to be landed by submarine at St. Margaret's Bay with the first assault wave. Upon landing this English speaking regiment would be divided into two groups. The first would mount bicycles and ride to the gun positions and capture all artillery batteries. A second group would cycle to Dover, take out all the defences in and around the harbour, and above all prevent the sinking of a block ship which was stationed ready at the entrance.

Even before the war the Cinque Ports (Fortress) Royal Engineers had regular meetings and parades at Archcliffe Fort. As the start of hostilities loomed ever closer their training covered many aspects of defence including drill, weaponry, searchlights and even gas mask training. During the war a medical room was set up to provide medical assistance for the batteries on the Eastern side of the Harbour, Pier Turret and the Southern Breakwater Battery. The sick or injured were ferried across by a launch known as *The Seymour Castle* which, before the war, was a pleasure craft running from Dover to Dungeness. The Royal Engineers Repair Unit was based at the fort for the installation and maintenance of the diesel generators used to power coastal defence searchlights.

The politicians and the Government thought that the Germans, after the defeat and subsequent retreat of allied forces from France at Dunkirk, would mount an invasion. They considered the need to empty the coastal towns of civilians thus preventing the problems which occurred in Europe when huge numbers of people clogged up the roads as they fled, hampering any attempt of a counterattack. The Government had drawn up a plan for the evacuation of about twenty towns ranging from Great Yarmouth on the Norfolk coast to Hythe on the Kent coast. Notices were put up by the police on 20 June, telling the population to be ready at 12 hours' notice to move.

It is understood that the British Generals had informed Winston Churchill to expect a landing between Thanet and Pevensey of many thousands of enemy troops, followed by mass landings of gliders and parachute troops. Even the code word 'Cromwell' was prepared for the imminent invasion threat. Winston Churchill in a letter to General Ismay, urged for plans of *'sheets of flaming oil'* to be put in place in one or more of the suspected invasion harbours.

Plans were also drawn up so that in the event of the Germans gaining a foothold and Dover being cut off on the landward side, regiments of infantry would withdraw into the Castle, the Citadel on the Western Heights, and Fort Burgogne. These units would become completely self-contained, able to operate seawards, and remain a strong point behind the enemy's lines.

After Dunkirk it was only three weeks before the French Government capitulated. The eyes of the world were firmly fixed upon the fate of this small island, just a small leap across the water. The big question was would Hitler attempt to invade our Sovereign Isle. From our perspective it was likely to occur sooner rather than later due to the powerful conquering German war machine gathering on our doorstep just 19 miles (30km) away. We did not know the answer to this question but had to consider all the possibilities in a defence strategy.

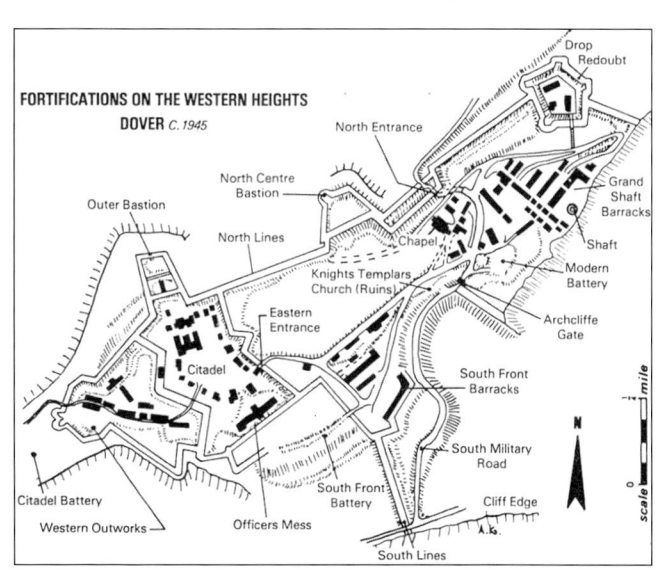

During June, Churchill visited the beach at St. Margaret's Bay to check on the defences. It is understood that the Prime Minister was **not** impressed by what he saw. He found that there were only three anti-tank guns covering 4 to 5 miles (6.4 to 8km)

of vulnerable coast. Speaking to a senior officer he found out that they had only six rounds of ammunition for each gun, and had to resist firing a test round to see if the weapons were operative. This was hardly a reassuring situation for the Prime Minister and the country at large.

From captured enemy documents after the war it can be seen that the German Admiralty had made all their plans for an invasion, planning to cross the narrow waters of the English Channel, never considering an alternative invasion route. This was designed to be perfectly straightforward. Under the cover of continuous shelling of our defences by their long-range guns and an all-out attack by the Luftwaffe, a concentrated invasion fleet would embark through a narrow corridor at the narrowest point of Channel. However, this plan was soon in difficulties and dismissed because the German navy would have found it difficult to protect such a large fleet, and the army was reluctant to trust itself without complete assurance of protection from the navy and the Luftwaffe. From their initial perspective they quickly realized they required more time to organize the domination of both sides of the Channel with their superior air and navy power, and have a fleet of special high speed landing-craft which could land thousands of troops, tanks and heavy armour on our beaches quickly. Furthermore they would need to maintain an enormous supply system to successfully secure a decisive victory.

With hindsight it took us four years of effort and planning, coupled with a massive amount of aid from the United States of America to put in place and undertake the D-Day landings.

From early on in the war Germany recognized the importance of propaganda. They broadcast false messages to non-existent agents, and dropped groups of parachutes and other equipment to give the impression that they had enemy agents in their area. German broadcasts attracted large numbers of the British public to their programmes. It was estimated that about a quarter of the population listened to Lord Haw-Haw, forcing the BBC to counter this propaganda by rescheduling their most popular programmes.

William Joyce (Lord Haw-Haw) was a notorious Nazi propagandist. His announcement 'Germany calling, Germany calling' was a familiar call across the airways, introducing threats and misinformation from his Hamburg base. He broadcast on the Reichsrundfunksgesellschaft (RRG) German radio and used it as a means of propaganda overseen by Joseph Goebbels.

William Joyce was born in America, the son of a naturalized American, and had grown up in Ireland but claimed to be British. For that reason his value to the Third Reich was as a supposed Britisher. In 1945, he was captured and returned to Britain where he was later hanged for treason at London's Wandsworth Prison.

The fear of invasion prompted the authorities to evacuate children of school age out of southeast Kent. One such scare occurred when the War Office issued an alert on 12 May that an airborne attack was considered imminent. In the Dover area nearly

3,000 children were sent to Wales on trains departing from Priory station on Sunday 2 June, for a new safe life far away from the fears of war. A mother in Eastry said that her son was evacuated to Wales and despite this being wartime his clothes were posted home for washing every fortnight. Those, whose parents decided not to allow their children to be evacuated, were faced with no formal education as all the Dover schools closed. A few days later on the 6 June, the children of Thanet followed the mass evacuation by train.

As a cautionary note the Prime Minister warned the Chiefs of Staff against being complacent and not to underestimate the enemy. As the threat was there farmers were asked to leave farm machinery out in the open and, whenever practicable, to build their ricks across the middle of a field to act as an obstruction to any landing of enemy aircraft. '... *regarding deterrents against enemy aircraft landings, the Regional Commissioner is now informed that a broadcast appeal may be made on Monday or Tuesday evening for volunteers to undertake this work. It is hoped that local authorities will be ready to make immediate use of all offers of service which may be forthcoming.*'

The following letter dated 1 June 1940, with the heading **CIVIL DEFENCE** in large letters, was received by the Town Clerk in Sandwich demanding urgent action to be in the position of quickly erecting obstructions to disrupt any enemy airborne attack.

A similar document must have been sent to the Elham Emergency Committee; because they reacted and distributed a leaflet to residents in their area advising them what to do should an invasion take place. A portion of this document stated :

> Conveyances will, if possible, be provided to collect and carry the aged, infirm, and young children and those in charge of them only, and all others must proceed on foot. All children under five years old must be **labelled**. All articles unnecessary for subsistence to be left behind.

The Wiltshire Regiment arrived in the area to take up coastal defence duties, installing scaffolding and pile driving lengths of railway line into promenades to form anti-tank barriers. Vulnerable beaches had to be protected with a variety of concrete and steel anti-tank obstacles, minefields, barbed wire entanglements, flame weapons, infantry and

---

CIVIL DEFENCE

No. 12 (South Eastern) Region

BREDBURY,
MOUNT EPHRAIM,
TUNBRIDGE WELLS.

S E C R E T.

1st.June,1940

Dear Sir,

I am directed by the Regional Commissioner to say, for the information of your Authority, that it is necessary for the purposes of the Defence of the Realm to carry out in the Region a number of works of a Military nature, and he has been in consultation with the Military Authorities regarding the procedure for the direction of these works. It is essential that they should be executed with the greatest possible speed, and in carrying them out it will in some circumstances be necessary to invoke the assistance of Local Authorities. All works on highways, including the construction of new or improvement of old road blocks and obstructions against air landing, will be undertaken by the Ministry of Transport (Divisional Road Engineer, Ministry of Transport, Gaywood House, Great Peter Street, Westminster, S.W.1: Telephone, Abbey 2262) and Local Authorities will be expected to undertake all field and foreshore defence works. Powers exist under the Defence Regulations by which Local Authorities may be required to undertake

artillery fieldworks, and 'pillboxes'- small reinforced concrete blockhouses sited to cover road junctions with machine gun fire. Open areas and large fields considered suitable for enemy troop carrying aircraft were systematically obstructed. Streets in many towns and villages were protected by their designation as anti-tank islands or fortified settlements at major road intersections. By late summer 1940, the defences were springing up everywhere, their construction in the hands of a workforce of hundreds of thousands executed under the Army's Home Forces command. In the village of River near Dover, a villager recounts the story about an octagonal pillbox which had been constructed when some villagers got together to add a thatched roof, and painted the walls to depict a timber framed cottage with hollyhocks growing up. This disguise was fine in the summer months but the winter? Along the seafront at Deal and at Folkestone Harbour there are old photographs showing kiosks and other unlikely seaside buildings, and bus shelters converted into armed blockhouses including one disguised as a crane.

In June orders were given to arm the Dover promontory with heavy artillery capable of firing across the Channel. Winston Churchill, on a tour of inspection, visited the Dover area several times during this anxious time, and with the Commanding officer inspected the rapidly improving defences. Along the coast towards Romney Marsh the old Martello Towers and the old Redoubt on the Dymchurch Road were rearmed and reactivated.

The Prime Minister inspecting a static mounted 15 inch naval gun at Wanstone Battery.

The following coastal guns were installed in Thanet. At Fort Crescent in Margate 2 x 6 inch (152mm) naval guns were sited ; Ramsgate 2 x 6 inch (152mm) were installed opposite Wellington Crescent ; 4 x 4 inch (102mm) quick loading guns at Kingsgate Battery, Broadstairs and a further 4 x 5.5 inch (140mm) breech loading naval guns positioned near the North Foreland Lighthouse.

Winston Churchill in a letter dated 20 June 1940, indicated he was in favour of a means of hiding our industrial targets and regarded it as of the highest importance. Such was the fear of an imminent invasion the Ministry of Home Security issued the following statement stating:

> 'That it is desired that, as a matter of urgency, arrangements should be made for all industrial works to produce as much extra black smoke as is feasible, without incurring too much waste. This retrograde step is now regarded as imperative in the national interest which renders industrial targets less definable from the air should be taken forthwith'.

On the 23 June at 6.15 pm, a BBC broadcast by the Minister of Home Security, Herbert Morrison announced:

> *'Since last September three Fighting Services have been in action. Now the fourth, the new Civil Defence Services are going into action. Air raids have begun in earnest. To-night I have the opportunity of speaking to all of you men and women who belong to those services; Very many of you on duty; I am proud of this chance, for in these dangerous days you are in the Front Line'.*

Such was the need of manpower it was announced that persons of French nationality who may wish to resume service or apply to enrol in the Civil Defence Services could be accepted for service. Within a fortnight the Minister confirmed to the Town Clerk of Sandwich, that the establishment of full-time personnel engaged on the local emergency fire precautions arrangements in consequence of the compulsory evacuation of the District, be increased to 44 Auxiliary Firemen.

The Civil Defence Services went into 'overdrive'. Police were armed to shoot parachutists, and members of Deal Fire Service visited the rifle range in accordance with the popular 'learn to shoot' movement as the counties in the south east were alive with rumours of parachute landings. With army units stationed in the vicinity there was a need for training and rifle practice. A range was hastily set up in the chalk pit near Eastry South railway station. There was a moving target on steel wires where all types of hand-held weapons could be used.

Areas of open ground such as parks, sports fields and golf courses were dug up and cluttered with large obstacles to prevent gliders landing. Road and railway signs were taken down or defaced, along with many other signages in an attempt to confuse the enemy should they come. Those in Whitehall were convinced that from the speed of the German progress across Belgium and France, the next battle would most likely take place across Southern England, but unknown to British intelligence the Germans were not ready to launch an invasion.

With the increased threat of enemy air raids, the residents of this part of the county became concerned about the lack of proper protection. *The East Kent Mercury* reported that village schools were not to be equipped with air raid shelters, the reason being the labour required and the material and cost involved but precautions were to be taken against flying glass viz. to apply sticky tape to windows.

The Ministry stated that the stock of Anderson Shelters had been exhausted, and materials were needed for more important usage such as building tanks but shelters were to be redistributed from the areas which had already been evacuated. The Ministry also issued a pamphlet entitled *'Your home as an Air Raid Shelter'* for guidance of those householders not entitled to free domestic shelters who had not yet taken any steps to provide for their own protection.

Over Sandwich the first bombs were dropped missing the town and falling mainly on marshland and nearby Richborough Camp. Evacuation of the town was considered with families being advised to move out of the danger area, and by the end of the year only those involved in maintaining essential services remained.

The Government's advice to the people of this country in the event of an invasion seemed to be more about what we should do after the enemy had gained a foothold and to make his advance as difficult as possible. For example a public information leaflet issued in June 1940 stated:

**Do not give any Germans anything – Do not tell him anything
– Hide your food and bicycles.**

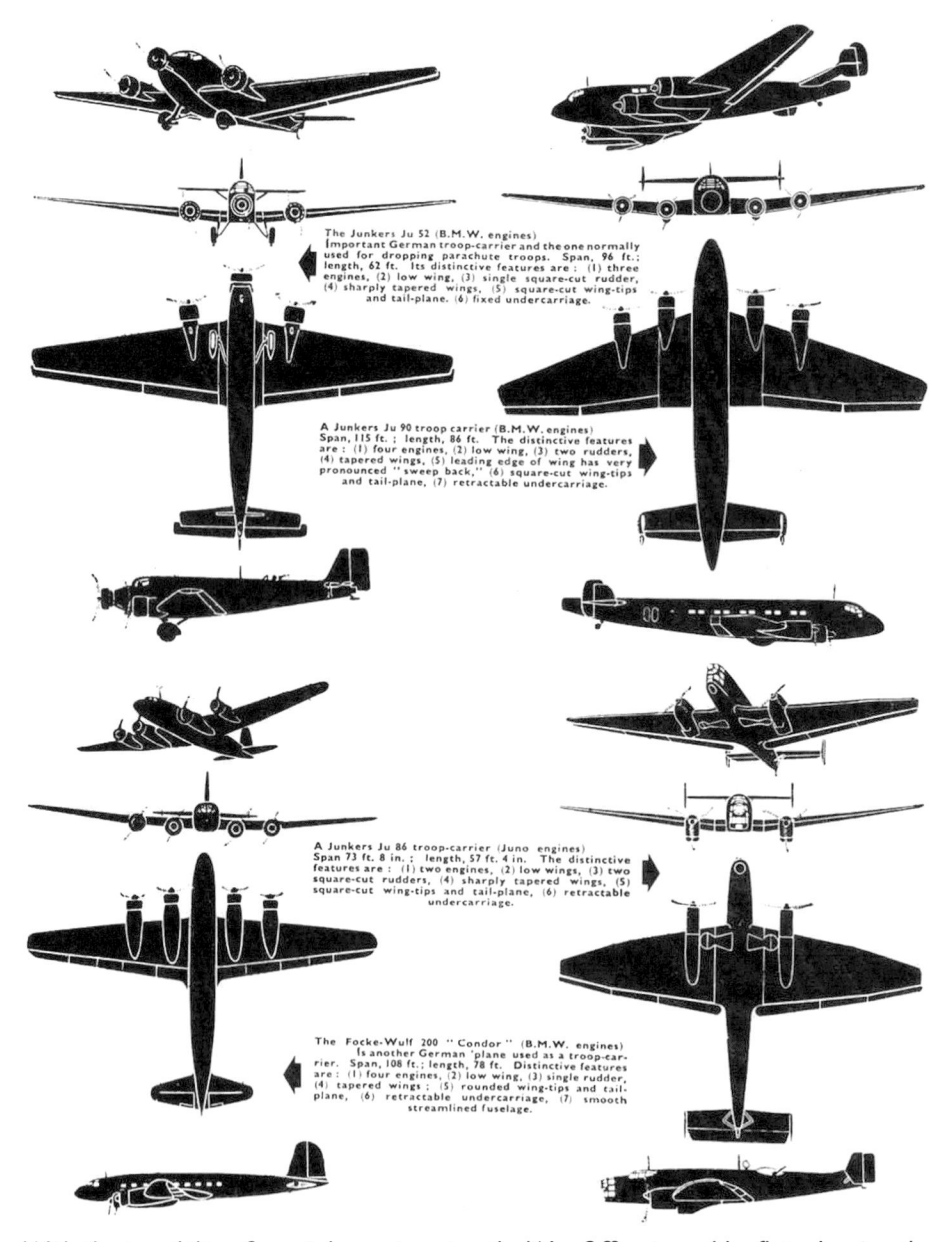

The Junkers Ju 52 (B.M.W. engines) Important German troop-carrier and the one normally used for dropping parachute troops. Span, 96 ft.; length, 62 ft. Its distinctive features are: (1) three engines, (2) low wing, (3) single square-cut rudder, (4) sharply tapered wings, (5) square-cut wing-tips and tail-plane. (6) fixed undercarriage.

A Junkers Ju 90 troop-carrier (B.M.W. engines) Span, 115 ft.; length, 86 ft. The distinctive features are: (1) four engines, (2) low wing, (3) two rudders, (4) tapered wings, (5) leading edge of wing has very pronounced "sweep back," (6) square-cut wing-tips and tail-plane, (7) retractable undercarriage.

A Junkers Ju 86 troop-carrier (Juno engines) Span 73 ft. 8 in.; length, 57 ft. 4 in. The distinctive features are: (1) two engines, (2) low wings, (3) two square-cut rudders, (4) sharply tapered wings, (5) square-cut wing-tips and tail-plane, (6) retractable undercarriage.

The Focke-Wulf 200 "Condor" (B.M.W. engines) Is another German 'plane used as a troop-carrier. Span, 108 ft.; length, 78 ft. Distinctive features are: (1) four engines, (2) low wing, (3) single rudder, (4) tapered wings, (5) rounded wing-tips and tail-plane, (6) retractable undercarriage, (7) smooth streamlined fuselage.

With the possibility of an air-borne invasion the War Office issued leaflets showing the silhouettes of troop carrying aircraft.

A poster issued by the Ministry of War Transport gave details on immobilizing vehicles, and failure to act would provide the enemy with transport. Advice for owners of petrol driven vehicles was – Remove distributor head and leads, and empty the tank or remove the carburettor. Hide the parts removed well away from the vehicle.

National Registration Identity Cards were issued to all civilians over the age of 16 years. Those under that age had a special one marked 'under sixteen years'. These cards stated the person's name, age, sex, occupation, residence, marital status and any reserve organizations such as the civil defence they belonged to. Everybody had to carry them and be ready to show them to the police, the military or members of the Home Guard in uniform on demand. These cards also assisted in the introduction of rationing.

People accepted the huge package of new restrictions telling them what to do if the enemy came. As spy fever grew roadblocks and checkpoints proliferated all over the countryside in a landscape with all the place names removed or obliterated. The Ministry of Information introduced more *'careless talk'* propaganda. It was designed to prevent the spreading of rumours, troop-movements and other security matters. **Even good news was suppressed!**

Before the war this country had been heavily dependent on food imports. This reliance had to be quickly reduced due to the enemy attacking our ships and by increased agricultural production. The emphasis switched from animal husbandry to arable farming, increasing the area of land under cultivation by about 50%. This radical change was assisted by the government providing subsidies to farmers as a reward for certain types of production. One such crop was flax. When Belgium was overrun by the Germans the products produced from flax such as all types of webbing, parachute harness etc., were difficult to obtain. The Ministry of Supply decided to introduce this crop in this country, employing men to advise farmers how to cultivate and harvest this. In addition the fact that flax requires to be pulled from the ground rather than being cut meant special machinery had to be developed to harvest it

Much agricultural land had been made over for growing potatoes which was a great success and farmers found this crop very much to their liking and produced good prices. Problems happened when the Prime Minister proposed to reduce the acreage of potatoes for the production of sugar beet which had a lower profitability. Churchill put his foot down and said *'measures should be taken to ensure that sufficient beet is produced, if necessary at the expense of potatoes.'*

In view of the threat of incendiary bombs instructions were issued to farmers detailing how they could protect their crops from being burnt and ruined in the following ways:
   (1) To prevent the fire from spreading, cut firebreaks lanes about 30 feet (9m) wide.
   (2) The lanes might be ploughed after cutting to increase protection.
   (3) Corn in stooks to be set in rows as far apart as possible.
   (4) It will be all to the good if the vacant stubble could be ploughed over.
   (5) Ricks should be separated from each other and from loose straw.
   (6) Farmers should be sure of having supplies of water ready during dry weather period.

(7) During the danger period, farmers should provide watchers to keep a lookout during day and night for outbreaks of fire.

(8) Farmers would do well to co-operate with their neighbours in the provision of watchers.

On the 5 June, the Kent Agricultural Wages Committee agreed a minimum wage and new holiday conditions for agricultural workers:

Workers 21 years and over at 48s. (240p) per week, with 50s. (250p) for specialists and proportionate increases for males under 21 years.

Female workers of 16 years and over are to receive ½d. an hour extra.

Overtime rates are to be 1s. 1d. (5p) an hour, with 1s. 2d. (6p) an hour on special days such as Good Friday and similar holidays. Men under 21 will receive pro rata rates. Holiday remuneration is to be increased by one sixth. Hours of work are to remain the same.

By July hop-growers in the surrounding area were getting anxious about picking. In most places there was not enough local labour to get in the crop and farmers felt that war restrictions may prevent London hop-pickers from entering restricted areas to gather the harvest. There were suggestions that soldiers should be used but that was mere speculation. Other questions were raised such as feeding and rationing arrangements for the pickers. The blackout was considered another problem in view of the pickers' fondness for lighting fires and the lighting arrangements in the camps would have to receive careful consideration. Such was the dilemma! However with the shortage of pickers local people, who would normally refuse to do this sort of work, rallied round to help. Many thought that their labour could be usefully turned into cash for the war effort, in particular for the Red Cross Fund.

Another dilemma was a restriction on the number of agricultural workers who could be employed at farms and nurseries. At Poison Cross Nurseries, Eastry, the Martin family ran a small agricultural business and they were forced to shed one of their number as they exceeded the specified quota. The Ministry of Agriculture decided that one of their sons should move with his family and take over the running of nearby Betteshanger Nurseries.

The Folkestone Herald reported that the Ministry of Food had given an order for the price of eggs to be increased in price by 3d. (1p) a dozen, to 2s. 9d (14p) for Grade 1 eggs. A ban was also imposed on making or selling iced cakes and the manufacture of candied peel and crystallized cherries, thus ending the making of traditional wedding and Christmas cakes.

By the 20th July *the Kent Messenger* carried a Ministry of Food announcement concerning the registration for Cooking Fats:

'From next Monday, July 22nd. Margarine & Cooking Fats will be rationed. You must now fill in the particulars on the 'Cooking Fats' page of your Ration Book, and also inside the front cover. Then take the Book to a retailer **immediately** for registration. With the coupons marked 'Butter & Margarine' you will be able to buy a total weekly ration of 6oz.(170gm).

With the coupon marked 'Cooking Fats you can buy 2 oz.(57gm) per week of lard or compound lard, or, if you wish, 2 oz.(57gm) of margarine. Dripping and suet are not to be rationed at present.

Tea is now rationed 2 oz.(57gm) per week. You may buy from any Shop you like - no registration is necessary, and may buy one week in advance'.

A couple of days later a slogan appeared in the press that said -

Help win the war on the kitchen front

We should use less tea. If each of us gives up one teaspoonful in every four, we shall save shipping space for 50,000 tons of war material in a year. This is a war contribution which one and all should make.

In a circular a few days later, the Minister of Food stated:

'It's desirable of making the greatest possible use of the ample supplies of fresh vegetables which are now available. Every possible step should be made for their consumption instead of tinned vegetables, in order to avoid any waste of valuable foodstuffs.'

I saw three ships a-sailing
But not with food for me
For I am eating home-grown foods
To beat the enemy
And ships are filled with guns instead
To bring us Victory

'Wanted urgently' notices were produced by the Ministry of Supply asking the public for their binoculars. They explained that owing to the expense of manufacture and the urgency of the need, it was thought the public would consider gifting or selling them as part of the war effort. The reason for this request was the urgent need for optics for gun sights and other vital war instruments. On a lighter note in Dover the 'B' Company of the Green Howards stationed in the town appealed in the *Dover Express* for the loan of a piano to liven up their off-duty hours.

The policeman's responsibilities at the outbreak of the war appeared endless. The Home Office announced that in view of the vital importance to Civil Defence of the police, the Government decided that the strength of these services must not be allowed to decline, and that wherever necessary they must be increased. This prompted the recruitment of Special Constables and War Reserve Constabulary. This new force, made up of many retired policemen, was given the responsibility of enforcing blackout restrictions and lighting regulations on vehicles. In addition they were required to round up aliens and in this area, with so many harbours along the coast, they helped immigration officers to check foreign nationals and to capture enemy spies before they gained entry.

It had become apparent that Germany's objective was to obtain a quick victory by the autumn or early winter of 1940. The British Government realized that before the

German Army could land it was necessary to destroy our coastal convoys, to sink or immobilize such units of the Royal Navy as would disrupt its landings, and above all to drive the Royal Air Force and our allies from the sky.

By the 18 June all the British forces had withdrawn from France. Both the RAF and the Luftwaffe had lost many aircraft and trained crews during the campaign and needed a while to replace their losses. During this time Britain built new fighter aircraft, trained pilots and brought them into service in readiness against the attack everyone knew was coming.

The lull, was vital to the British armed forces as it gave them time to prepare. By the beginning of July the RAF had built up its strength to 640 fighters as against the enemy who had about 2600 fighters and bombers. The stage was set. In the skies above southeast England the future of the nation was about to be decided.

The following is a short résumé and day by day accounts of actions occurring during the period, culminating in the battle in the skies known as the 'Battle of Britain'.

Whilst this battle was being fought day by day people in this area went about their business without appreciating fully what was happening overhead with hundreds of aircraft flying at speeds often in excess of three hundred miles an hour. On other occasions the sound of aeroplanes skimming over the houses and the rattle of machine gun fire brought people rushing out into their gardens. In the press *The Kent Messenger* ran a morale building article:

An RAF Spitfire.

> Dogfights on all sides, the roar of cannon and the rat-tat of machine gun bullets together with descending parachutes of men who had baled out were but a few of the exciting incidents which broke the quiet of the countryside in East Kent on Sunday.
> Columns of smoke arising from enemy machines already brought down in flames and the whine of still more falling to earth also contributed to a spectacle which all who saw it said they would not have missed for anything.

1 July – Several German Dornier Do.17 bombers were shot down by anti-aircraft guns around Dover.
3 July – Enemy bombers attack Hawkinge airfield. Little damage, as many bombs miss target. Dogfights between RAF and Luftwaffe fighters took place over Dover.
At about 4 p.m. sirens sounded in the Deal area with bombs falling at nearby Kingsdown. There were no casualties but a large amount of structural damage to property.
4 July – Dogfights over Manston airfield area with an RAF Hawker Hurricane Mk1 being shot down at St. Margaret's Bay, in which the pilot was killed. Another Hurricane was forced down at Manston with some damage.

5 July – A Super Marine Spitfire Mk1a limps back to Hawkinge airfield after being shot up in a dogfight with enemy fighters.
A German Heinkel He.11P was shot down in the sea off Lydden Spout. Some bombs dropped close to defences on the harbour breakwater at Dover.
6 July – Five bombs dropped on Dover by loan raider flying at high altitude in the early hours, resulted in some damage in the Buckland area.
7 July – Five bombs dropped in Dover Harbour. Later the same evening there was an aerial battle over the town involving approximately 50 aircraft, three enemy aircraft shot down, and a Spitfire Mk1a crashes in flames in a wood at Hougham. The pilot was killed.
8 July – In and around Dover, anti-aircraft guns were in action during the morning in which the RAF loses three aircraft and two pilots. In dogfights over Dover during the afternoon a RAF Spitfire Mk1a was shot down crashing into the sea. The enemy losses were three aircraft during this attack. A Messerschmitt Bf.109E fighter was shot down crashing in a field at Buckland Farm, near Woodnesborough.
9 July – Morning and afternoon enemy air raids took place over Dover with the local anti-aircraft guns in action.
Spitfires patrolling the North Foreland in the evening forced down a Heinkel He.11P bomber and accounted for four of the accompanying Messerschmitt Bf.109E fighters. Unfortunately three Spitfires were lost, one crashing into the sea off Dover and two being shot down near Manston.
A damaged Heinkel He.59 seaplane was captured whilst stranded on the Goodwin Sands. It was towed ashore at Walmer and later moved to Dover Harbour.
10 July – About 70 German aircraft attack a convoy off Dover. During this battle clusters of bombs fell around the ships with one smaller vessel being sunk The RAF lost three Hawker Hurricanes.
11 to 13 July – Intermittent air raids occurred in the area with little damage reported.
14 July- German Stuka dive bombers attack allied convoys in the Channel. Three ships were damaged (one with an unexploded bomb on board) and brought into Dover Harbour. There were five seamen killed and a number injured during this exchange. As this was happening the harbour was dive-bombed and a Norwegian merchant vessel hit. Several aircraft from both sides were lost.
German bombers attack Ramsgate Aerodrome which was at the time being used as a satellite airfield for Manston which was out of action due to constant air attacks.
15 July – In the early hours, Langdon Battery and the Duke of York's School were hit by incendiary bombs, resulting in some fire damage. Two 250kg bombs were dropped close to the accommodation buildings at the battery killing one soldier and injuring five others. After this attack the men began sleeping underground beneath the battery.
16 July – More dogfights out to sea, one enemy aircraft shot down near the French coast.
18 July - The Luftwaffe switched their attention to shipping and the Channel Ports. The coastguard station at St. Margaret's was also bombed. The Prime Minister Winston Churchill visited local coastal defences and inspected the 14 inch (356mm) naval guns at St. Margaret's.

19 July – A couple of enemy dive bombers attacked Dover Harbour during the day, were engaged by RAF fighters. It was estimated that ten enemy Stukas were shot down. One RAF Boulton Paul Defiant Mk1 fighter was shot down crashing at Elms Vale. Both the pilot and the gunner were killed.

20 July – Further attacks on Dover Harbour and on a convoy just outside. Twenty Stukas dive bombers attacked around tea time and a British destroyer was sunk. Further bombs were dropped near Admiralty Pier and in Snargate Street. Twenty RAF Hurricanes and Spitfires engaged a large number of German fighter aircraft who were escorting the dive bombers. Many aircraft on both sides were destroyed.

21 July – More enemy attacks on convoys in the Channel, one enemy fighter-bomber shot down.

24 July – After a lull in enemy activity for a few days due to bad weather, a minesweeping fleet came under attack and a couple of vessels sunk outside the harbour. Two enemy fighter-bombers were destroyed by RAF Spitfires.

25 July – During the morning a large number of enemy bombers and fighters attacked the Radar Station at Swingate. One enemy fighter was shot down with a light machine gun. Then in the evening four bombs were dropped close to the radar station but without causing much damage.

Most of the action was taking place out in the Channel with attacks on an allied convoy off Lydden Spout. During this attack four ships were sunk, two damaged and one ran aground beneath Shakespeare Cliff. The convoy was being escorted by two Dover based destroyers, both of which were so badly damaged that tugs had to help them back into the harbour. It was estimated that 300 to 400 aircraft were engaged in a daylong series of dogfights, finally the enemy withdrawing at dusk. The RAF lost six Super Marine Spitfires but the enemy lost a similar number of aircraft in the battle. Dover was also shelled with one missile falling in Market Street in the centre of the town causing a great deal of damage. Fortunately nobody was killed.

26 July – A RAF Hawker Hurricane Mk1 fighter operating out of Hawkinge was shot down possibly by friendly fire?

27 July – Two enemy air attacks were made on Dover Harbour during the afternoon with bombs being dropped on Marine Station. The destroyer HMS Codrington lying alongside HMS Sandhurst, a Royal Navy supply ship, moored alongside the Eastern Arm was attacked by a number of Heinkel He.111P bombers.

28 July – At about 2pm 100 bombers and fighters were engaged by four squadrons of RAF fighters over Dover without a bomb being dropped. The RAF lost two aircraft to the seven lost by the Germans.

29 July – About 80 Junkers Ju.87Bs with an escort of Messerschmitt Bf.109Es made a concentrated dive-bombing attack on Dover Harbour. Harbour installations set on fire. During the morning the Stores Depot Ship *Sandhurst* was set on fire alongside the disabled *HMS Codrington*. Two enemy dive bombers were shot down by the harbour batteries and four other enemy aircraft were destroyed by RAF Spitfires. The RAF lost a Spitfire and a Hurricane in the raid.

30 & 31 July – A 'balloon barrage' was installed and was promptly attacked by enemy fighters. They were engaged by Spitfires from Manston. After a dogfight the German airmen shot down two Spitfires and damaged another which landed in France with a wounded pilot. A Spitfire glided back to Manston after being shot up by Messerschmitt Bf.109Es off Folkestone.

During July it must be mentioned that the RAF were undertaking regular night and day raids on the French Channel Ports, and the explosions could be heard in the coastal towns.

Early in August the Ministry of Information in Whitehall issued a document headed **Air Raid Warning System**. It stated that whenever enemy aircraft approach this country, their movements are continuously reported by trained observers stationed around our coasts. All reports are sent to Fighter Command Headquarters, where the course of the raider is plotted on a chart.

As a rider a note was added *'The Government will do all in their power to protect the civilian population, but everyone is in the Front Line this time.'* The reason for this was due to the enemy aircraft deviating from the plotted course and bombing districts that had not been warned of an imminent attack.

Orders from German High Command gave the directive, that the assault on Britain would begin on 5 August, but there were several delays due to bad weather. **Eagle Day** as it was called was set for 13 August, when the Luftwaffe began its campaign to eliminate the Royal Air Force.

3 August – The Prime Minister visited the large guns being installed at St. Margaret's to find them almost complete. A section of 468th Searchlight Company Royal Engineers was established at Upton Wood at Shepherdswell.

5 August – During the morning bombs were dropped at Guston and at Whitfield. Others aimed at the searchlight installation at St. Margaret's missed, falling in the sea. Shipping was attacked in the Channel during the day by enemy aircraft. Super Marine Spitfires Mk1a and Hawker Hurricanes Mk1 fighters accounted for several enemy aircraft during various encounters.

8 August - During the hours of darkness the British Navy attempted to run a convoy of 25 merchant ships through the Strait, protected by barrage balloon ships and destroyer escort. When it became light the Luftwaffe launched the first of a series of mass air attacks which lasted for several hours. This was the beginning of ten days of dogfights. The drama was witnessed by hundreds of men and women in the towns and villages, as it took place high up against the background of a clear blue sky in a fierce and prolonged life and death battle. A Spitfire Mk1a crash-landed near Capel le Ferne due to engine failure.

9 August – The Swingate Radar Station attacked again by enemy bombers, buildings badly damaged but the radar towers remained intact.

12 August – Some of the first cross channel shells fell on Dover. Some fell at Buckland wrecking four properties, another behind the gas works killing two civilians, and another on Noah's Ark Terrace. Two shells missed the town exploding in Minnis Lane, River. Altogether twelve people were injured.

In the early morning the enemy began their attack by launching about two hundred aircraft in eleven waves against targets in the Dover area. Swingate Radar Station was again attacked causing slight damage to the towers. Langdon Battery was machine gunned by enemy aircraft.

In Col. Arnold's book *Conflict across the Strait* he stated:

> 'The balloon barrage was repeatedly attacked during this period. Also the harbour batteries were subjected to continuous machine-gunning. On the Eastern Arm, two planes regularly machine-gunned the battery between 8-9 am. each morning.'

The aerodromes of Hawkinge and Lympne were heavily attacked. At Manston two Bristol Blenheim Mk IV fighter bombers of No.600 Squadron were destroyed on the ground. Other bombs damaged the gas and water supplies to the airfield. A damaged Messerschmitt Bf.109E fighter was forced to land on farmland just north of Margate.

13 August - During low level night flying training, a Mk. III Spitfire crashed in the Eastry area killing the pilot. During the day a German fighter bomber was shot down crashing at Coldred.

A Dornier Do.17Z bomber was engaged by several Hawker Hurricanes off Whitstable and was forced to land at Stodmarsh, the German crew of four being captured.

Manston aerodrome was patrolled by No.11 Group fighters while the airfield was being repaired.

14 August – RAF Manston aerodrome was dive-bombed by Messerschmitt Bf.110Cs during a heavy air raid. On the ground four aircraft hangers and three Bristol Blenheim Mk IV fighter bombers of No.600 squadron destroyed. Two enemy aircraft were shot down by the air field's machine-gunners.

St. Margaret's was again attacked by enemy bombers. Bombs fell at Reach Road and in the churchyard causing damage to the church.

Enemy planes also attacked the balloon barrage in Dover Harbour.

15 August – A further mass attack by enemy aircraft accompanied by many dogfights over a large area. Local anti-aircraft guns shot down eleven enemy aircraft and the RAF also accounted for another three or four but lost a couple of Hawker Hurricanes.

In a document issued by the Ministry of Health, the district council was informed.

> Where the body of an enemy airman if found in your district it is your duty to attend to the burial of the body. The Clerk should first inform the nearest RAF unit who would remove the body to the local mortuary. Any effects found upon the body must be carefully preserved and handed over to the RAF officer. A report on finding the body a short statement should be sent to the Prisoners of War Information Bureau, with an indication of the RAF authority to which the body - effects had been handed over.

The airfields of Hawkinge and Lympne heavily attacked by enemy Junkers Ju.88A and Bf.109Es bombers. The main aircraft hanger and a small accommodation block were severely damaged.

A German Messerschmitt Bf 109E.

Both airfields remained out of operation for a couple of days. RAF Manston attacked again at midday by a dozen Messerschmitt Bf.109Es with cannon and machine gun fire, destroying two of No.54 squadron's Spitfires.

16 August - Enemy aircraft were intercepted over Eastry. Two fighter aircraft collided; the RAF pilot was killed, but the enemy Messerschmitt Bf.109E landed in fields nearby. Two other Super Marine Spitfires of No 266 Squadron were also shot down, one landing in a field near Adisham. A further Spitfire limps back to Hawkinge aerodrome after being damaged by friendly fire over Dover. An enemy raider was shot down in the Channel. This was part of the five to six hundred aircraft attacks the Germans made against our airfields in the southeast.

RAF Lympne, a First World War airfield, was also heavily bombed and many aircraft destroyed.

18 August – Enemy bombers passed over Dover making for inland airfields but encountered RAF Hurricanes and Spitfires. During the battle a Hurricane was shot down but six enemy aircraft were also accounted for. Around midday there were several bombs and incendiaries dropped in the Castle Avenue area of Dover and at Langdon but there was little damage or casualties.

During the evening 30 bombs were dropped on Deal by enemy aircraft. Fortunately there were no fatalities, just a few injuries. Fourteen houses were destroyed and about 300 were damaged, some seriously. Later in the evening more bombs were dropped at Mongeham, Sutton, Nonington and Elvington. No casualties reported.

RAF Manston again attacked during the afternoon by a dozen Messerschmitt Bf.109s, raking the airfield with machine gun and cannon fire. Two Spitfires of No. 266 squadron were destroyed on the ground and one airman and fifteen ground crew injured. A Hawker Hurricane which had been forced down during the morning was also destroyed in the raid.

It is estimated that in the first ten days of the battle the Luftwaffe lost over six hundred aircraft. Over the same period we lost about one hundred and fifty. The pace of battle was too hot to last. The German High Command called a halt and gave the Luftwaffe a rest period of five days.

19 August – A lone German bomber slipped in undetected as enemy fighters attacked Dover. Two bombs were dropped in a field between the Castle and Connaught Barracks, killing 10 military and navy personnel and injuring 14 whilst they were playing a football match. More bombs exploded in and around the Castle. A landmine killed a young soldier from the searchlight battery at Farthingloe, west of Dover.

20 August - The Prime Minister presented the House of Commons with a review on the progress of the war. He was speaking at a time when the battle was still taking place. Referring to the war in the air Mr. Churchill said:

> 'The gratitude of every home in our island and indeed throughout the world, except in the abodes of the guilty, goes out to the British airmen, who, undaunted by odds, unwearied in their constant challenge and mortal danger, are turning the tide of world war by their prowess and by their devotion. **Never in the field of human conflict was so much owed by so many to so few.**'

21 August – One soldier wounded at Langdon Battery by enemy machine gun fire.

22 August – A convoy was dive-bombed off Deal. Ships in the convoy engage enemy aircraft. A further convoy in the morning was shelled from enemy batteries at Gap Gris Nez.

Shelling continued during the day with the town of Dover, the Harbour, Buckland, River and St. Margaret's receiving shells. Two naval officers were killed in Maison Dieu Road. Many civilians were injured and taken to hospital during this barrage. Of the two 14 inch ex-naval guns 'Winnie & Pooh' manned by Royal Marine Siege Regiment on the old St. Margaret's Golf Course, one returned fire at the enemy's batteries across the Channel.

RAF Manston aerodrome attacked during the evening by enemy bombers and fighters. Fortunately there were no casualties and little damage to report.

23 August – Enemy shelling continued during the day destroying a building at the Dover Gas Works which affected the town's gas supply for a couple of days.

The search light unit at Kingsgate was machine-gunned during the night by enemy aircraft, which in turn, were engaged by anti-aircraft guns at Joss Bay.

24 August – The shelling of Dover continued virtually all day. The village of Temple Ewell in the Dour Valley received about 30 shells. Today enemy air raids were again more intense after a period of bad weather. There was considerable activity in the air for most of the day with raids by over 100 enemy fighters and bombers, which were engaged and driven away by several squadrons of RAF fighters. During the morning a RAF aircraft crashed into a field at Hammill on the outskirts of Eastry due to the pilot losing control of his aircraft after being attacked by enemy fire and being injured by a bullet wound through the ankle. Dogfights continued into the afternoon over a large area. A Spitfire was shot down near Shepherdswell and the pilot taken to hospital with considerable injuries. Three German fighters destroyed off Dover, one blowing up over St. Margaret's Bay, another crashing at East Langdon. A RAF Hawker Hurricane came down in Dover Harbour. An unspecified German aircraft was shot down in flames near Kearsney Railway Station. Two Spitfires were shot down, one near Deal and the other near Sandwich.

It was reported that four unexploded bombs had fallen near the searchlight battery at Littlebourne, and a further two at Snowdown Colliery in the evening. It was reported that the two at the colliery exploded later.

RAF Manston aerodrome was bombed three times in the space of five hours causing a great deal of damage. Aircraft hangers and aircraft destroyed and the field covered with craters. Allied fighters claimed five enemy bombers and two fighters for the loss of three of our fighters.

During the afternoon Ramsgate was attacked by a formation of German bombers targeting the town centre, Gas Works and Municipal Offices with high explosive bombs and incendiaries. Many houses destroyed and roads blocked, and gas and water mains fractured. Over 30 people killed and approximately 60 seriously injured. It was fortunate that a warning had been given and a great proportion of the town's population had managed to find shelter in the underground shelters.

The small airstrip used by Ramsgate Flying Club was attacked. A damaged Messerschmitt Bf.109E fighter was forced down at Northdown, Margate.

The Kent Messenger carried a story regarding air ace, Stanford Tuck, who had been attacking a formation of Junkers Ju.88As when his Spitfire was hit and came down at Lord Cornwallis's home at Horsmonden. The paper continues- The weary airman was allowed to rest. 'When the pilot awoke, Lord Cornwallis was able to tell him that he had the money to buy him a new plane.' His Lordship told a reporter he had had a telephone call from a gentleman who wanted to give £5000 toward the Spitfire Fund.

25 August – RAF Manston aerodrome was again attacked, and it is understood several aircrew were killed and several accommodation buildings badly damaged.

Wing Commander Robert Stanford-Tuck.

A Super Marine Spitfire crashed at Sandwich after being attacked by an enemy aircraft over Dover. During the afternoon a tragic accident occurred to the Earl of Guildford's son, Lord North, and his sister whilst out picnicking were killed by stepping on a mine at Sandwich Bay.

26 August – Dover continued to be shelled by the enemy's long-range guns but fortunately with many shells falling in the sea and in the fields surrounding the town. At midday about 150 enemy aircraft crossed the Channel near Deal, attacking the balloon barrage at Dover and Folkestone Harbours. Three enemy aircraft were destroyed; one crashing near Kearsney Railway Station and another near Sandwich, and a third was brought down by a balloon cable in the sea off Dover.

27 August – Enemy long-range guns shelled Dover again during the early morning causing much damage in the town. As darkness fell in the evening 'Winnie' our long range gun at St. Margaret's opened up, shelling the German gun positions on the French coast.

28 August – The Prime Minister visited Dover, RAF Manston aerodrome and Ramsgate during the day. Churchill's visit to Ramsgate coincided with the town being heavily bombed.

Barrage balloons attached to barges in the Dover Harbour were attacked by an enemy fighter. An RAF Boulton Paul Defiant Mk1 fighter was shot down near the town, but later two Messerschmitt Bf.109Es were destroyed during an afternoon raid. An RAF pilot was killed when his Spitfire was shot down near Deal, also

The Prime Minister during his visit to Ramsgate.

another two enemy aircraft were shot down, one landing at St. Margaret's and the other near Goodnestone.

Suspecting that the enemy was about to switch to more night raids a circular was sent from the Minister of Home Security stating, *'that in view of recent developments he is no longer able to permit the use of low intensity street lighting in any Borough, Urban District or Parish any part of which is situated within twelve miles of any part of the South Coast'.* The following day the Town Clerk of Sandwich replied rather sharply to the Ministry, stating that there is no street lighting in the Borough and no plan to install any.

A barrage balloon being taken out to a dump barge to protect the harbour entrance.

29 August – Large number of enemy aircraft flew over the coastal towns early in the morning to bomb inland airfields.

30 August – Electricity failure at the radar station resulted in non-detection of incoming German aircraft. Enemy aircraft attempted to bomb Deal Railway Station but resulted in bombs falling on Mill Road, Blenheim Road and Park Lane where two people were killed and several injured.

An enemy Heinkel He.11P bomber was shot down by Spitfires of No.242 Squadron near Manston.

31 August – Twenty of Dover's barrage balloons were shot down during an early morning attack but were replaced by lunchtime. In the evening there was a further attack on the balloons.

Citadel Battery overlooking the harbour engaged enemy E boats in the Channel.

A Dornier Do.17 bomber which had been shot up and damaged by ground fire crash-lands in Sandwich Bay. All the 4 crew captured. Another German bomber was recorded to have crashed at Eastry just after lunch.

An enemy aircraft dropped more bombs in the same area of Deal as the day before, this resulting in much damage but no casualties. Radar stations in the area also attacked.

Enemy aircraft formations attacked by RAF planes over St. Margaret's where there were many dogfights and much anti-aircraft and machine gun fire from local batteries. During the evening the RAF carried out attacks on German gun positions on the French coast.

1 September – Many enemy aircraft came over the coastal towns during the day to attack inland targets. In the evening more barrage balloons shot down at Dover.

2 September – Flights of enemy aircraft passing overhead to attack inland airfields. A German bomber crashed at Venson Down, near Tilmanstone, at midday killing all members of the crew.

An aircraft with a Polish pilot crashes near Elvington. During the morning a Hawker Hurricane Mk1 was shot down near Dover and later a Messerschmitt Bf.110C was forced down near St. Radigund's Abbey. Reports stated that the plane's observer had baled out but the pilot was captured close to where he had landed. Then at teatime another Hurricane lands north of Dover after an engagement with enemy fighters. At the same time the town of Herne Bay is bombed and a Spitfire Mk1a shot down close to the town.

3 September – A vast number of enemy formations passed over in the early morning to bomb inland targets. A Hurricane MK1 crashes near Snowdown Colliery. An enemy Bf.109E fighter shot down off Dover. A bomb was dropped between Hammill and Selson, Eastry, late in the evening.

Dogfights occurred over Margate where a Spitfire Mk1a was shot down. The pilot was later rescued by Margate lifeboat.

4 September – An RAF fighter crashes near Eastry in the morning after the pilot baled out.

Langdon Battery engaged an enemy seaplane, believed to be photographing the defences.

By midday large formations of enemy fighters and bombers had crossed the coast to bomb inland targets, in particular airfields.

5 September - At about 10am the first big enemy raid of the day started, firstly bombing Dover Harbour and docks on the way to bombing inland airfields. A Spitfire Mk1a was shot down by an enemy fighter near Dover during the afternoon.

6 September – An enemy Bf.109E fighter was forced down to land at Vincent's Farm, Manston.

7 September – Several bombs dropped near Deal Castle damaging several houses. The Germans again switched their attacks from fighter airfields to industrial and other targets, also making London their main bombing objective. Then, on their return trip, bombs were dropped on Dover Harbour and on fields to the west of the town. Two enemy aircraft shot down in a dogfight over the sea off Dover. A Hawker Hurricane Mk1 fighter crash-lands and explodes on impact at the top of Cowper Road, River. Four enemy aircraft shot down by anti-aircraft fire near Ramsgate.

An invasion alert issued during the evening.

8 September – The *East Kent Mercury* records an enemy bomber being shot down over farmland near Eastry. Eighteen bombs dropped at midday on the outskirts of Dover and the sea. One casualty reported.

During the evening enemy bombers attack Dover Harbour, and No.2 Citadel Battery emplacement damaged. Bombs dropped on Whitfield Hill, very little damage recorded.

9 September – Big air battles developed during the afternoon and included a heavy anti-aircraft barrage by the Dover guns, one enemy bomber shot down into the sea. During the early evening the town was heavily shelled, four civilians and one military person killed.

Bombs dropped at St. Margaret's in the evening 20 houses damaged, and a few people injured.

It should be remembered that throughout the battle the enemy made use of night as well as daytime bombing. The invasion ports along the French Coast attacked by RAF bombers.

10 September – Bombs dropped on Broadstairs during the evening, very little damage reported.

11 September – Today turned out to be one of the heaviest attacks on the town of Dover when 16 persons were killed and over 60 seriously injured requiring hospital treatment. It was also shelled between 6.30 and 11.00 in the evening, and a number of bombs landed in heavily populated areas causing much damage. The balloon barrage was attacked again by enemy fighters. The RAF brought down a German aircraft over the Western Heights but lost a Hurricane Mk1 over the sea.

Heavy enemy bombing also occurred at Deal, and two bombs were dropped near Worth. A major bombing incident at St. Margaret's was reported when two 500 kg bombs exploded along with several incendiary fires. A 250 kg bomb was dropped on the village of Guston during the evening.

The RAF again attacked the French harbours crowded with invasion barges during the night.

12 September – Our defences along the coast held on high alert.

The Prime Minister, Winston Churchill, arrived at Kearsney Railway Station to see the bomb damage for himself, and to check on the progress of anti-invasion defences. He was met by car at the station and chauffeured to the casemated headquarters beneath Dover Castle and later to carry out inspections of various batteries being built around the town or to the cross Channel guns at St. Margaret's.

Winston Churchill and General Bernard Montgomery on a tour of inspection of Fan Bay Battery.

13 September - Seven bombs were dropped in the Eastry district. Dover again attacked, enemy aircraft dropping bombs in the Elms Vale and Markland Road area during the afternoon, with six properties being totally destroyed and about 80 houses damaged.

Bombs dropped at Cliffsend, near Ramsgate, during the evening, properties slightly damaged.

14 September – Three bombs were dropped by enemy aircraft landing in the harbour area at Dover.

Two Hawker Mk1 Hurricanes were lost in dogfights during the day.

15 September – Early in the morning after the mist had cleared over the Dover Harbour, enemy aircraft were spotted and the town's air raid sirens started wailing. This attack was repelled and was all over by dinner time with the enemy in full retreat to their bases in Northern France.

There was a lull of about two hours before enemy aircraft reappeared in about the same strength as employed that morning. This time the German formations were quickly intercepted by squadrons of RAF fighters whose superiority was immediately established. This major encounter was described by Winston Churchill as the most brilliant and fruitful of any fought upon a large scale by fighters of the Royal Air Force. Dogfights taking place over a large area from London to the south coast. It was estimated that the enemy had lost several hundred aircraft in a single day.

One crashed at Adisham and two more were shot down by anti-aircraft guns at Dover.

Three bombs hit Langdon Battery close to No.1 gun. Two further bombs hit barracks injuring eleven soldiers.

16 September – At breakfast time nine bombs were dropped in the Elms Vale area of Dover, and later during the day the town was again shelled.

During the evening several bombs were dropped on Ramsgate seafront, little damage was reported.

17 September – Large formations of enemy fighters and bombers passed over to bomb inland targets, in particular, London. On their return in the evening some bombs were dropped in the area of Minster.

18 September - Large formations of several hundred enemy aircraft passed over Eastry making for Chatham and London. Two RAF Spitfires were seen to attack a German bomber which eventually crashed and burst into flames in a field behind Mill Bank Cottages at Eastry. Three of the crew managed to bale out, one being arrested at Heronden and another at Felderland, whilst the body of the third member of the crew was found in Knowlton Woods.

Three enemy aircraft shot down, one at Deal, another at Ash and the third at Worth. In the evening many bombs were dropped in the marshland near Ash, killing some animals. Just before dark three bombs were dropped near Sandwich close to or on St. George's golf course.

19 September – During an early morning raid incendiary bombs were dropped at Shepherdswell. There were occasions when the enemy jettisoned their heavy bomb loads before reaching their objective having come into contact with our fighters. On one such occasion ten bombs were dropped in a line from Farthingate, Eastry to Woodnesborough. Fortunately there were no casualties only broken windows. Mrs.V. Donaldson (writing from U.S.A) recalls this attack:

> 'My paternal grandparents were landlords of the Jolly Gardener (now The Blazing Donkey) during WWII, I remember the day one of the ten bombs on that location and the enormous bomb crater. Luckily nobody was hurt and today there are accommodation rooms built over the crater.'

One unexploded bomb was reported north of *The Lynch* in Brook Street and another in the fields east of the Church. The one near *The Lynch* buried itself in a bank which turned out to be a dud. It is said that one elderly lady was not so sure so she spent nights in a friend's house returning to her home each morning to see if it was still there!

20 & 21 September – Over the next two days our heavy guns at St. Margaret's bombarded the German batteries around Calais Harbour area.

In the air there was little activity except for enemy bombers passing overhead in the evening to bomb airfields around London. There were several dogfights overhead in which two RAF Spitfires and an enemy Messerschmitt Bf.109E fighter were shot down, and another Bf.109E was claimed by Dover's anti-aircraft guns. During the action a damaged RAF Spitfire landed safely at Manston.

22 September – Invasion alert (code name Cromwell) issued in the area during the day.
Four high explosive bombs were dropped near Waldershare Park, one of the bombs failed to explode. At Dover six soldiers serving with the Royal Artillery were killed when a mine exploded behind the Castle at Broadlees.

23 September – During the morning a 'stand down' invasion alert issued.
A German aircraft brought down in the sea off Kingsdown. 'Winnie' the heavy gun at St. Margaret's carried out another bombardment of Calais Harbour facilities.
Seven bombs dropped to the west of Dover during the day causing little damage.

24 September – In the early morning a lone bomber dropped three bombs at Great Farthingloe, near Dover, without causing any damage or casualties.
The batteries at Langdon and the Citadel were both in action against enemy shipping in the Channel.

25 September – Late in the afternoon four bombs were dropped at Sandwich, one blocking the railway line near the railway crossing on Woodnesborough Road. This caused some disruption.
Two bombs were dropped in fields between Tilmanstone and Guston followed by three more at West Langdon.
Towns in Thanet were heavily bombed during the day. Many bombs were dropped in the Margate district causing a great deal of damage, particularly in the Cliftonville and Northdown areas.

26 September – Four bombs dropped in the early hours in the Betteshanger area, little damage except that the electricity supply and telephone lines were put out of action for most of the day. A salvo of four shells fell in the Market Square area of Dover killing two people and injuring 18 others.
At Minster three high explosive bombs dropped in the adjacent marsh land killing some sheep.

27 September – Mass enemy attacks in Kent as formations of aircraft advanced against London. A damaged German fighter-bomber crash-lands in Northbourne Park.
One bomber attacked Dover dropping four bombs in the Maison Dieu Area. This was followed by some shelling later in the day centred in the Connaught Park area of the town.
Dogfights continued, three Messerschmitt Bf.109Es shot down over Dover but the RAF also sustained some losses.

28 September – Large formations of German aircraft crossed the Channel between Deal and Dungeness. Two RAF Hurricanes shot down, one pilot killed. During the morning five bombs and incendiaries dropped in the Frith Farm area of Dover, causing little damage but small fires.
The Folkestone Herald reported that a local man had swum out to rescue a German airman who had been shot down into the sea off Folkestone.

29 September – A morning of enemy bombing at Dover mainly in an area behind the castle near Connaught Barracks.

30 September – Just before midday Dover was again shelled causing a great deal of damage to about 60 properties. There were two civilians killed and 11 injured.

During the afternoon towns in Thanet attacked again, very little damage reported.

A war damaged street in Dover.

2 October – Enemy aircraft bombed Dover, resulting in casualties in the Clarendon Street area of the town.

4 October – Eight people were killed in Middle Street and Union Street, Deal, when a single enemy aircraft dropped bombs destroying the *Victory* public house and four other properties.

6 October – The final stage of the battle began. The enemy's strategy and method of attack changed completely. He withdrew nearly all of his long-range bombers and tried to achieve his end by means of fighter and fighter bombers. These fighter-bombers were Messerschmitt Bf.109Es fitted with a makeshift bomb carrier enabling them to take a pair of bombs and travel at 300 mph. The enemy preferred to send the major bombing force over during the hours of darkness, and this he did in increasing numbers.

9 October - Another rather amusing event is recorded, when an enemy fighter crash-landed at Venson Farm, Eastry. Apparently the pilot's life raft accidentally inflated in the cockpit making him lose control and crash. The pilot was unhurt in this extraordinary incident.

18 October – A shell fell on the Sergeants' Mess of the Pier Turret Battery in the harbour, killing two soldiers and wounding three others.

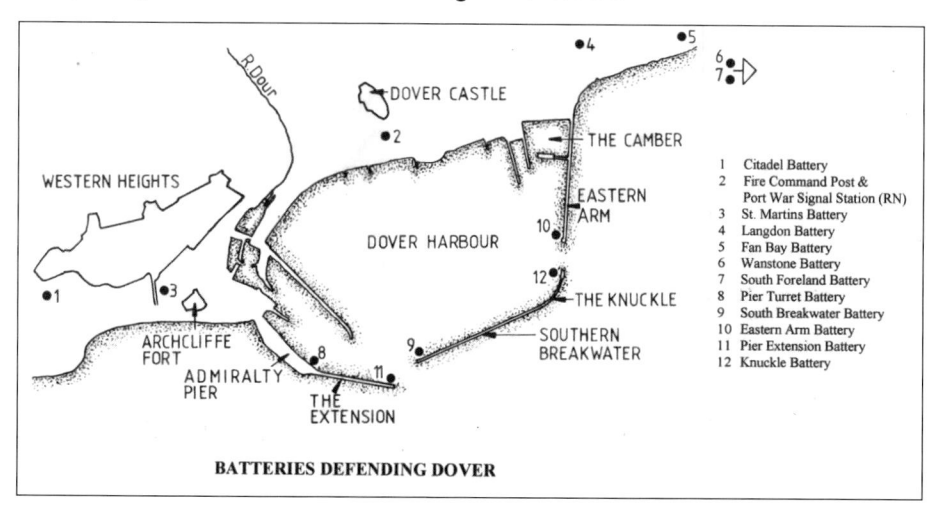

1 Citadel Battery
2 Fire Command Post & Port War Signal Station (RN)
3 St. Martins Battery
4 Langdon Battery
5 Fan Bay Battery
6 Wanstone Battery
7 South Foreland Battery
8 Pier Turret Battery
9 South Breakwater Battery
10 Eastern Arm Battery
11 Pier Extension Battery
12 Knuckle Battery

BATTERIES DEFENDING DOVER

28 October – Dover again was attacked. Three bombs exploded harmlessly in Crabble Athletic Ground, just damaging the cricket pitch.

30 October – Three shells landed in front of the Observation Post of Langdon Battery injuring six soldiers. A dozen shells hit the Western Heights close to Citadel Battery, destroying the bridge across the moat and badly damaging the old Officers Mess.

31 October - This phase of the battle was over. From the beginning of October raids tended to peter out as the weather conditions worsened. It did not cease immediately but bitter experience had at last taught the enemy the cost of daylight attacks causing them to revert to mainly night attacks. However some intermittent daylight attacks continued, concentrating on what was called hit-and-run tactics which involved one or two fighter bombers coming in at tree top level, attacking the coastal towns and installations in East Kent.

What the Luftwaffe failed to do was to destroy the fighter squadrons of the RAF which were indeed stronger at the end of the battle than at the beginning. Command of the air space above the Channel and the beachheads was vital to the German plan, and as supremacy had not been established this meant a tremendous setback denying Hitler the chance of successfully invading and securing this Island when we were at our most vulnerable. Any ideas of an invasion would have to be postponed until 1941. From these accounts it can be seen what a tremendous strain was put upon service personnel on both sides, and at what cost. Between the 8 August and 31 October, 2,375 German aircraft are known to have been destroyed. The allied air force lost 375 pilots killed and 358 wounded and many aircraft.

This was the price; such was the Battle of Britain!

By now the RAF and their allies had asserted their mastery of the air in southeast Britain. In addition the Canadian Army Corps was positioned between the capital and the channel ports. Vast intricate systems of fortifications, blockhouses and pillboxes stretched as far as the eye could see, and the coastline bristled with masses of artillery pieces.

During August the bodies of about 40 German soldiers were washed up at various points along the south coast, which led to a widespread rumour that the Germans had attempted an invasion and had suffered heavy losses. The British Government deliberately took no steps to contradict such rumours knowing that the enemy's loss of life was probably due to RAF bombing of invasion barges, practicing embarkation along the French coast.

During the first week in September, four German spies were captured after landing from a rowing boat on the Kent coast. When interrogated they confessed to being spies, and had been instructed to report on movements of troops in the Home Counties and the east coast area.

With the moon and the tides favourable for an invasion on the nights of the 8th to 10th September, it was considered possible that the enemy would attempt an invasion on the southeast coast, so the Chiefs of Staff concluded that the defence forces should go to battle positions. All leave was stopped and those on leave were ordered to return immediately. So the code-word '**Cromwell**' which signified '**invasion imminent**' was issued on the evening of 7 September to both Eastern and Southern Commands. This activated the Home Guard who immediately blocked roads and manned their positions. Church bells were rung out over a large area intimating that the enemy had landed or were at least on their way. This led to more rumours of enemy parachutists and landing craft nearing the coast.

It was likely that the next morning there were plenty of red faces amongst the Chiefs of Staff when it was realized that no invasion attempt had been made during the hours of darkness. Although this overreaction served as a useful rehearsal for all concerned, the chiefs did establish that 'Cromwell' was rather a clumsy procedure and new orders had to be issued. These orders were:

Stand To – Would indicate conditions favourable for an invasion. Troops to be in a state of readiness. All posts and road blocks manned.
The Command Reserve would be at 3 hours' notice to move.
Action Stations – On this order the Reserve would be at 1 hour's notice.
Command headquarters would then be in the position to issue specific orders as and when needed.

The Home Guard was instructed that even when the code-word 'Cromwell' was issued, they would not be called out except on specific tasks. The instruction to ring church bells was given to the local Home Guard member only to ring them when he personally spotted a large number of parachutists about to land and not because he heard the next parish's bells ringing.

This invasion alert lasted until the 19 September when the authorities considered the threat had passed. Those troops still in Southern Command were ordered to a new state of readiness, with all beaches to be patrolled during the hours of darkness.

The military authorities realized that boredom could be a major problem in static defence, and to overcome this advanced training was introduced which included getting to know the area being defended. They made it the responsibility of every officer to keep their men alert and well prepared in the event of an invasion.

A poster printed in readiness should an invasion occur but never displayed.

The presence of a 'fifth column' (sympathizers or hostile infiltrators) which would assist the enemy was feared by our Government, and was complicated by the large numbers of refugees and foreigners fleeing from the advancing Germans on the continent. In a confidential document entitled *'Powers of the Armed Forces engaged in Active Operations'* sent to the Sandwich Town Clerk, it was made clear that in the event of an invasion the Military Authorities would have such powers as the Military needed and the situation required, in dealing with an invasion or 'armed insurrection' without any declaration of Martial Law. The mention of an armed insurrection would today be considered very unlikely but during the first couple of years of the war it was an outside possibility.

Sir Oswald Mosley's 'Blackshirts' or the British Union of Fascists, had a local office in Strand Street, Sandwich, and he used to stay at Lady Pearson's house in Sandwich Bay. Lady Pearson was known as a keen supporter making all her staff belong to the BUF, and stand in the streets of the town on Saturdays selling the movement's literature. Mosley's organization had, in the years leading up to the war, attempted to establish a substantial Fascist presence in this country but was reliant on foreign powers such as Mussolini, and the support of right-wing aristocrats residing in this country for funding.

Sir Oswald Mosley with his black shirted supporters.

Another right-wing extremist of the BUF and close associate of Mosley was Captain Robert Gordon-Canning. M.C. who lived on the Sandwich Bay Estate. It was said that the Prince of Wales, before his abdication, met there at weekends to play golf at St. Georges. In 1938 he broke with Mosley becoming a member of the anti-war group, the British Council for Christian Settlement. He was later detained under 18b of the Defence Regulation until 1943.

By the mid 1930s the BUF had 50,000 members but Moseley's attempt to radicalize British workers failed. Late in 1936 the Government, in an attempt to recover the situation, passed a Public Order Act banning the wearing of paramilitary uniforms, together with slogans likely to cause a breach of the peace. Even so British intelligence was aware of at least 20,000 organized German Nazis living in England at the time. Beneath the surface the tension remained but Mosley's dream of a fascist nation in line with German propaganda was dashed, and when war was declared Mosley and his major supporters were rounded up and imprisoned.

During the summer and autumn months the erection of German gun emplacements between Calais and Boulogne could clearly be observed from the cliffs around Dover. This caused Winston Churchill much concern who felt that some positive action was needed. In a memo sent to the First Sea Lord the Prime Minister suggested that the old monitor ship, *HMS Erebus*, mounting two 15 inch (381mm) guns, be used to bombard these installations. For unknown reasons this action was never authorized.

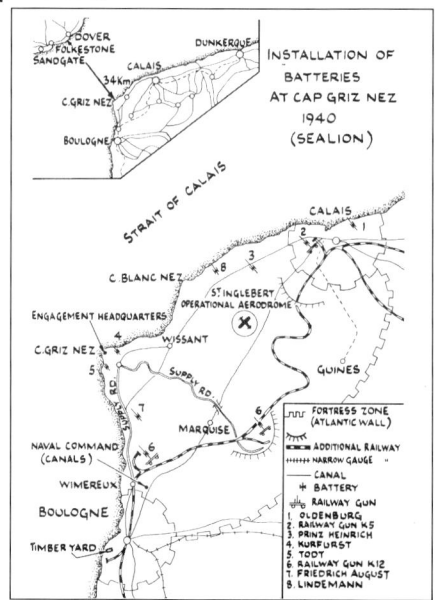

In addition, the Germans assembled a number of railway mounted guns, capable of firing across the Channel. It was reported that they had taken the large weapons from captured French naval warships.

When by September one of the largest German batteries was ready for action, the British had no answer to such a barrage, and any reply would only be a token gesture by a couple of static guns at St. Margaret's east of Dover Harbour.

Whilst all the aerial activity against British targets continued, the proposed 'Invasion of England' was being filmed for German newsreels. On the 1 and 2 September a mock invasion took place in Antwerp Harbour and on beaches close by representing beaches on the south coast of this country. For two days troops and light tanks went ashore firing at imaginary targets creating filmed footage and stills for publicity purposes and for propaganda. Hitler was so convinced that an invasion was possible that sets of postage stamps were designed and proofed ready for issue.

To counter a threat that was developing on the south coast General Brooke, now Commander-in-Chief Home Forces, announced he was able to provide sixteen divisions, three of which were armoured divisions, all of which were additional to local coastal defence units and could be ready for action at great speed in the event of an enemy landing.

By the end of the year conditions for the county's Fire Brigades and Auxiliary Fire Service (AFS) had improved with derelict sub-stations made serviceable and supplied with suitable towing vehicles for their pumps. These services were issued with guidelines if called to the scene of an aeroplane crash fire:

Identification : It is very important to differentiate between a bomber or a mine carrying plane, particularly if carrying a live load.

Rescue : Every effort should be made to rescue members of the crew if at all possible. If a bomber containing live bombs crashes in the open where the explosion could do little or no harm, it should be allowed to burn out but only if there was no hope of saving the crew.

Attacking the fire : Speed in getting water or foam on the fire is of the utmost importance. Police, Air Raid Wardens and others should be advised to warn persons in houses within 200 yards (183m) to leave.

The Fire Brigade is responsible for extinguishing the fire and endeavouring to save life. Directly this has been done the Royal Air Force authority should take charge.

A circular from the Home Office (Fire Brigades Division.) headed –**'Fires and the Blackout'** arrived on the Sandwich Town clerk's desk. It stated:

'…a number of enquires have been received as to the obligation of a fire authority to extinguish a fire, where it may be open to doubt whether any substantial danger to life or property is to be apprehended from the continuance of the fire and the principle reason for its extinction is that, if not extinguished, it will continue after dark and act as a beacon to hostile aircraft. In certain circumstances outbreaks on heaths and common land, fires in hay ricks, rubbish dumps and the like would be instances

> of such fires, and doubts have been expressed whether the obligations imposed under the Fire Brigades Act, 1938, extend to their extinction'.

The Home Office Minister gave the following order:

> ' any fires which, by reason of the display of light therefrom, would involve an offence under the Lighting (Restrictions) Order 1940'.

In a circular addressed to the Fire Service and marked **SECRET** there were instructions relating to unexploded parachute mines. It stated that:

> Houses should be cleared within 200 yards (185m) of a mine and persons advised to open windows and keep clear of glass within a distance of 500 yards (462m). The Police have been instructed that wheeled traffic should not be allowed within 400 yards (369m), owing to the risk of detonating the mine by vibration. Fire fighting, rescue work and first aid should continue, but Fire Brigades should bear in mind the risk of explosion due to vibration and it is dangerous to operate a fire pump within 200 yards (183m) of an unexploded mine.

Even before the sustained bombing of the towns and cities inland, the coastal towns and particularly Dover with its port facilities, became a magnet to enemy bombers. The town's fire service had also to deal with many stricken and blazing vessels which had been attacked whilst sheltering in the harbour. The destruction wrought on the coastal towns was continuous between September 1940 and October 1941.

Town	No. of Raids	Property Severely Damaged
Dover	53	9,000
Margate	47	8,000
Ramsgate	41	8,500
Deal	17	2,000
Folkestone	42	7,000

The air sea rescue vessels operated out of Dover and Ramsgate Harbours and were clearly marked. Their task was to patrol the channel especially after dogfights or after some of our planes had been on raids on the Continent. Ditched airmen of all nationalities were picked up. In addition there were rescue buoys anchored in a line about five miles apart and about seven miles off our coast. These contained survival kits, blankets and bunks, and were visited each day by our air sea rescue craft.

It was said that enemy bombers flying at 20,000 feet could clearly see a light shining from a small window. In rooms where people needed to switch on a light the windows had to be covered with thick curtains. Some people made wooden frames fitted to the shape

An Air Sea Rescue vessel picking up a British airman from a rescue buoy.

of the window and covered with special blackout material, and if removed during the day had to be refitted each evening. It was part of the air raid warden's duty to patrol the streets and knock on the doors of any houses showing a light. Of course, with no street lights on during blackout the only light on a clear night came from the moon. A full moon with no cloud was nicknamed 'A Bomber's Moon', and people did not venture out.

With so many problems caused by the blackout the Prime Minister suggested that perhaps some consideration should be given to 'decoy lighting' and 'baffle lighting' in open fields and at suitable distances from vulnerable points in an attempt to confuse German aircraft.

During this period it had become apparent that some regulations regarding the blackout were being flaunted. By order of the Regional Commissioner of Police, under the Defence Regulations, all public houses, clubs, cinemas and restaurants must close by 10 o'clock at night on and after this Saturday 21 September. The premises mentioned in the order must close as stated and remain closed until half an hour before sunrise the next morning.

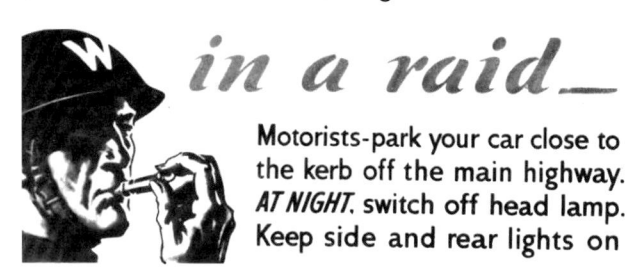

in a raid —
Motorists-park your car close to the kerb off the main highway. *AT NIGHT.* switch off head lamp. Keep side and rear lights on

A poster instructing motorists how to park during a blackout.

In 1940 nine out of ten families did not own a car so most people got about on foot and public transport. For many people the blackout was the source of grumbling; getting lost or tripping over something and getting hurt trying to get home after dark. Cars were fitted with headlight masks of an official design but only one headlight could be lit at a time and one bulb was removed. Motorists, who parked their cars on the road at night, had to keep side and rear lights on to prevent accidents. Driving a car or lorry was a nightmare particularly at night as there were no signs or white lines so a 20 mph speed limit after dark was introduced in an attempt to combat the high number of road accidents. One horrendous accident happened on the Thanet Way during the night, when two doctors and one of their wives were killed when their car hit a concrete road block.

At the same time fire brigades were concerned about vehicle lighting in air raids during hours of darkness. The Minister issued details of permitted lighting:
    1. One masked headlamp and the other with distinctive 'Fire' illuminated sign.
    2. The side and rear lamps dimmed in the prescribed manner.

In a collision on Crabble Hill between a Rescue Squad vehicle and a lorry going to the Auxiliary Fire Service station at *Woodlands*, a Dover Councillor was injured. The accident was caused by one vehicle not showing lights in accordance with the instructions of the military.

In a circular from the Home Office in September the Minister thought that Observation or Watching Posts would prove useful in detecting and locating fires, exploding bombs or other incidents caused by enemy action, or occurrences such as the illicit use of signal lights or other signals being given to enemy aircraft. He said that in a small town a single post may suffice if it could be sited in a position commanding a clear view. The Town Council in Deal introduced training courses under the 1940 Fire Watchers Order for aeroplane spotters. Another important consideration that had to be tackled urgently was the locating and extinguishing of incendiary devices before they had set fire to buildings as these would serve as a beacon for further enemy attacks.

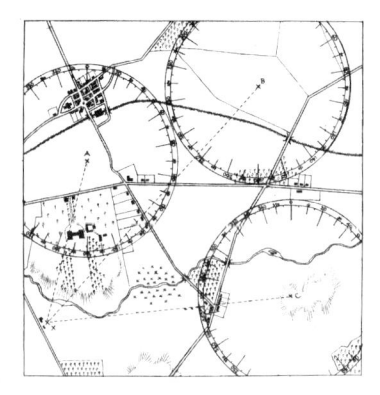

DIAGRAM OF MAP AT KEY POST ILLUSTRATING BEARINGS TAKEN FROM POSTS A, B, & C OF INCIDENT AT X

A document showing how to pinpoint an incident.

The Minister of Home Security in a circular refers to the *'arrangements which have been made with representatives of various churches, whereby selected ministers may be allowed the freedom of the streets during air raids'*. They would be given a distinctive armlet and a pass. The selected clergymen were advised to make themselves known to the wardens and first aid posts in their area.

In another circular the Minister, writing to town clerks, stated that with a view to enabling air raid wardens to carry out their duties more efficiently, arrangements have been made with the Post Office to provide additional telephone facilities.

A humorous commercial advert with the caption 'There's been a serious incident, somebody's swiped the OXO'.

It was announced by the Government that a supply of ear plugs was available to those who wished to have them. They suggested that the recipients should tie them together and hang them up so they would not get mislaid as there were no replacements! It was also announced that the Ministry of Supply was arranging the massed production of a composition helmet for air-raid protection. These so called 'Rag Hats' would provide a measure of protection against falling metal splinters, and was to be a temporary arrangement until steel helmets could be manufactured.

Sleep while wearing **Aurax** Ear Protectors
The only anatomically designed ear plugs

With so many no-go areas in the district it became a major problem where delivery lorries were to park and off-load their materials. On one occasion a lorry driver from Dover was killed by a land mine. At the inquest it appeared that he and a companion began to unload in an area that appeared to be outside a restricted boundary barbed wire entanglement when the explosion occurred. During the investigation it was established that the boundary moved in strong winds exposing the area where the materials were being unloaded.

It was reported that the Ministry of Supply expects that many windows would continue to be broken during air raids, and during the winter months glass may become scarce. They advised utmost economy in replacing broken window glass recommending that some might be boarded up as full-sized glazed windows could not be guaranteed. All glass should be removed and stored when hot-houses were not in use and replaced only when needed.

The Kent Messenger did their best to keep the county smiling. There were many witty quips published in the newspaper which were meant to act as a morale booster. *'It might have been worse' laughed a woman whose house had been shattered by a bomb…'We are alive and that's something. The house was not worth anything, it ought to have been pulled down long ago. The furniture was not paid for, so you see we can still keep smiling'.*

'A woman was busy engaged in making Christmas puddings when a bomb exploded in the garden. She was unhurt but the Christmas puddings completely disappeared.

A woman had a narrow escape the other day when she was reading by a window during an air raid and a fragment from a shell flew through the window and cut her book in half. She was unhurt but wiser after the event.

A white cat was asleep in a box when a bomb fell within yards of it. The cat disappeared. When it returned five hours later – it was a black cat!'

As shortages and rationing increased a strange piece of graffiti appeared chalked on walls, it was called 'Mr. Chad'. This mythical cartoon character appeared looking over a wall with a slogan that said *'Wot, no sugar ?'* or *'Wot, no ciggies ?'*. Another attempt to keep people smiling was the introduction of supplementary petrol coupons. These could be claimed for extra domestic or business needs in the government's *'Help Your Neighbour'* free lifts scheme.

It was the fear of looting as much as anything that made people unwilling to leave their damaged properties. The offenders, when caught, also caused the authorities a headache as to how to administer appropriate punishment. The Prime Minister, writing to the Home Secretary in late November, also had a dilemma with the great disparity in the sentences the courts were handing out, and he thought it was about time there was a standardization of punishment.

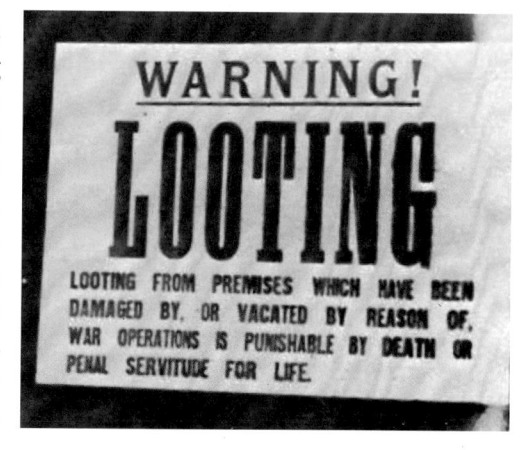

People must be made to realize that looting was stealing. The bombing and destruction of property together with the blackout provided a form of cover for all sorts of criminal activities from the worst crimes to people making false claims for the loss of ration books.

It was said that in Dover and, most likely in other towns which experienced the blitz, damaged homes were boarded up prior to the owners moving to a safe area during the summer when invasion looked likely, but upon returning home found their homes had been stripped bare of everything remotely portable. Such wilful theft would have compounded their misery.

On a different scale in late September at Ramsgate a First Aid worker was prosecuted for removing a machine gun as a memento from a Heinkel He.11P bomber which had crashed on the foreshore.

Shelling of Dover Habour by German long-range guns occurred during the latter months of the year with reports of damage and casualties to the batteries in the harbour area. On 27 November the Eastern Arm Battery was heavily shelled and an operator on the adjacent searchlight emplacement was killed. The South Breakwater Battery experienced sustained shelling during December. One shell damaged the cookhouse, three searchlight emplacements were hit and the battery observation post damaged. In all six servicemen were wounded.

In the *East Kent Mercury* as autumn gave way to thoughts of winter the Borough Engineer of Deal offered small quantities of firewood free of charge to householders. Warnings to householders in the Boroughs of Deal and Sandwich were ordered not to order more than a ton of coal and to save as much fuel as possible for the winter.

The Ministry of Information made a plea to people writing letters to Prisoners of War at Christmas, not to be careless in giving the enemy valuable information such as making mention of air raid damage, locations of factories, camps or aerodromes, movement of troops or anything that may be of use to the enemy.

The Ministry of Food issued a couple of circulars on 3 December. Firstly they wished to draw people's attention to the need for stringent economy in the use of liquid and tinned milk in the present circumstances. Secondly, in consultation with the Minister of Health they announced:
> In the interest of public health and that the best possible use may be made of all available foodstuffs, that no carcasses or portions of carcasses or offal should be condemned, unless there is definite evidence that it is unfit for human consumption.

In late December, Churchill wrote to the Home Secretary expressing a feeling that it was about time to refine treatment of internees who had been arrested and held in custody at the start of the war. He felt that the action was initially justified but retention was at variance with British Liberty (*habeas corpus*), and should be relaxed. For example he asked is it right that the wife of Oswald Mosley is not permitted to see her young baby?

On the 21 December the Ministry of Health wrote to the clerk of Eastry Rural District Council regarding arrangements for the provision of accommodation for persons rendered homeless by enemy bombing. He stated that the situation had been assisted by homeless persons being looked after by other householders in the neighbourhood, and he had decided to issue a billeting allowance at the rate of 5 shillings (25p) per week for each adult and 3 shillings (15p) per week for each child under 14 years, payable to the householder providing the accommodation.

Railway mounted guns were positioned at Lydden and Guston tunnels on the Dover-Deal line. The old colliery sidings which had a direct railway connection with the main Dover-Canterbury line at Stone Hall, Lydden, were to be used as a 'Gun Park' for the maintenance and repair of 13.5 inch (343mm) railway mounted guns. The guns would be hidden in the tunnels together with their ammunition wagons when not in use.

The Prime Minister inspecting one of the railway guns in its firing position.

The East Kent Light Railway which had derived most of its income before the war from the movement of coal from Tilmanstone Colliery had, by the end of 1940, been equipped with massive railway mounted guns controlled by the military. The 5th Super Heavy Battery manned their 12 inch Howitzers south of Eastry at Shepherdswell and at Eythorne. In addition the 12th Super Heavy Battery took up positions at Poulton Farm in the village of Ash, and at Staple Station which is said to have fired only twice in practice. During the war years the small railway had a significant upturn in freight as large quantities of ammunitions and other pieces of equipment were transported to the various sites in the area.

To address a serious manpower shortage the Home Security Ministry issued a circular in which it highlighted the necessity to take swift action in view of serious deficiencies in the Police and Auxiliary Fire and First Aid Services. So it had been decided that men over the age of 30 registering under the National Service Act between the dates 11-18 January next, and who are not in reserve occupations, shall be given the option of applying for full-time service in one of the above services. Also men and women between the ages of 16 and 60 have been ordered to register for part-time Civil Defence work.

King George VI encouraged his subjects in his Christmas broadcast on the radio. He said:
> 'Remember this if war brings separation, it brings new unity ….. The future will be hard, but our feet planted on the path of Victory and with God's help we will make our way to Justice and Peace.'

The second wartime Christmas must have felt very strange with many families fragmented and not knowing what was going to happen next. It was **Xmas on the ration**, with food rationing having been a part of everyday life for almost a year. By this time weekly rations were 4 ozs. (113 gm) of bacon or ham, 6 ozs. (171 gm) of butter or margarine, 2 ozs. (57 gm) of tea, 8 ozs. (227 gm) of sugar, 2 ozs. (57 gm) of cooking fats and meat to a value of 1/10d. (9p.), although a week before celebrations were due to start the Government doubled the tea ration and increased the sugar ration to 12 ozs. (342 gm). There were still some non-rationed foods available, however, at a price. Gifts for Christmas were still available. The more practical ones were in vogue such as gardening tools, seeds or a bag of fertilizer but the most popular present for adults was bars of soap.

On 27 December, the Minister of Home Security issued his New Year message thanking the Civil Defence:

> The year that is now ending has given the Civil Defence Services a very severe test. All who belong to those services may justly be proud of playing their part in a task that has been well done. Under heavy and constant attacks thousands of brave men and women who sacrificed their leisure and trained themselves in various branches of the Civil Defence have undergone the ordeal by fire and bomb.

1941 The Prime Minister made a surprise visit to Dover in January to find out for himself the reasons why some of the new batteries had not been completed. On his return to London he wrote to General Ismay expressing his concern over the delay. He found that the weapons had been ready-mounted but lacked sights and control instruments which had not been delivered. There were problems regarding the lack of shuttering timber, inefficient labour and, of course, the weather. Churchill concluded that the batteries needed to be completed quickly and a weekly report should be forwarded to him.

Since this country was a democracy fighting a war against totalitarianism, any censorship of the press was voluntary (in theory, at least). On 28 January the British Communist Party's newspaper *The Daily Worker* was shut down by order of the Home Secretary because the paper was publishing anti-war propaganda, and later threatened the *Daily Mirror*. Editors of newspapers were required to submit reports which might have security implications to the censor.

The Prime Minister made it known that he wanted greater security in all matters relating to the war, and suggested that a new set of posters cautioning against gossip and idle talk about Service matters should be produced.

By early 1941 the shortage of skilled labour became critical. By March the Government passed a bill called 'Essential Work Order' which required all skilled workers to register. This legislation was able to prevent workers from leaving jobs designated as essential such as munitions, mining and agriculture. The Minister of Labour and National Service,

Ernest Bevin, was able to suspend trade practices by promising to restore them after the war. This was achieved at the time because the trade union movement had become directly involved in government. Union participation was assisted by the prominent part Labour politicians played in the wartime coalition government. There was also an appeal for 100,000 women to sign up for munitions work.

Nationally the food situation was becoming a major issue so on 25 February the Food Minister, Lord Woolton, announced steps to reduce food consumption. He announced as from 10 March no meal consisting of more than one main course of either fish, meat, poultry, game, eggs or cheese may be served to any person in a catering establishment, institution or residential establishment.

> 'Only one egg may be served with bacon. In general, provision has been made that not more than one egg may be served to any person as part of the same meal, though this will not apply to an omelet or scrambled eggs.
>
> **Penalties for offenders :** Any person contravening the order will be liable on summary conviction to 3 months' imprisonment or a fine of £100, or both, and on conviction or indictment to 2 years' imprisonment or a fine of £500, or both. Where necessary the regulations may be modified to meet the needs of patients in hospitals, sanatoria or nursing homes.
>
> **More Meat for Works Canteens :** They are being allotted double the amount of meat per meal served in hotels, as they are considered of greater national importance. Other food news is:
>
> **Milk :** In some industrial areas, there has been some difficulty in meeting demand during the last week or two. The position is not serious and will right itself in a few weeks.
>
> **Oatmeal :** Public demand for oatmeal and rolled oats has increased greatly, and in the last few weeks there have been shortages in some parts of the country. Steps have been taken to put matters right.'

During the early months of the year, the Eastry Rural District Council's Offices were moved from Sandwich to St. Alban's, the Nonington Training College, after the students had been evacuated. Due to its relocation and the shortage of transport, the move created some problems of accessibility to outlying communities as the offices were also used for a Food Office dealing with the issuing of ration books and other related matters, as well as being a centre to monitor air raids. However, in some communities food rationing restrictions were felt more than in others. For example in rural areas eggs, milk, meat such as rabbits, and fresh vegetables could be obtained easily without coupons. This obviously upset people residing in large towns and cities who did not have such access.

It interesting to note that in Sandwich the air raid warning system consisting of a steam driven siren had by now been replaced with a new one which was dependent on dry cell batteries for operating the starting mechanism. However, this also proved to be a problem due to the difficulty of obtaining replacement batteries, and had to be fitted with control gear powered directly from the mains.

The local authority also announced at this time that the construction of water reservoirs was being completed for use in fire emergencies.

By now schools had their own air raid shelters constructed. The Board of Education announced in January that the cost of constructing and equipping them would be reimbursed in full on the understanding that such shelters would be made available, when required, as public shelters out of school hours.

Public shelters in general did not have a good name as most offered no seating, light or sanitation and were extremely cold. They were built as protection against daylight air raids which were of a short duration, and to protect the occupants from shrapnel and flying debris. In most cases they were constructed to government standards but it was reported in the press that some local authorities produced them on the cheap. It was proved that a powerful blast close by could turn them into a death trap, and nicknamed a *'Morrison Sandwich'* when the heavy roof collapsed on to the occupants.

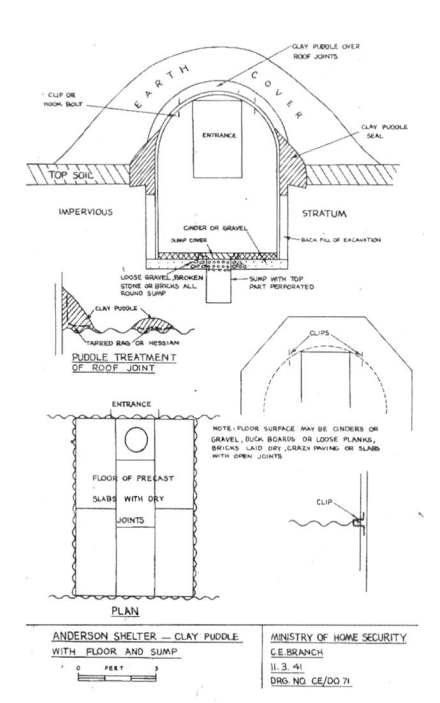

The distribution and the erection of Anderson shelters had now been completed in Eastry Rural District. In April, a circular addressed to the local authority, warned that in spite of repeated instructions and publicity, many preventable casualties continue to result to occupants of Anderson shelters through the insufficiency of cover and problems of flooding. The illustration is one of a variety of methods that the Ministry felt should be adopted.

Problems regarding eligibility of free shelters persisted and in December 1941, the Government issued new criteria:
(a) Persons compulsorily insured under the National Health Insurance Acts. This includes all manual workers and all persons employed in non-manual occupations earning less than £250 a year, but from 5 January 1942 non-manual and manual workers earning up to £420 a year.
(b) Persons mainly dependent on earnings (or pension) not exceeding £350 a year. If there are more than two children of school age in the household, this limit may be increased by £50 for each child in excess of two.

In January the 'dining room table shelter' went into production. This was the Morrison Shelter and was a rectangular steel mesh cage measuring 2 x 1.2 x 1 metres. It proved to be more popular than the Anderson as it was situated indoors and very effective against falling masonry. It could accommodate two recumbent adults and two small children, and could be used as a table. A year later a new form of indoor shelters was announced:

> 'In order to meet a demand for an indoor shelter of a larger capacity than the Morrison table type, a two-tier shelter has been designed. This shelter will also be available to householders in exchange for the table type where the latter is too small to accommodate the family as it contains two beds one above the other. Sale price of the two-tier is £9.15s. and the one-tier £7. It is essential that production should be adjusted to the demand and closed down as soon as it is met.'

Enemy aircraft frequently attacked the town of Sandwich with incendiaries. Some damage was done to Manwood School but those that fell on the town were generally dealt with by the Corporation's Air Raid Wardens and the Fire Service. The residents went about their day-to-day activities and occupations the best way they could but were unable to escape events on their doorstep. Looking back to those awful days and nights it is remarkable that there were so few serious fires in the town's narrow streets and timber framed buildings.

During February and March various circulars arrived on the Clerk's desk, warning members of the ARP to be very careful in dealing with the different forms of incendiary bombs being dropped by the enemy. In air raids it had been noticed that a proportion of the standard 1 kilo incendiaries contained an explosive charge. When this type of bomb exploded it scattered molten magnesium and steel splinters for considerable distances causing lethal wounds. Whilst burning these bombs behaved in the same way as the ordinary bomb until it exploded. The explosion was designed to take place in about 2 minutes after the bomb started to burn. In general if the bomb could not be tackled within half a minute from the time it fell, it should be left for 2 minutes, after which it could be covered with a sandbag or left to burn out.

The ARP were informed on 7 March that the 'Practice Incendiary Bomb' which was a firework made to simulate the Magnesium (Electron) device used for training personnel, had to be modified by substituting another ingredient for Potassium Chlorate which was now required for vital war purposes. However the new practice bomb could be obtained at a price of 8½ p. from various firework manufacturers.

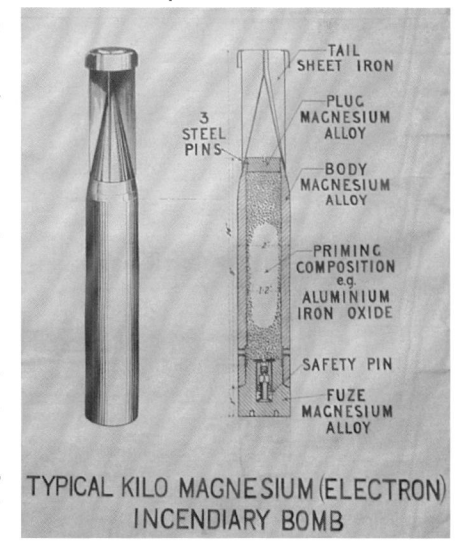

Then in the autumn warning came to be on the lookout for what was known as 'incendiary leaves' dropped by enemy aircraft for the purpose of setting fire to growing crops and woodland. These so called 'leaves' were dropped in a wet condition, and upon drying out burst into flames. The idea was that when dropped at night they did not ignite until the dew had evaporated the following morning. They came in different shapes and sizes and the Ministry pointed out that they were especially dangerous to young children should they pick them up. *'The leaf is a potential fire raiser in the countryside, particularly in corn growing areas. If found should be kept under water.'*

The East Kent Mercury reported in February that the town of Ramsgate was shelled for the first time. Three shells landed but doing little damage.

A Spitfire MKII of No.74 Squadron crashed on the parade ground of RAF Manston Aerodrome on 10 April whilst attempting a 'victory roll' after shooting up a Bf.109E over Canterbury, which ultimately crashed at St. Nicholas-at-Wade. On 14 April, a parachute mine was dropped at *Five Ways* at Sholden which caused a considerable amount of damage.

During this period, however, the whole of southeast Kent appears to have been taken over by the military. Life in the small village of Eastry went on much the same. Vehicles and weapons of every kind trundled through the High Street, and each day soldiers marched backwards and forwards from Walton House to Eastry Court for meals or to their billets at Brook House. The Royal Corps of Signals was based at the old Eastry Isolation Hospital, and the Village Hall was commandeered by the troops for dancing and other shows organized by the various Services.

Cromwell or Cruiser tank.

An extract from David Phillips' account of a visit to the village on 21 April 1941, recounted in the *Eastry Parish News* some fifty years after the event:

> 'A motor cyclist in full war paint of a dispatch rider dashes down the street and pulls up at the newsagents. He walks smartly into the shop and a moment later emerges with a newspaper sticking from his hip pocket. Smartly he mounts and dashes away.
>
> A distant strident horn, unlike the note of any vehicle known to us, fills us with expectancy. It is followed by a faint rattling sound which rapidly increases to a clanging din; and down the village street, surely exceeding the limit allowed for cars, darts an ungainly

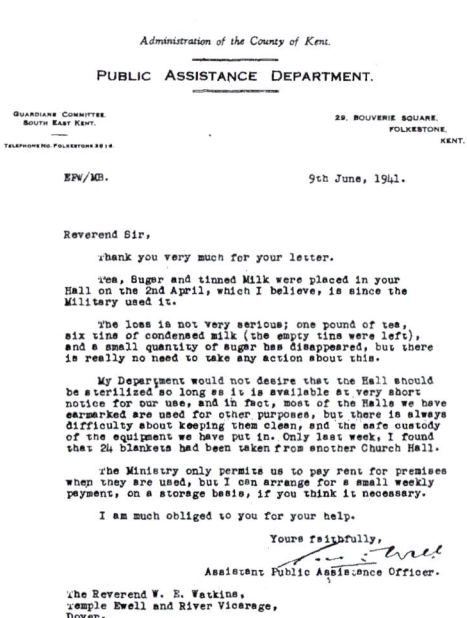

```
                    Administration of the County of Kent.

                    PUBLIC  ASSISTANCE  DEPARTMENT.

GUARDIANS COMMITTEE
 SOUTH EAST KENT.                              29, BOUVERIE SQUARE,
                                                    FOLKESTONE.
TELEPHONE NO. FOLKESTONE 2618                           KENT.

EPW/MB.                                        9th June, 1941.


Reverend Sir,
        Thank you very much for your letter.

        Tea, Sugar and tinned Milk were placed in your
Hall on the 2nd April, which I believe, is since the
Military used it.

        The loss is not very serious; one pound of tea,
six tins of condensed milk (the empty tins were left),
and a small quantity of sugar has disappeared, but there
is really no need to take any action about this.

        My Department would not desire that the Hall should
be sterilized so long as it is available at very short
notice for our use, and in fact, most of the Halls we have
earmarked are used for other purposes, but there is always
difficulty about keeping them clean, and the safe custody
of the equipment we have put in. Only last week, I found
that 24 blankets had been taken from another Church Hall.

        The Ministry only permits us to pay rent for premises
when they are used, but I can arrange for a small weekly
payment, on a storage basis, if you think it necessary.

        I am much obliged to you for your help.

                            Yours faithfully,

                            Assistant Public Assistance Officer.

The Reverend W. E. Watkins,
Temple Ewell and River Vicarage,
Dover.
```

The correspondence continued

> tank. Everyone keeps well to the side of the road, for on the smooth, hard surface, this animated box of steel looks capable of a sudden and devastating skid. Even the soldiers gaze after it admiringly, as with an air of performing the improbable, avoiding pavement and wall, rather than keeping to the highway, it trundles swiftly down the hill and vanishes with the bending road.
>
> At night, the village school, itself formerly a block of works buildings, is transformed into a canteen and dance hall. Until 10 pm music floats down the street; then the night is filled with loud conversation and laughter, firefly cigarettes dance and jog in the darkness and the faultily blacked doorway spills shapes of light, to the dismay of the inhabitants.'

In the village of River near Dover, the County Council had earmarked the Church Hall as a 'Rest and Feeding Centre' for people rendered homeless due to enemy action, but the Public Assistance Department considered it could be more useful as a military canteen and rest centre. When the vicar heard that dances were being held in the hall he was surprised but had to concede to the military.

A very controversial problem the Government had to consider was the possible use or counter use of poison gas should an invasion come. The British Government had ordered 2,000 tons of mustard gas in October 1938, and had it put into store just in case. On 27 March, the Secretary of State for the Home Department, Herbert Morrison, answered questions in the House of Commons on the use of poison gas. He is reported as saying:

'The use of gas is abhorrent to His Majesty's Government, and this country will in no circumstances be the first to employ the gas weapon.

Unhappily, we cannot put any faith in statements which the enemy has made, that he will not use gas. On the contrary, his whole past record shows that he will stop at nothing, and that if he conceives the use of gas to be of military advantage to him; he will use it. For that reason it is essential that the country should be prepared'

A circular was received by the Medical Officer of Eastry Rural District Council advising him of precautions needed in the event of an enemy gas attack. To keep a small stock of anti-gas ointment in each medical post and public shelters and to ensure people to be in a 'proper state of preparedness', and to advise the public of the dangers and the importance of having their respirators (gas mask) with them and to practice putting them on and wearing them. To encourage young children to wear

MINISTRY OF HOME SECURITY

BLISTER GAS ANTIDOTE

The pails contain Bleach Cream which prevents skin burns from Blister Gas

If you suspect that **liquid blister gas** has fallen upon your bare skin (for example upon your face, neck, hands or forearm), or has soaked through thin clothing such as stockings to the skin beneath, you can prevent or greatly reduce blistering by the **immediate** application of Bleach Cream to the skin.

Instructions for the Use of Bleach Cream.

Put some of the cream into the palm of one hand and rub it well into the contaminated skin for one minute. Allow the cream to remain on the skin for one more minute and then wipe it off or wash it away with water.

If the face is contaminated, take care not to get any of the cream into the eyes. Close the eyes whilst applying the cream.

the skin is contaminated with a **large drop of blister gas**, or has been splashed with liquid blister gas, mop up the liquid **immediately** with a rag or handkerchief and throw this away before applying the cream. If no cloth is available do not waste time by looking for one, but apply the bleach cream at once.

10372 Wt, 43508/379 19,000 2/41 K.H.K. Gp. 8.

Instructions on how to apply Bleach Cream, an antidote against Blister Gas.

one a Mickey Mouse design gas mask was produced but a child of five and above had to wear the standard grotesque model. People found gas masks very uncomfortable to wear and found reasons why they would not use them. Those with respiratory troubles had real problems but fortunately this was rectified by installing an outlet valve. This new updated version, identical to the standard model, was obtainable by taking a medical certificate to the local authority and surrendering the old gas mask.

The Prime Minister in August warned that the danger existed and we must expect gas warfare on a tremendous scale, and it could happen at any moment. Later in September he asked his Chiefs of Staff whether they were satisfied with our means of retaliation if necessary in regard to offensive and defensive measures in chemical warfare. Churchill is quoted as saying: *'The enemy may use gas, but if so it will be to his own disadvantage, since we have arranged for immediate retaliation'.*

In a circular sent to local councils regarding the replacement of essential clothing or footwear lost in war damage, special additional coupons would be issued without having to surrender the standard allocation. However, the description of essential clothing excluded dress suits but in special cases, such as a concert artist, extra coupons would be considered essential.

At the same time, a Government department stated the importance of keeping all brickworks in operation, supplying enough bricks to meet demand. It continued:

> *'The Minister understands that the maximum extra cost due to the use of local bricks would be £1 per thousand. The Ministry of Works and Buildings have reached an agreement with the manufacturers to standardize the sizes of brick to a British Standard Spec. – Thickness 2.375 inches in the South and 2.875 inches (Commonly known as 3 inch) in the North.'*

The National Service Act this year introduced conscription for women. All unmarried women aged between 20-30 years were called up for work. This was later extended to include women up to the age of 43, including married women. The Prime Minister wanted to encourage voluntary recruitment of women for the Services, and to increase the existing powers for directing more women into the munitions industries. During May there was a concerted effort to encourage more women into war work. Letters had gone out to women born in the 1920s, inviting them to attend their local Employment Exchange for an interview. Large number of women would be added to a National Work Register including those available for work of national importance. Women who had a conscientious objection to making or handling munitions would be offered employment on some other essential service.

In the army women joined the ATS. Like soldiers they wore a khaki uniform. The recruiting posters were glamorous and many joined believing they would lead a life of glamour but they were to be disappointed. One such lady who received the call was Joan Ratcliff of Eastry. She was recorded as saying *'that with the outbreak of war our lives changed from a sheltered life to venturing into the unknown, but felt she was doing her bit for her country'.* As a raw recruit she enlisted with a friend at Canterbury barracks and June, 1941, saw the two of them posted to Worcester for 6 weeks' training. Joan said that their first task was to fill a mattress with straw to have something to sleep on; next we were marched off to the stores to be fitted with a uniform. The next day we were given our inoculations. This was followed by weeks of lectures, square bashing etc., before we were fully-fledged Auxiliary Territorial Service (ATS) girls ready for posting and going our separate ways.

Conscripts to the ATS did not get the glamour jobs. They acted as drivers, worked in mess halls, acted as cleaners and even worked on anti-aircraft guns. For a young girl, to embark into an unknown military environment in time of war required a great deal of nerve and courage. Joan just laughed it off, saying *'I loved the life, the comradeship was wonderful.'*

It was soon revealed that the financial requirements to fund the war effort was crippling the country, and soon the government was facing bankruptcy as all saleable assets such as gold reserves were exhausted. An effort to control inflation was to ration commodities at fixed prices, either by a coupon system which applied to basic foodstuffs or a points system that allowed flexibility, within limits, in the purchase of goods. However, at the same time people were generally protected from price increases by food subsidies.

Each year communities were encouraged to compete with their neighbouring town or village to raise the most money for the war effort. Fund raising initiatives continued in the Eastry Rural District during the May, with one particularly being favoured for donations. This was entitled *Wings for Victory*. The District Council set a target of £80,000 to purchase a Sunderland Flying Boat, a Mosquito and two Typhoons, and much to everybody's amazement people rose to the challenge and raised a magnificent £144,000, which at the time was an extraordinary effort. This was followed by other campaigns such as *Warships and Tanks for Attack and Salute the Soldier* Funds. Campaigns were usually for one week's duration, and their aim was to raise enough money through special events. Fund raising parades, usually involving the military or youth groups, were considered good for morale. In a letter from the Mayor of Sandwich and chairman of Eastry Rural District Council it referred to the forthcoming *War Weapons Week* on 17 to 25 May :- *'Let us now in Sandwich and Eastry show what can be done in an area already evacuated by much of its normal population and where no war industries exist. Will you help by lending to the Country every shilling that you can lay your hand upon.'* This first annual National Savings promotion raised £50,170. A tremendous effort!

This competitiveness was demonstrated in March 1942 when during *Warship Week* in Deal, in an effort not to be beaten by their neighbours in Sandwich, a sum of £91,500 was raised compared to £36,340. Exhortations to buy National War Bonds appeared in the press. It stated that we should *'Save to the Limit'* as some £40 million a week was needed from the people to lend to the Government for the duration of the war.

Squander Bug was a propaganda character created by the National Savings Committee to discourage spending, and was widely used in poster campaigns throughout the war. The savings committee became concerned that inflated prices were being paid for scarce consumer goods, and believed that the money would be better spent on savings certificates to finance the war. The character eventually was drawn covered with swastikas depicting the enemy within.

As Germany began achieving victories in Europe the American President, Franklin D. Roosevelt, began seeking ways to aid this country. Constrained by the Neutrality Acts, Roosevelt found a way round the Act by declaring large quantities of United States weapons and ammunition as 'surplus' to requirements, and authorized shipment to Britain. He also negotiated to secure 99 year leases on some naval bases and airfields, and agreed to supply 50 surplus American destroyers to the Royal Navy and Royal Canadian Navy.

Seeking to involve the United States further and to have a more active role in the conflict, Roosevelt wished to provide Britain with more assistance and aid to shorten the war. On 11 March 1941, the Lend-Lease Act was signed. In effect, it authorized the transfer of military materials to this country on the understanding that we would pay for or return them if we were not defeated. With the cessation of the war Britain needed to retain much of the equipment and supplies for postwar use, and an agreement was signed through which this country agreed to purchase the items. The total value of the loan was around £1,075 million. The final payment on the loan was not concluded until 2006.

During May a circular from the Ministry of Home Security arrived at Sandwich the title of which was rather frightening; reading –

Duties of Local Authorities in the event of invasion

If fighting should break out in the area, members of the authority, their officers and members of the Civil Defence Services will be expected to stand firm and carry on with essential activities. There must be no paralysis of local services.

There may, however, come a stage when it is necessary for the military authorities to take charge, and the military have by Common Law such powers as the military needs and the general situation require. There is a general duty on the civil population to assist in repelling attack by conforming with any necessary orders.

They should do what they can to continue civil administration for as long as possible, but should avoid any action which would assist the enemy, and any secret papers or maps likely to be of assistance to the enemy should be hidden or destroyed.

For Civilian Action in the event of an invasion see 8 June 1942.

On 7 June, the *Dover Express* reported that the RAF and the Luftwaffe had been engaged in a dogfight over Whitfield and Dover Town, when seven enemy aircraft swept in around midday.

An unusual and somewhat unexplained event, which must have been thought at the time to be a sign that some Luftwaffe pilots were becoming disillusioned, was when a new type of Messerschmitt Bf.109F landed undamaged in a field near St. Margaret's on 10 June. But nothing more regarding this incident has been recorded.

Two days later the *Dover Express* reported that a parachute mine had destroyed a whole street, killing 16 people and injuring another 43. A lone enemy aircraft had flown in low over the town, apparently targeting the Dover Gas Works in Union Road. Rescue workers were soon on the scene. The Home Guard and soldiers of the Royal Sussex Regiment helped the ARP in the rescue.

To assist RAF bomber pilots to find their way home after bombing missions on the Continent, searchlight units in the Dover area illuminated sections of the balloon barrage. Although this was extremely useful for our pilots it also assisted the enemy bombers and their long range guns but considered to be a good compromise!

During June, the Ministry of Works and Buildings sent a circular to all local authorities stating that it had been decided nationally the conditions under which Sunday Working would be limited and strictly applied. It is likely that the Minister had recognized how people were being pushed to the limit and needed some respite:
  (1) Air raid damage repair and services, war factories and essential house repairs after a blitz.
  (2) Work of exceptional urgency in the war effort, such as work in connection with the Battle of the Atlantic, defence against invasion etc,.
  (3) Any work requiring to be carried out as a result of a serious local emergency.
  (4) The repair of plant and equipment which might hold up important work.
  (5) Railway work where weekend work is necessary and the unloading of railway wagons.
  Note: These arrangements are subject to the Government's right in the event of national emergency, such as invasion, to take whatever action may be found necessary.

The Government must have realized that there was a need to have control on the number of hours that employees were expected to work and the need to allow additional time off to recover. Where Sunday Working was permitted the 60 hour working week was adhered to.

During July the Parliamentary Secretary to the Ministry of Food was asked whether it was possible to have a more efficient arrangement so that pay days could be staggered to assist workers? Their hours of work had become restricted because of the length of time spent in food queues. He said he would look into the problem.

The allied Chiefs of Staff were still expecting some form of German invasion or at least a Commando style attack during the summer months. On 20 June the Prime Minister, Winston Churchill, visited the area around the south east channel ports to check up on the anti-invasion defences. This was the second visit he had made in the past ten months. Writing to the Secretary of State for Air, he pointed

The remaining two radar masts on the cliffs above Dover.

out that it's the responsibility of the Air Force to defend aerodromes. Every man in uniform ought to be armed with something be it a rifle, Tommy gun, or pike etc., and without exception should do an hour's drill and practice every day. It must be understood by all ranks that they were expected to fight and die in the defence of their airfield.

On the 18 June there was a rather unusual disclosure in The Daily Telegraph. The article revealed **'the best kept secret of the war'**. This propaganda announcement was made by the Chief of Coastal Command who declared that 'radio location or RDF' was Britain's secret weapon against the German bomber. It is a system, he said *'whereby rays which are unaffected by fog or darkness are sent out far beyond the limits of our shores. Any aircraft or ship in the path of this ray immediately sends back a signal to the detecting station, where people are on watch'*. The article continued to say that this remarkable weapon helped us win the Battle of Britain last autumn. This new technology, later called 'radar', was situated at sites called Air Ministry Experimental Stations at Dover and Dunkirk, north of Canterbury.

Due to heavy air raids in some parts of the south of England it was found necessary to reorganize the Civil Defence messenger service, providing messengers for long distances with motorbikes, and locally with bicycles. The service would be on a part-time basis, and to recruit young members of the public who had left school to fill these roles. Male messengers would remain in the service after reaching the age of 18, whilst waiting to join H. M. Armed Forces. It was not proposed to extend the service of young women over 18 as it was considered that at this age they could be more usefully employed in other Civil Defence forces.

Restaurants were exempt from food rationing which led to resentment as the rich could supplement their food allowance by eating out. To restrict this anomaly rules were introduced; no meal could cost more than 5/- (25p.); no meal could consist of more than three courses; meat and fish could not be served at the same sitting.

Establishments known as British Restaurants came into being supplying meals for the masses. These were greatly appreciated and created a new eating experience away from home. At first they were unpopular with café proprietors and restaurateurs, naturally suspicious and jealous of their government aid. They were run by local authorities and the first food outlet called 'A British Restaurant' was opened early in June in Canterbury. The press announced that customers could purchase a three course meal for only 9d. (approx.4p.), and further establishments were planned in every town in Kent. By the end of the war there were around 2000 of them serving half a million meals a day in the whole country.

Everyday items of clothing were given a value and controlled by coupons in response to the shortage of material to make clothes. A new kind of clothing 'utility clothing' was introduced using cheap materials and using a minimum amount of cloth. Every man, woman and child was given 66 coupons to last a year. The quantity required varied according to the size of the garment. For example a woman's overcoat needed 14 coupons, whilst a man used 13 for a jacket and 8 for a pair of trousers. The need for coupons was overcome by the number of second-hand clothes shops that were established.

Furniture also expressed the spirit of the times. Indeed emergency furniture provided an example of state control over the supply of scarce materials in standardized designs at fixed prices. The CC41 utility symbol became one of the best known of all symbols in this time of austerity.

National newspapers announced that from the 4 July the supply of coal, coke and any other solid fuel for households was limited, as was gas and electricity. The intention was to conserve as much fuel as possible for industrial use. The only good thing at this time was that sausages were not rationed but difficult to get hold of!

During July the Post Office began introducing wartime issue postage stamps. These were in pale colours as part of a cost cutting exercise, and included King George VI definitives ½ d. 1d. 2d. 2 ½ d. 3d. 2/6d and 10/- values.

In a circular from the Ministry of Health, the Minister delivered a hard sell stating that National Wheat Meal Flour was now available to bakers:

> This flour contains the greater part of the germ of the wheat, with some of the finer bran, but excludes the coarser bran. It thus contains not only most of the vitamin B1, but also most of the remainder of the vitamin B complex, as well as valuable mineral

Sack labels from Mannering's Buckland Flour Mill in Dover, showing various grades of National flour which had been manufactured at the mill.

elements which are removed in producing white flour. This flour has a high nutritional value and is valuable at times when there is restriction upon the availability of other foods from which these vitamins and minerals could be obtained.

On 9 July Parliament approved under the Food and Drugs Act, 1938, that on account of the urgency, the following regulation should come into immediate operation ie., use of the special designation 'Pasteurised Milk'. This Milk and Dairies Act specified that:

> The milk in relation to which the special designation is used shall be retained at a temperature of not less than 162 degrees Fahrenheit for at least 15 seconds and immediately cooled to a temperature of not more than 55 degrees Fahrenheit.

At this time the Government considered it prudent to introduce this Act as Tuberculosis was on the increase, and introduced this process of heating milk to destroy harmful microorganisms. It was Bovine TB that was spreading mostly in children through milk from infected cattle that prompted this move. Lord Woolton, the Food Minister, in conjunction with the Board of Education, intended to press the case for an increase in the number of children receiving milk in schools as in some areas the scheme had not yet been adopted. The Ministry of Food confirmed that unless there was an unreasonable run on the country's stocks, condensed milk would be sold without restriction. The amount of liquid milk available may vary in which case the basic quota would be altered. A Ministry official jokingly said, 'It all depends on the cow'!

On the 2 July the Secretary of State for War was asked whether it was necessary to release miners from the armed services for a period in order to assist in coal production. The scheme, similar to agricultural workers serving at home, meant that workers would be released for periods up to 28 days in a year to return to their former farms to help at times of seasonal pressure. The Secretary said the suggestion was not considered necessary at present.

From the 15 July, alterations to the reserved occupation conscription list were made. The age of reservation for school masters was raised from 30 to 35, and for pharmacists from the age of 30. Various other measures were introduced in the autumn by the Ministry of Home Security due to the manpower shortage. In August a scheme to allow volunteer Conscientious Objectors and Aliens to serve in the Civil Defence were outlined. The first circular read:

> The Ministry hitherto, by reason merely of their conscientious objection to military service, regarded them as unsuitable candidates. The increasing pressure on the nation's manpower in itself provides the strongest of reasons for utilizing in the Civil Defence their services.

A second circular, titled Aliens in Civil Defence Services, stated in the following extract:

> The Minister is anxious that no obstacle shall be placed in the way of employment in Civil Defence work (whole time paid or part-time unpaid) of suitable and reliable foreigners who are willing to assist the war effort, whether they are men or women and whatever be their nationality, including Germans, Austrians and Italians who are friendly to the allied cause.

By mid 1941, the emblematic use of the letter **'V'** had spread through occupied Europe, and on 19 July Winston Churchill put the government's seal of approval on this symbol, and the British 'V' for Victory campaign was born. Churchill from this point in the war continually promoted this in every way he could including making the 'V' sign when moving about in public or inspecting the forces. This was a constant morale booster!

On 29 July, the Prime Minister disclosed to the House of Commons that in this war we have within two years reached the level only achieved in four years in the First World War. He was also able to give encouraging news of progress in fighter-aircraft performances and of the increased loads and ranges of our bombers. These statements were greeted with loud bursts of cheers from the assembled members but he was careful to add a warning against undue optimism, saying:
'The invasion season is at hand. All the armed forces have been warned to be at concert pitch by 1 September and to maintain the utmost vigilance meanwhile.'

Later in the month as a measure of controlling the consumption of rubber the Minister of Supply announced an order banning the sale of car tyres until 13 February the following year. The order listed various ways to effect economy. This included the running of tyres at pressures 15% above normal stating this should give extra mileage although at the expense of comfort, and also to make full use of the remoulding facilities only when the tread was smooth in the centre of the tyre. The reason for this was the fall of Singapore to the Japanese Army and the loss of our supply of raw rubber. The invasion of Malaya by Japan meant they took control of 40% of the world's output of rubber and about 60% of the world's tin production.

During August the British Political Warfare Executive (PWE) was created to produce and disseminate propaganda with the aim of damaging enemy morale and sustaining the morale of occupied countries. The main forms of propaganda were in the form of radio broadcasts, often from clandestine radio stations and printed documents. The organization was governed by a committee made up of Anthony Eden (Foreign Secretary), the Ministers of Information and of Economic Warfare and others. The PWE included staff from the Ministry of Information, propaganda elements from the Special Operations Executive (SOE) and from the BBC with its Headquarters at Woburn Abbey. By early October the Ministry of Information and other government departments assumed control of the home and overseas news propaganda. A government adviser to the BBC assumed the responsibility for home news programmes under the direction of the committee.

It was reported in *The Daily Telegraph* on 27 August that there was better news for housewives. Difficulties of preparing a breakfast menu, which had suffered the most from rationing, was to be relieved by increasing supplies from the United States under the Lend-Lease Act. These will include canned meats and fish and breakfast cereals transported in bulk.

Beginning in late September the Ministry of Food have arranged for a larger allocation of sugar and fat to bakers and manufacturers of these products. It was on condition that production must be increased in the output of cakes and biscuits of inexpensive varieties, at least in proportion to the increased allowance of fat and sugar. It was also announced that the harvest of oats in the country promises to be so good that it is expected there will be adequate supplies of oatmeal throughout the winter months. A little bit of good news.

In May the Home Secretary, Herbert Morrison, announced that Parliament had passed the Fire Services (Emergency Provisions) Bill, and all regular fire brigades and the Auxiliary Fire Service (AFS) would be reorganized and formed into the National Fire Service (NFS), with the independent fire authorities being swept away on 28 August. Despite the early difficulties the Service quickly settled down and a standard uniform introduced. By the end of the year the NFS was ready for anything the Luftwaffe was about to throw at them.

On 15 August at Broadstairs an enemy bomber dropped a series of bombs on the town killing five of the local fire brigade. This would have been badly felt by the Brigade as their men daily faced the threat of serious danger.

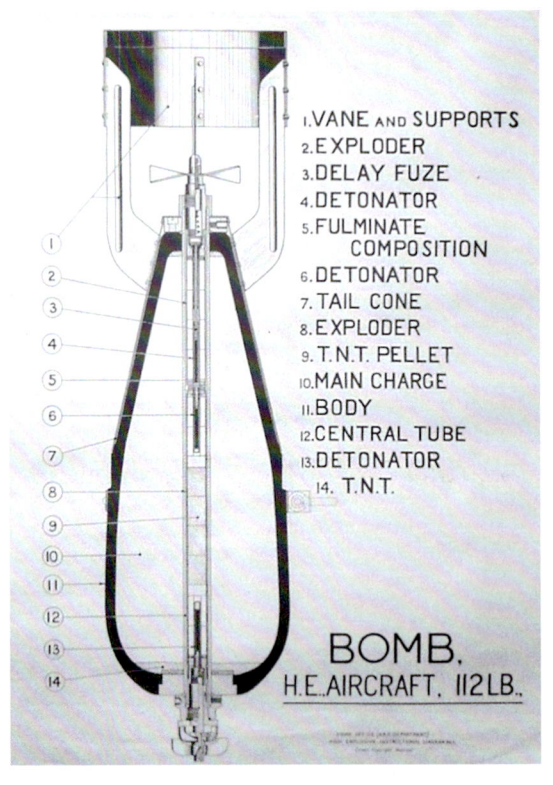

During the night of the 7 September a lone enemy Junkers Ju.88A dropped five bombs which hit the old Burlington Hotel in Dover killing three people. It was fortunate that only a handful of people still resided in this large building otherwise there would have been many more casualties. This was followed later in the month by bombs being dropped in the Charlton Green area of the town destroying many houses, killing three people and seriously injuring five more.

The Daily Telegraph printed an article in September from their Industrial Correspondent saying that the Government was about to set up industrial courts, with full judicial powers to impose fines or even imprisonment to deal with evasions of the Essential Work (General Provisions) Order which had been applied to most of the vital war industries when it was introduced in March. The Correspondent pointed out that there have been complaints that the policy set up is being abused and is not completely effective. The intention of the order was that workers should be 'tied' to their jobs, employers should not discharge them without permission of a National Service officer, and persistent absenteeism should be dealt with. Where penalties had been imposed, magistrates and justices needed clearer guidelines, particularly as they have not been sufficiently familiar with conditions operating in industry.

Problems arose in industry when the Amalgamated Engineering Union had their claim for an increase of 4d. (1½p) an hour turned down. They pointed out that skilled men were earning less than £3. 10s. (£3.50) per week. These wages were contrasted with those 'skilled wartime' workers in factories. A spokesperson for the Union, denounced this disparity, saying, *'fabulous sums being earned in the aircraft industry by butchers, bakers and the rest who do not know one end of a lathe from the other'*. He pointed out that people who have spent 30 years in a trade are being put on the same basis as trainees who, after 6 months, have the audacity to call themselves skilled engineers. The Union felt helpless as any direct action would damage the war effort and would only help that 'mad dog' who brought Nazism to Europe.

As Dover's anti-aircraft guns were being moved during the first week of October, the town came under attack by enemy dive bombers which killed and injured many civilians and military personnel. At the time the residents were angry and there were rumours that the enemy had been informed that the town had been left undefended.

With a lull in enemy bombing the RAF proposed sending 8000 skilled technicians on loan to production facilities for about six months but in an emergency such as heavy air raids, they would return to their duties. This would also apply to the army who had been assisting in getting in the harvest. The Prime Minister writing to the Secretary of State for War said:

'come the spring we shall require all our men to be in a high state of readiness and your responsibility is to have them ready like fighting cocks'.

General de Gaulle chats to a Free French pilot of No.615 Squadron during his visit to RAF Manston in October 1941.

This period of inactivity of the enemy worried the Prime Minister and his cabinet so they needed to be ready should circumstances quickly change. They addressed a possible scenario of a spring invasion. As the German forces had pushed the Russian armies back, Hitler might suddenly take up a winter position as he was advised to do. Should he do this it was considered that 20 or 30 divisions could be diverted for this invasion idea. So we will have to be ready for them.

In the event of invasion voluntary food officers will be chosen by the Government and will be responsible for the equitable distribution of food supplies. *The Daily Telegraph* stated in October that all food stores named by the military authorities would close for stocktaking. They would re-open when the food officer decided on military advice, and a set amount distributed to each person preventing panic buying.

Deal District ARP personnel at the Regional Training School during October 1941.

News of the Russian people's plight as the German forces advanced towards Moscow, caused the people of this country to raise money to provide medical equipment and supplies for their needs. Mrs. Churchill was invited by the British Red Cross and St. John's to chair an appeal called 'Russian Aid Fund', with a target of one million pounds which was a colossal amount at that time.

The Daily Telegraph on 22 October reported that all women born in 1913 would be required to register at their local Ministry of Labour office at the weekend unless exempted. The Ministry of Labour announced the withdrawal of women in the retail distributive trades aged from 20 to 25, except those handling food, was to be extended to other industries in the near future. The official view was that this big reserve of labour must be transferred to the Service Auxiliaries or munition factories. Young women would be offered the Services as a first choice. In the case of factory work there was to be a much '**firmer attitude**'. Unless the women had good reason to remain at home they would be directed to take war work. The newspaper also reported that by the end of the year they expected that registration would be extended to women up to the age of 40. Employers were to be encouraged to take on women over the age of 40 to replace the younger ones.

During November the War Cabinet began to discuss how to get more men into the Services:
>Raise by 10 years the age for compulsory military service to 51. This would release younger men from non-combatant duties to frontline service.
>Call up young men at 18 instead of 19. It was considered that this measure would make a substantial contribution.

Those planning the Christmas dinner were told in the press that the allocation of dried fruits such as vine fruits, prunes, figs, dried apples and apricots would be doubled to 12 oz. (336 gm) per head for the rest of the month. After November the allowance would return to 6 oz. (168 gm). In addition the Ministry of Food announced that the maximum price for leeks would be fixed at 5d. (2p) per lb. (450 gm).

On the 1 December when it was felt that the government had run out of ideas along came a new twist in food rationing. A points system was introduced whereby canned meat, fish and vegetables were restricted items. In this each person had 20 points which had to last four weeks but could be spent at any shop which had the items wanted. Other food products such as margarine, dried fruit, rice and biscuits also became difficult to purchase. Women frequently queued for hours and had to be very careful with their ration quota, often doing without small pleasures.

The Ministry of Supply issued an order introducing the urgent need to conserve the use of paper needed for munitions and other essential purposes. They highlighted the great number of articles purchased from shops which had wrapping paper. This was to be stopped immediately and customers purchasing items were advised to take their own form of wrapping paper. Where it was practicable sales outlets would be encouraged to sell cigarettes loose, saving on packaging. All sweets would only be sold loose and without any wrappers.

Manufacturers producing foodstuff in jars would in future print the description of the contents on the lid rather than producing a separate label. In mid November the Ministry of Supply announced that for the duration of the war this would be the last Christmas that Christmas cards would be available due to the urgent need to save paper. Most cards were very plain in design with a standard greeting 'Wishing you A Merry Xmas' in black letters.

Reports appeared in the national press regarding timber felling companies denuding many of our woodlands for profit. When the Prime Minister saw this he wrote to the Forestry Commission saying that due consideration should be given to the appearance of the countryside, and there was no reason why a number of trees should not be left and surely we must continue to replant a couple of trees for every one cut down.

On 2 December the Prime Minister announced to Parliament that 1,700,000 unmarried women between the age of 20 and 30, and 70,000 youths between the age of 18½ and 19 would be affected by the Government's new conscription plan.

Unmarried women could be called up for service in the ATS, NFS, full-time Civil Defence forces and the police war reserve. They would have the same rights as men to obtain exemption as conscientious objectors to combatant duties. In a letter to the Secretary of State for War, Churchill wrote that great responsibility rests on you to see that all young women are not treated roughly, particularly those compelled to join the ATS. He realized that there was a bias against women being connected with lethal work which must be eliminated.

A member of the ATS accurately plotting targets and checking accuracy of shelling for our coastal artillery batteries.

The age of military service was to be lowered from 19 to 18½, but permission to send youths abroad had yet to be approved by Parliament. The reservation system was to continue for some occupations including the Merchant Service, full-time Civil Defence, Royal Observer Corps, Vets, Lay Evangelists and men in certain student occupations. The proposed call up of 10,000 young farm workers for military service might be deferred with most being compulsorily transferred to farms short of labour. Boys and Girls between 16 and 18 are to be interviewed by youth committees of the education authorities. Special arrangements will be made for students and apprentices in this age group. An existing system was to continue for those studying for the medical or dental professions, and those apprentices in industry.

The Government had for some time been looking at how to integrate more women into front line civil defence duties. On 19 December the Minister for Home Security, Herbert Morrison, announced that membership of the Women's Voluntary Service did not of itself exclude a woman from the liability of being called up. He said:

> 'In view of the present serious manpower position it is essential that no mobile woman should be employed on work that can be done by immobile women, nor should younger women be employed on work that can be done by older immobile women.'

Later an announcement was made from the headquarters of the Women's Voluntary Services saying that they had decided to institute a scheme of simple basic training in Civil Defence for all their members. The course would cover first aid, anti-gas, fire fighting and elementary ARP. It was hoped that additional civil defence workers provided by the WVS would be realized after completing their training.

On the 20 December the Minister of Home Security sent seasonal greetings to all the Civil Defence Services. In his message he conveyed his appreciation of what had been achieved and hope for the future. The following is a short extract.

> I would like to couple with my sincere greetings to all members of the Civil Defence Services for Christmas and the New Year an expression of my warm appreciation of the Services they have rendered during the past year.

He also noted that the respite from heavy enemy air raids had given the services an opportunity for recuperation, and of improving civil defence organization in ways shown by experience to be necessary.

Yet Christmas 1941 was a time of optimism particularly as we were no longer alone to fight against Hitler as the United States of America had entered the war. In the public view there was no doubt that the allied forces would eventually win. Also at this time a growing number of evacuated children began to return home. The Government introduced compulsory part-time education starting in the New Year.
Rationing was at its height: 3 ozs. (84 gm) of cheese, 4 ozs. (112 gm) of jam or preserves (including mincemeat), 2 pints (1.14 litre) of milk a week and 3 eggs a month. Meat was obtained on a points system (viz. 1 month's points would get you 1 lb. (450gm) of luncheon meat). There were no turkeys available.

Children's toys were in short supply. Often they were handmade or old presents renovated. People were encouraged to spend their money wisely and to give National Savings Certificates or a savings book with a few stamps attached. Families did their best to make their homes as 'Christmassy' as possible.

1942 On the 6 January, President Roosevelt appeared before Congress declaring that the United States land, air and sea forces would take up stations in the British Isles which would *'constitute an essential fortress in the world struggle'* and bring the battle to the enemy on his own home ground. The President continued by saying, *'That this time we are determined not only to win the war but also to maintain the peace which will follow'.*

'Austerity' was the buzz word in towns and villages throughout the country during 1942. In February soap rationing began with housewives being allowed 4 ozs. (113 gm) of household or 2 ozs. (57 gm) of toilet soap per person per month. The Government introduced campaigns like *'Make Do and Mend says Mrs. Sew and Sew'*, encouraging women to knit more, and to get their needles and cotton out to mend or darn worn-out clothes. With clothes already rationed, the Board of Trade introduced a new *'Utility'* scheme which had a philosophy that 'every little helps'. For example, a gentleman's suit from a small range of materials would be manufactured with fewer pockets and with trouser turn ups banned. Even shirts were so short they did not tuck into the tops of trousers. Women's garments were to be produced without elastic waistbands, hemlines would rise again and the heels on shoes limited in height.

Cosmetics, if you could get them, were produced in small ranges to make production more efficient. With the summer season approaching women were asked to dispense with wearing stockings in order to conserve stocks for the winter months.

With all the restrictions and shortages it is interesting to note that Prime Minister Churchill when writing to the Minister of Food, was upset that his department had prohibited the manufacture and sale of ICE CREAM. He thought it was not worth implementing and in any case a decision should not have been taken without the Cabinet having a chance to express an opinion.

A letter addressed to District Councils in the area during late March highlighted the need to conserve water supplies. The document stated that due to rainfall being below average and materially less than the preceding year, we should be cautious about the depletion of supplies, and the usual steps for restriction must be considered. Measures were necessary to avert any future shortage jeopardizing the fire-fighting service. A directive was sent by the Ministry of Health regarding the necessity of preventing mosquitoes from breeding during the months of April to September in collections of water stored for fire-fighting purposes. Necessary measures were to be taken by the National Fire Service regarding all such water tanks for which they were responsible.

After a signal had gone out for the Royal Marines to volunteer for hazardous duties, the first group began to arrive at the North Barracks in Deal in February. The Royal Marine Commando volunteers went through exhaustive medical checks and very demanding training programmes. This training included hand-to-hand fighting, swimming and 20 mile (32km) marches. Bombed out buildings in the town were used for street fighting exercises.

The coastal towns and airfields continued to be attacked by enemy aircraft. During May the 8 inch (203mm) coastal defence guns at Capel Battery near Folkestone were installed and ready for action. They provided a useful anti-aircraft (flak) barrage against enemy aircraft, and they later were to come into their own when the V1 'doodle bug' threat came.

On the 23 March, nine members of staff of the East Kent Road Car Company were killed in St. James Street, Dover. This tragedy took place when the air raid shelter they were taking shelter in was struck.

Early on 1 June, Canterbury was subjected to a massive enemy bombing attack, when wave after wave of aircraft dropped thousands of incendiaries and high explosives on the historic city, reducing large areas to burning rubble. Fierce fires swept through the city and the glare could be seen for many miles. The chief damage was to shopping and business premises and to the buildings in the narrow streets. Fire Service crews from all over Kent rushed to the city to help fight the inferno. When the smoke settled a total of 4,000 buildings had been either destroyed or badly damaged. During the raid the bombers were met with anti-aircraft fire and RAF fighters. Three enemy aircraft were destroyed. The *Kentish Gazette and Canterbury Press* paid tribute to the ARP messenger boys who cycled around the burning city distributing instructions and advice to the residents, often with punctured tyres. Others went on foot.

On 2 June Herbert Morrison, the Minister of Home Security issued a message to all Civil Defence workers, he wrote:

> 'The terrible blows struck by the RAF at Germany bring to our minds the possibility that the enemy may not only continue but increase his counter blows so far as he is able.
> Let all services look to every detail of their organization and make sure that they are fully ready. Any night now the call may come.'

Following a period of relative inactivity by the Germans in the previous winter months, the Prime Minister was prompted to make statements pertaining to a possible invasion ploy in the spring. Following this the Ministry of Home Security began formulating a strategy to be put to the civilians of this country should the unthinkable happen. The following is an extract of a circular issued by the Ministry on 8 June 1942. It was accompanied by a letter addressed to the Town Clerk at Sandwich:

> *'I am directed by the Minister of Home Security to send a short statement which has been prepared for publication on the general character of the plans for civilian action in the event of invasion…'*

PLANS FOR CIVILIAN ACTION IN AN INVASION

The following statement of plans for civilian action in case of invasion has been prepared, not because His Majesty's Government wish to indicate that invasion is imminent, but because it is important that we should be fully prepared and that as far as possible everyone should know what he is expected to do when, if ever, invasion comes.

1. CIVIL ADMINISTRATION IN EMERGENCY CONDITIONS.

Since the beginning of the war much of the work of government has been regionalized and the Regional Commissioners, in addition to their immediate responsibility for civil defence, have the duty of seeing that the plans of all Departments and local authorities in regard to all matters connected with civil defence are properly co-ordinated. At present the regional representatives of Departments are responsible to their respective Ministers but in the event of an invasion, Regional Commissioners will assume all the functions of the central Government in their region at any time when reference to the central Government becomes impracticable, and the regional representatives of the various Departments of State will operate as the governing centre of a self-contained community. Detailed arrangements have been made for the setting up of War Zone Courts to administer justice in time of emergency.

2. RELATIONSHIP BETWEEN THE MILITARY AND CIVIL AUTHORITIES.

Under the common law in an emergency which threatens the safety of the realm, any member of the armed forces may claim the help and obedience of civilians and, simply because the emergency exists, it is their duty to respond. There need not be any 'proclamation of martial law.' Obviously orders should not be accepted without verification if there is any suspicion that they are being given by mere busybodies or by enemies or fifth columnists masquerading as police or as members of the armed forces of the Crown. Everyone must be on his guard and if in doubt consult a policeman, warden or Home Guard whom he knows.

Wherever possible, the military (or naval or air force) authorities will work with and through the civilian authorities. Plans have been made, of which some account is given below, to enable this to be done efficiently and smoothly. Civilian authorities will, of course, carry on with their duties as long as possible without waiting for orders from the military.

3. CONSTITUTION OF INVASION COMMITTEES.

In most of the larger towns the Civil Defence Emergency Committees formed the nucleus of an Invasion Committee on which the officers of the civil defence services, local officers of State Departments, the police, National Fire Service, the WVS, and other voluntary agencies, and the military can meet together and work out plans of action in advance. Each civil and military member of this Committee has his instructions but only local contact and discussion can secure that all these instructions are welded into a smoothly working plan of local action. In other towns, villages and rural centres, where Civil Defence Emergency Committees do not exist, contact between the military and the various civilian authorities is achieved through specially constituted Invasion Committees. These work in exactly the same way as the committees in the larger towns which are described above.

In most places where special preparations are needed the committee takes one of the above forms but there are naturally wide variations to suit the circumstances of the different regions. For instance, in some areas the Emergency Committee may be able to act without the formation of a special Invasion Committee. In others preparations are being organized by a small committee of three consisting of a local authority representative or other suitable person, the military commander and the police representative. In other Regions again a special official may be selected to co-ordinate the preparations. It is for the Regional Commissioner, in consultation with the Army Commander, to decide where and in what form these special invasion arrangements are to be made.

4. FUNCTIONS OF INVASION COMMITTEES.

At this stage the task of Invasion Committees is to plan and prepare. The representatives of the civil and military authorities on the committee will carry out the plans, each in his own sphere, under his ordinary executive powers. In the event of an invasion action will have to be taken at short notice, and the more the Committee has done by way of preparation the less there will be for it to do if invasion comes.

The work which the Committee can do now covers a wide field varying according to local circumstances and includes the following:

(a) Co-ordination of civilian plans with the military scheme of defence.

(b) Enrolment of volunteers and allotting to them various tasks which would help the military if invasion comes, eg., digging trenches and earth walls, clearing or blocking roads, removing debris, or first aid work.

(c) Ensuring that an efficient messenger service is available in the event of a breakdown of telephonic communication, using for this purpose young persons on foot or on bicycles.

(d) Ascertainment of local sources of drinking water in case the usual supplies are interrupted.

(e) Plans for the cooking and distribution of food to the military or civil defence services, and distribution of food to civilians as directed by the Ministry of Food.

(f) A census of the tools available for any labouring work and of stirrup pumps, sandbags and so on.

It will obviously be necessary that the existence and location of the Committee should be made widely known in the neighbourhood and that volunteers should be instructed where to offer their services.

If invasion comes the Committee will be a focal point to which the civil population can look for guidance. It will meet to co-ordinate any necessary action which affects a number of Services. It will deal with any urgent matter for which no existing Service is responsible and, if need be, will provide through its Chairman or other selected member a channel of communication between civil and military authorities.

If there is need the compulsory enlistment of civilian labour for work of military importance in invasion conditions will be carried out by the Ministry of Labour and National Service.

Normally, if a town or village is cut off, the Military Commander will be in control and it will be the duty of the civil authorities to undertake any work which he considers necessary. But if circumstances make it impossible for the various civilian Services to obtain orders from their official superiors or from the Military Commander, the Chairman of the Committee will be responsible for seeing that any necessary action is promptly taken, and if casualties occur he will take steps to see that the Service affected continues to carry on.

5. WHAT SHOULD THE CIVILIAN DO NOW?

(a) He can join the Home Guard and be trained to make the best use of himself as a fighter. If he is in work that can stop during invasion he will be listed immediately available and put in list I: if he is in work that must go on he may be accepted for list II and will not be called out until fighting is imminent in the neighbourhood. In either case he will be given the full Home Guard training. Later on it may be possible to arrange to take into the Home Guard under special conditions men who cannot spare the full time now prescribed for Home Guards.

(b) Without joining the Home Guard he can volunteer for emergency duties of urgent military importance under the auspices of the Invasion Committee (see para 4 b). In modern war, while some soldiers are using weapons in the front line, many others are doing necessary military tasks, many of which are very similar to the work which civilian volunteers will have the opportunity of performing.

6. WHAT SHOULD THE CIVILIAN DO IN THE EVENT OF AN INVASION?

(a) He will be expected to stand firm, and, if he is in the Home Guard or has been allotted some civilian duty, to carry out his duties with energy and resolution.

(b) If stray enemy marauders or small parties of enemy soldiers are moving about in an area not in the effective occupation of the enemy the Government expects that every stout-hearted citizen will use all his powers to overcome them.

(c) Needless to say, a civilian should not set out to make independent attacks on military formations. Such a course of action would be futile and, worse still, might actually impede the operations of our own forces. He must obviously do nothing which would be of the slightest help to the enemy but on the contrary hinder and frustrate him by every means which ingenuity can devise and common sense suggest, and if his help is asked by the military, as it may well be, it is his duty to answer whole heartedly any call however exacting, that may be made upon him.

7. MISCELLANEOUS INSTRUCTIONS.

There will be drastic restrictions of all kinds. Instructions on particular points will be issued to civilians by the civil authorities at appropriate times, dealing with such matters as travel, the use of roads by cars and cycles and the closing of schools, cinemas, theatres, etc.

Instructions for the immobilization of all cars and motorcycles except those essential vehicles, the owners of which have been specially warned, will be carried out where and when the civil authorities in each area give the word. Cyclists should immobilize their bicycles by removing essential nuts and bolts when there is a risk of them falling into the enemy's hands. In connection with military operations certain roads may be closed by the police to all civilian use, and this may from time to time affect even the users of the essential vehicles referred to above. Such closure will take place to enable military movements to be carried out and will not necessarily be permanent.

Emergency stocks of food have been provided in such form and in such places as will best serve the needs of the civil population during invasion. Supplies will be available even if enemy military action has dislocated normal transport. As far as possible local retail distribution of food will continue as usual but, if necessary, emergency measures can be brought into operation and will be announced locally.

As long as it is at all possible news and official instructions will be made known to the public through the normal channels, chiefly the press and BBC. If these fail, emergency measures for which provision has been made will operate.

8. POLICE, NATIONAL FIRE SERVICE AND CIVIL DEFENCE SERVICES (INCLUDING FIRE GUARDS).

In the situation envisaged it will be of paramount importance that these specialist Services should concentrate on performing the essential functions for which they have been equipped, organized and trained.

As regards the Police, their most important function is the maintenance of public order and the control of the civil population – functions which must be carried out efficiently so as to avoid any interference with the proper performance by the military authorities of their duties. Any failure on the part of the Police in carrying out these primary duties might seriously impede the military operations of our own forces. The same holds true of the other Services in their own specialist spheres, but all these Services alike, when not engaged in the discharge of their essential duties, have the same responsibilities as civilians as defined in paragraph 6, but because these Services are disciplined bodies they will be specially qualified, and will be expected to provide an example and leadership to the general body of private citizens.

9. DENIAL OF RESOURCES TO THE ENEMY.
On this subject all that can publicly be said is that plans have been made and have been or are being communicated to those concerned, but they are of a kind to which obviously it would be unwise to give publicity. They will, when required, be carried out solely with the view to national defence and without regard for private interests of any kind.
Civilians should do what they can to keep their own stocks of food or other useful things out of the enemy's hands, but they should not set out to destroy plant or communications, to block roads or anything similar except on the definite orders of the military, the police, or wardens.
The scheme for denying our resources to the enemy has been carefully balanced with the needs of our own forces. Independent action by civilians may have the most serious results on our military plan, and is forbidden.

From spring round to autumn Betteshanger Colliery near Deal was targeted by German fighter-bombers in hit-and-run raids. The first was on 26 April when the colliery was bombed by a couple of modified BF109s. They successfully destroyed the power house, injuring nine men on the surface, and preventing the miners underground from being lifted. A further raid took place on 18 May when two bombs were dropped, neither exploding. Then in September the colliery was again targeted. In this attack damage occurred to the winding gear preventing miners at the coal face being brought to the surface for 17 hours, and the mine was shut for several weeks. Two men were killed and many others injured in this raid. Then on 31 October during heavy bombing raids on Canterbury, two Focke-Wulf Fw.190s bombed the colliery. Other planes strafed the villages of Mongeham, Nonington, Eastry, Woodnesborough, Ash and Staple with machine gun fire, and bombs dropped at Richborough, Sandwich and Worth. Local anti-aircraft batteries returned fire, and a Fw.190 was brought down, landing safely near Stonar Lake, Sandwich. The pilot was taken captive. The German aircraft were challenged by allied fighters scrambled from Hawkinge Aerodrome resulting in losses on both sides.

Langdon Battery high up on the cliffs was in continuous action throughout the war protecting the harbour entrances and attacking enemy shipping. They were on the receiving end of much enemy shelling, and the following is a small example -

> On 13 July, seventy rounds of shells fell in the vicinity of the battery. No serious casualties, but some damage. A further sixteen rounds were fired from the French coast around 9 o'clock in the evening on 16 August. On 10th and 11th December nearly fifty rounds were fired at the battery.

A Bofors gun positioned in Thornton Lane, Eastry. Residents recollect that the crew lived in tents and local children often ran errands for them to buy cigarettes at the village shop.

The two 15 inch (381mm) static guns 'Jane' and 'Clem' became operational at Wanstone Battery, St. Margaret's in August. These were manned by the Royal Artillery and could attack both land and naval targets in all kinds of weather using 'radar plotting'.

The Luftwaffe continued to attack and bomb Manston Aerodrome, and it was at times impossible for the ground staff to keep it open for RAF operations. Winston Churchill made a surprise visit to the airfield in August, and later in a letter to the Secretary of State for Air, he stated he was not best pleased with what he had found. He pointed out that although there had been an attack four days previous many of the craters on the landing area had not been filled in. He was angry and said that they should all have been filled in within 24 hours, and should there be a problem outside contractors must be engaged. Then he added –

> 'ps. Perhaps when they have been filled, camouflage might be added to pretend they had not been'.

On 11 August eight people were killed in Deal when bombs hit the gas works, station and elsewhere in the town. On another occasion on 22 October fifteen were killed by three bombs, one landing on shops in the High Street.

Several residents of Eastry mentioned the horror when an enemy bomber was shot down in September. The aircraft came down immediately behind the Eastry Mill and caught fire. The crew had all baled out except for the pilot. It was very fortunate that his bomb load appeared to have been used otherwise there would have been many casualties from resulting explosions. Four enemy aircraft made a low level attack on Sandwich strafing the town with cannon and machine guns, damaging the toll bridge, causing major damage to Manwood Court and destroying two houses in Fisher Street. Surprisingly in this attack there were only a few minor human casualties and furthermore the bridge was back in use the following day.

In September an urgent circular from the Home Security arrived on the Town Clerk's desk in Sandwich, giving advice about 'explosive incendiary bombs':

> Instruction is to be given to the general public which outweighs the claims of security, since by now the enemy are probably generally aware of the measures which are being taken to deal with the new explosive incendiary bombs (IBs). At the end of July the

enemy brought into use new types of incendiary bombs; one was a phosphorus oil bomb and the other a modification of the 1 kilo incendiary having a more powerful explosive charge. The newest types of German IBs have greater penetrative powers and can go through several floors before igniting.

Shortly after the above circular arrived, news was circulated that the new form of incendiary device had been dropped by enemy aircraft. This new bomb known as IBEN had a more powerful explosive charge than the previously used 1 Kilo magnesium incendiary. Civil Defence Services were warned that it was liable to explode any time up to 7 minutes after it had fallen, and should not be approached until after that period when water could be played on the fire.

On 15 November, church parade services were held throughout the country to mark Civil Defence Day. This celebration had been approved by the War Cabinet to be a day of national remembrance and thanksgiving for the defeat of the German air attacks on this country in 1940-41 and the work of the Civil Defence Services. The day chosen fell on the anniversary of the first great raid on the City of Coventry.

In December a dedicated unit called Royal Marine Boom Defence Scaffolding Unit was formed at Deal. They were engaged to build various types of coastal defence systems, including 'sea fire', which would cast flames on the surface of the sea should the enemy attempt to land. Around this time Kingsdown Holiday Camp was taken over by the army becoming a Weapon and Tactical Training Camp.

Two elderly dazed residents survey their wrecked home.

A circular from the Ministry of Health referred to the work of the Women's Voluntary Service and their ongoing work in handling large quantities of gifts of new and second-hand clothing from home and overseas. These were held in depots all over the country and were to be issued to persons made homeless and also evacuees. In a letter from the Ministry of Information concerning Utility Furniture, details were to be given as steps to be adopted by the Ministry of Health for the rehabilitation of those people who had been bombed out of their homes and the contents destroyed.

Shortages were the order of the day. To prepare for the festive season families had to start saving their points coupons or items of storable food months in advance. Alcohol was difficult to get unless you were a regular at the local pub! People prepared to enjoy the festivities with what they had. The Ministry of Food suggested that they created a Christmassy sparkle by dipping their sprigs of holly in a strong solution of Epsom salts which, when dry, became beautifully frosted.

A Yuletide message was sent to all Civil Defence Services describing this joyous season as being 'a work-a-day Christmas. But hope it will be a happy one all the same'. The message continued:

Like your comrades in the fighting forces you have a right to be of good heart this Christmas. In their glorious achievements you can feel that you have a very real share. Every sailor, soldier and airman knows that the Home Front is as important as any other, and it's in excellent keeping so long as the warden is on his beat, the fire guard at his post, and the whole Civil Defence machine at the ready in every village and on every street.

Shortly after wishing everybody a happy Christmas the Government announced that action would be taken against persons failing to register under Defence Regulations to Civil Defence Duties (Compulsory Enrolment) Order 1941. It was stated that local authorities should apply for prosecutions against persons who have failed to enrol. People were constantly being reminded of the country's commitment to this war.

1943 With the start of the New Year air raids continued, and on the 17 January two 250 kg high explosive bombs were dropped on the village of River. One landed in River Street, the other on the corner of Lower Road and Common Lane. Fortunately neither of them exploded. Some RAF personnel had a lucky escape when a bomb went through the verandah on a house where the men were standing throwing them into the bomb crater. Over fifty persons had to be evacuated from adjacent properties whilst the bombs were recovered and made safe. The task was made difficult because these bombs had sunk into the river mud.

Then on 18 January, during darkness, enemy aircraft attacked Dover with incendiaries and high explosive bombs, then heavily bombed Langdon Battery with six high explosive devices causing a great deal of damage and resulting in several casualties amongst the artillery men. In their log book there was an entry that confirmed that the battery's 'fighting efficiency was maintained'. Enemy aircraft on 8 February dropped mines in the harbour approaches but lost one aircraft which crashed into the sea near the western entrance.

On the morning of the 3 February, a formation of Lockheed Ventura bombers set out to bomb targets in Northern France. By mid morning they were attacked by Luftwaffe fighters. One of the allied planes was severely damaged but managed to turn around and limp back towards the British coast. A Tilmanstone resident recalls the event as the aircraft had crashed on his grandfather's farm at Poor Start. He remembers the wreck staying on the site for about a week before being transported away on a low-loader via Sandwich to RAF Manston to be repaired. It was at this time that an

A Fog Intensive Dispersal Operation (FIDO) system was installed to permit aircraft to land in poor conditions. This photograph shows the large fuel tanks required for this undertaking.

emergency crash runway was left clear at RAF Manston to allow aircraft returning home to land if they were low on fuel or severely damaged.

During the early months of 1943, the Board of Trade in a circular expressed their concern that small shopkeepers and traders should be made aware of the fact that if they did not insure their properties they would receive no war damage compensation. The document stated:

> Fixed property is covered under the War Damage Act, but movable property is not protected unless the owner insures. Stocks are insurable under the commodity insurance scheme. Plant and machinery and shop fittings are insurable under the business scheme.

With the great demand for materials in repairing war damaged buildings and replacing window glass, a circular was sent to local authorities asking them to advise builders to reduce the consumption of linseed oil and glazing putty wherever practicable. Shortages were being experienced in every direction. The Minister of Works announced that five hundred thousand gallons of paint was now available for the exteriors of private dwellings and civil properties, but distribution would be controlled by the 'Control of War Emergency Paint Order, 1943'. To prevent the nation getting too excited the circular pointed out that the paint was produced in only one colour, **dark brown**!
It was also announced that local authorities would hold a stock of stirrup hand pumps for resale.

With so many items being on ration or in short supply, Winston Churchill thought it was time to ease the gloom that hung over the country. So in a letter to the Ministers of War and Transport he thought it was inappropriate to ban the transport of flowers by rail. The letter continued:

> *'I ask that some effort should be made to ease up on this WAR on flowers, in which your department is showing an undue relish'.*

Furthermore Churchill wrote to the Chiefs of Staff saying he could not see why church bells should not be rung on Sundays to summon worshippers to church. I recommend that permission be given in time for Easter as invasion has become less likely.

In July a new use was found for the crumbling and silted up Sandwich Port facilities at Richborough which had been such a major asset during the 1914-18 war but allowed to decay. The camp then referred to as Richborough Camp became a Naval Shore Establishment and posting for the Marines, and was involved in landing craft construction and training. The camp was renamed *HMS Robertson*.

With the war in Europe coming to a close but spreading into the Far East the need for jungle training became very important, and to ensure that the Royal Marines were at least basically prepared, a miniature jungle was simulated at Eastry.

In a report to the Cabinet on 19 July covering a visit he had made to the Dover Garrison, the Prime Minister said he was worried that there was only one battalion in Dover and one at St. Margaret's Bay. He had posed the question to their Commander as to what would happen if a few thousand Storm Troopers came across in fast motor boats one night. Churchill said the Commander was not able to give him a very reassuring answer, and would look very silly if some of our valuable guns were blown up. A cause for concern, Churchill thought.

An interesting series of letters exchanged by the Prime Minister with Hugh Dalton at the Board of Trade in late July was in regard to the shortage of playing cards for use by the forces and industrial workers. Winston felt it was extremely important that some amusement in their leisure hours was provided and there was nothing handier than a pack of cards. He was so keen on getting extra packs of cards manufactured that he was willing to get 20 more workers and 100 tons of paper to produce them.

Two of Dover's famous wartime visitors, Winston Churchill and Field Marshal Smuts meeting the town's Civil Defence Officials.

In June the town of Margate experienced a terrifying daylight attack by a dozen Focke-Wulf 190 fighter bombers. A great deal of damage was done to the High Street and there were a number of casualties.

On the 31 August, a Spitfire developed an engine fault and crashed at Selson on the outskirts of Eastry. The airman tried to eject but his parachute did not fully open in time and he was killed. A few days later on 3 September, an enemy fighter bomber came in over Sandwich Bay. The searchlights at Knowlton picked it up and the anti-aircraft battery at Worth opened fire. The crew jettisoned a large bomb in trying to escape. This exploded above a group of trees in the grounds of Eastry House. Consequently a great deal of damage was caused to houses in the High Street, Gore Road and Mill Lane. Windows were smashed, roofs torn off and ceilings brought down. A resident at Forge House had heard the aircraft passing and the whoosh of the falling bomb followed by a mighty explosion. *'It gave the village a jolly good shake!'*, he said.

On Guy Fawkes Day, a twin-engine American Mitchell bomber crash-landed near Upper Venson Farm. It was piloted by Wing Commander Tait who later commanded No.617 Squadron on the remarkable Dam Buster raid.

On Sunday afternoon 4 December the town of Deal was shelled causing a great deal of damage. Then a couple of days before Christmas eight shells from German long-range guns were reported to have landed near Eastry. It is impossible to record the number of incoming shells fired from the guns across the channel. Fortunately many of these fell in the marshland between Deal and Sandwich.

During August, the National Fire Service held a major exercise in the county in conjunction with the military. It was held to test the Service's readiness in the event of an invasion attempt by the Germans. Hundreds of men and women and their vehicles took part in 'Operation Harlequin'. Emergency fire stations were set up in military camps and naval establishments with the fire crews coming under a military code of discipline. The NFS crews carried out detailed inspection of stores, ammunition, petrol dumps and the availability of emergency water supplies.

The exercise took several months and lessons learned were quickly put into operation. Under strict security the country was divided up into Red, Brown and Green areas. The Brown areas were those thought least likely to be attacked, and would provide reinforcements to the coastal areas designated Red. In the Green areas the fire force was to remain at the same manpower level. All seagoing fire boats were to be sent to the south coast, and the naval auxiliary boats were fitted with fire pumps and manned by the National Fire Service.

A decoy operation that went wrong, **'Operation Starkey'**, was originally planned as a large scale invasion hoax aimed at Boulogne in the Pas de Calais region of the French channel coast. By the time it was actually executed it was considerably downsized. From mid August to 9 September, elements of the British and Canadian armies, the Royal Navy, the Royal Air Force and the United States Army Air Force were involved in preparations in the southeast described as consistent with an assault on Boulogne. Much activity occurred in the surrounding area, with troop movements and transports aimed at making the enemy believe that an attack was imminent in the Pas de Calais area. At the same time squadrons of bombers attacked airfields on the other side of the Channel. On 9 September at 07.30 an armada of over 250 different sized ships sailed from Dungeness but without any troops. Noticeably the absence of Royal Navy battleships was the vital element, and was probably one of the main reasons why the Germans did not swallow the bait! At 09.00 hours the entire armada did an abrupt 'U' turn, and headed back to their English ports. The RAF and the USAAF proceeded to bomb targets in the Boulogne area, including airfields. A tragic result of all this bombing was the accidental bombing of the French village of Le Portel by USAAF B-17s which resulted in the killing of 500 French civilians.

Earlier in the year the government realized that conscription had taken many of its experienced coalminers into the armed forces. By then the industry had lost 36,000 workers and was desperate to attract men of service age into mining. Few accepted their offer. It was announced on 2 December by the Minister of Labour, Ernest Bevin, that one in ten men called up between the ages of 18 and 25 would now be ordered to work in the coalmines instead of going into the forces, and were called the 'Bevin Boys'. In an appeal he said:

'We've reached a point to which there are not enough miners to produce the amount of coal needed to keep the war effort going'... 'None of you would funk a fight with the enemy and I do not believe it would be said of any of you boys that you failed to respond to the call for coal upon which victory so much depends'.

Bevin organized a ballot to select the draftees. Each month for nearly two years his secretary drew two digits from a hat and all men whose National Service registration numbers ended with one of them were directed into coal mining. Many found the environment unfriendly, not only on account of the working conditions but also because of the hostility which the men encountered from the miners. Though most would have preferred to go into the Services, they faced jibes of cowardice. When the war ended they received no official recognition or received a medal as awarded to the Armed Forces.

The Ministry of Food estimated that only one in ten families would get a turkey or goose, and even rabbits were in short supply for Christmas dinner that year. A lot of food was referred to as 'mock' or 'fake'. Christmas recipes printed in the press included 'mock goose' or 'mock turkey' which was likely to be a disguised lamb joint if you were lucky! Presents again were 'make do and mend'. Popular magazines printed instructions for embroidered bookmarks, knitted slippers and gloves made from recycled wool from an old garment.

Then nationally the press announced that due to the changing role of women in society, the Church of England had relaxed its rules which insisted that they wore hats to church. At the time this was greeted as great news for women but not for milliners!

1944 At the beginning of the year things were still on the gloomy side of hopeful. The long range artillery pieces on both sides of the channel were engaged in a shoot-out. Our gunners were intent on 'softening up' the enemy positions prior to D-Day, whilst the German gunners were trying to destroy our weapon sites, radar stations and other installations.

During the early months of the year our military authorities suspected that the enemy might try some reprisal attack or some suicide mission in our area. They had been monitoring their airways and believed that a commando style raid might be made in the Sandwich Bay, Richborough area. So a Royal Marine detachment was deployed to defend and cover the radar installations in this coastal area in case a surprise attack was mounted but it turned out to be a false alarm. After the war it was established that German paratroops were to be dropped at Richborough Castle to destroy the radar station at Sandwich, and then make their escape by sea.

On 17 January the Footwear (Rubber and Industrial Directive) stated that rubber boots were only available for essential usage, and no trader could supply except on the production of a certificate issued by the Board of Trade. Furthermore coupons needed to be surrendered in respect of each pair of rubber boots. The directive also stated that very little rubber could be spared for civilian use so it was up to all of us who had rubber boots to make them last longer, getting them repaired as soon as they needed it. Reconditioned boots would not look quite as good as new but would be coupon-free and supplied at a price of 18s.6d (93p.) retail. (By comparison new boots cost £1. 9s (£1.45p.) and 6 coupons). The customer was urged to return his old boots as salvage material. It was also announced that there would be no further supplies of rubber soled plimsoles during the present acute shortage of rubber, and recently manufactured supplies were to be reserved only for the use of the Forces. A number of rubber hot water bottles are available only for Medical Supplies but stone or other alternative types should be used wherever possible. It was also suggested that wherever practicable that by using an adaptor, smaller bore rubber hosepipes should be used. This would result in a substantial saving of rubber. It can be seen every avenue was explored to conserve materials.

With so much military activity occurring in the coastal towns, Deal suffered their most tragic loss of life from shelling on 20 January from the German long range guns. Ten civilians were killed in their shelters and two more on the streets with another seventeen seriously injured. The following day the town witnessed prolonged shelling with extensive damage to properties in the High Street, College Road and the Beach Street areas. There were no reports of any casualties that day. Shells from the German long range artillery were aimed at the village of St. Margaret's and Westcliffe on 23 February but many fell short of their target, landing in the sea. Further sustained shelling was experienced on the 20 and 21 March when over 50 shells fell in the St. Margaret's area. No reports were made of any casualties.

As the war in Europe was concluding Mr. Churchill in a radio broadcast in March 1944 announced a plan for temporary housing. His vision was for the Ministry of Works to instigate an emergency programme to build 500,000 'new technology' prefabricated houses with a structural lifetime of between 10 and 15 years. This was to be started at the end of the war. It is interesting to note that this was envisaged to be a temporary fix to the housing shortage but in actual fact these 'prefabs' as they became to be known, were very sturdy and much loved by the tenants and lasted up to 50 years.
By May a prototype was on show outside the Tate Gallery in London. There was much discussion and debate over the design. By September the Prime Minister was getting annoyed over the lack of progress, and is on record as saying, *'if we are not careful we shall finish up supplying Nissen huts.'* This prompted him to write to the Minister of Reconstruction, saying that there must be no delay in ordering jigs and tools for these temporary houses for the provision of shelter for people whose homes had been destroyed. Through the use of wartime production facilities the programme got off to a good start but foundered through a combination of commercial rivalry, public concern and cost. In fact just over 150,000 were built. To confuse the issue the Ministry of Works introduced a design competition whereby over one thousand ideas were submitted. Some were approved and production began providing a confusing array of buildings. One of the most successful was 'Airey Houses'. These prefabricated buildings were made from precast concrete panels reinforced with metal recycled from obsolete military vehicles, and could be built using unskilled

A typical 'prefab' estate.

labour. A development of this type of house was built at Mill Green, Eastry, finally being replaced in 2001.

Putting on one side the shortages, the rationing and day-to-day problems the ordinary citizens of this part of England had been experiencing, on the big picture which had been going on for months all around us, allied planners had created '**Bodyguard**' in November the previous year. They had known for some time that the key to the D-Day invasion (**Operation Overlord**) was to deceive the Germans into thinking it would happen elsewhere and later than planned. Operation Bodyguard consisted of a number of sub-plans and was devised and managed by the London Controlling Section at the offices of the War Cabinet. Primarily a British Operation it was highly sophisticated and ambitious, London Control having been given considerable authority and autonomy. Their deception plans included spoof wireless traffic from dummy radio stations with the aim of making the German High Command think that we had plans to make an invasion attempt centered from the East Kent ports. The most significant part of Bodyguard was '**Fortitude**' where the aims were to ensure that the Germans did not reinforce Normandy and instead reinforced Norway and the Pas de Calais area.

This was an immense plan of deception which had started to be planned some 12 months previously. As D-Day approached hundreds of dummy landing craft were seen in Ramsgate, Dover and Folkestone Harbours. All over this part of Kent other methods of deception were being employed such as inflatable dummy tanks and aircraft, and large tented camps erected to confuse the enemy. The RAF even allowed German scout aircraft to penetrate the airspace of southeast England to see what appeared to be a build-up. Troop exercises were undertaken in the hope of being witnessed and reported by enemy agents who had been allowed to remain active, in addition to making use of double agents amongst many other tricks. Whilst all this was taking place all types of army vehicles and vast quantities of ammunition were being assembled and carefully camouflaged some distance away from the coast.

> **Author's Note:** As a child he was evacuated to north Buckinghamshire and remembers seeing the country lanes lined with camouflaged corrugated steel shelters with countless boxes of munitions. Then, almost overnight to his surprise they had all disappeared!

From radio messages intercepted by the allies, it was confirmed that the deception had worked and accredited by the German High Command until several days after the D-Day landings.

Early in the year Richborough Port in Sandwich became a Government Defence Area. The high walls concealed the workshops where parts of the allies' secret weapon, the **Mulberry Harbour**, were being assembled in readiness to be towed out to sea en route to the Normandy coast ready for the D-Day invasion. The area was a hive of activity with numerous lorries coming and going at the Port. It is said that even the local bus service had its windows 'blacked out' for journeys through the area.

Richborough was allocated the task of manufacturing the floating roadways that were connected with Mulberry, codenamed '**Whale**'. The Whale sections were, in fact, bridges supported on floats called '**Beetles**'. Each section consisted of six bridges, the whole section being some 500 feet (154m) in length. Each 36 ton bridge was carefully lowered onto a beetle. The fifty completed whale sections were towed downstream to the **Overlord** assembly areas ready to be transported across the channel to Normandy when the call came.

In a Press Release on 29 March 1944 the Secretary of State for War declared that certain areas of the coast were to be referred to as Military Protected Areas. This consisted of a coastal belt some 10 miles (16km) in depth extending from the Wash and round the east and south coast to Lands End, thus including the Borough of Sandwich and Eastry Rural District. At Richborough Port a haze of a smoke screen covered the area concealing the activities going on within its walls from aerial reconnaissance. The general effect of this order was to prohibit persons who were not resident from entering the controlled area. However, certain classes of person such as members of the Forces on duty, Members of Parliament, and certain Government officials on duty were exempt. Even if a person came within one of the permitted classes the Secretary hoped that he or she would refrain from entering, save in cases of real necessity.

In a letter to various Ministers, Winston Churchill said he was pleased to hear that the production of **'Mulberry'** was successfully completed on time. The final operational requirement for **'Phoenix'** had been met by 23 May, and the minimum operational requirement for **'Whale'** by the following day. As a result all the equipment is now in the hands of the Admiralty, and ready and waiting in the assembly areas on D-Day.

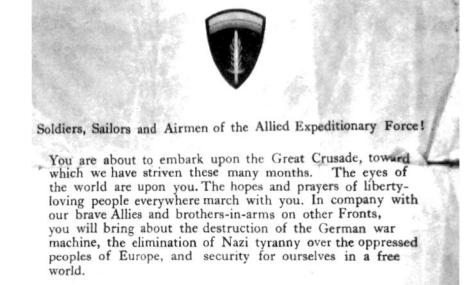

A good luck message from General Dwight Eisenhower, the Allied Supreme Commander before the epic D- Day battle.

'I congratulate you all for completing this complicated work.'

Operation Overlord (D-Day) began on the morning of 5 June, when minesweepers cleared ten lanes through the German minefields in the English Channel. They were followed on the 6 June by huge convoys of troopships, each escorted by all manner of vessels running the gauntlet of enemy dive bombers. At home the Home Guard battalions began manning sections of anti-aircraft and coast defences, often taking over many routine and security duties previously undertaken by the military thus releasing them for battle. From RAF Manston there were hundreds of sorties against enemy coastal positions, with space at the ready to receive back damaged aircraft making emergency landings. So the Allied invasion of

Europe had started. The Normandy landings were a massive joint services operation with naval, aerial and paratroop elements supporting the main amphibious assault. The successful outcome of the landings was a tribute to the planning and heroism of the men and women involved.

Sections of the two Mulberry harbours were towed across the English Channel to the Normandy coast by tugs at a speed of about 5mph. The 'Whale' sections from Port Richborough passing Dover Harbour on 6 June encountered a storm. Some units were anchored in Dungeness Bay and required some remedial repairs before they were towed into position off the Normandy beaches. By 9 June, just three days after D-Day, two harbours codenamed Mulberry A & B had been assembled by Corps of Royal Engineers. However a storm on 19 June destroyed the American harbour leaving only the British one, Mulberry B, which came to be known as Port Winston. This harbour in the 10 months after D-Day was used to land over 2.5 million men, 550,000 vehicles and millions of tons of supplies showing how important it proved to be.

Portions of Mulberry Harbours being towed along the coast in readiness to cross the English Channel.

A tentative warning about missiles appeared in the press as early as 26 April, asking the Police, Aid Raid Wardens and members of the Royal Observer Corp in southern England not to publish any report *'which would indicate to the enemy where his missiles may fall'*.

The successful landings in France did not mean that the war in southeast Kent appeared to be over. The summer months that year saw the enemy deploy a new form of attack with V1 flying bombs. In the early hours of 13 June, four 'pilotless aircraft' were spotted. Nothing further happened until late on 15 June when the Langdon Battery at Dover recorded in their log book at 23.30 hours, *'radio controlled plane or flying torpedo sighted from the French Coast'*. The Germans now started their campaign of 'Vergeltung' or Retaliation in earnest. The *Evening Standard* headlines on 16 June, stated -

Morrison announces New German 'Air Weapon'
Pilotless Planes now Raid Britain.

These were the first of Hitler's terror weapons. Londoners called them 'doodle bugs' or 'buzz bombs', from the sound of their engine. They were the first operational guided missiles designed to fly at 350 mph. at an altitude of 3500 feet (1077 m) and with a maximum range of 130 miles (208km) and came as a surprise to everyone. People were puzzled as they passed overhead. The realization soon set in that when the engine stopped these missiles plunged to earth in an indiscriminate way causing devastating loss of life and structural damage. The Ministry of Home Security issued the following advice:

'When the engine of the pilotless aircraft stops and the light at the end of the machine is seen to go out, it may mean that the explosion will soon follow – perhaps in five to 15 seconds : so take refuge from the blast.'

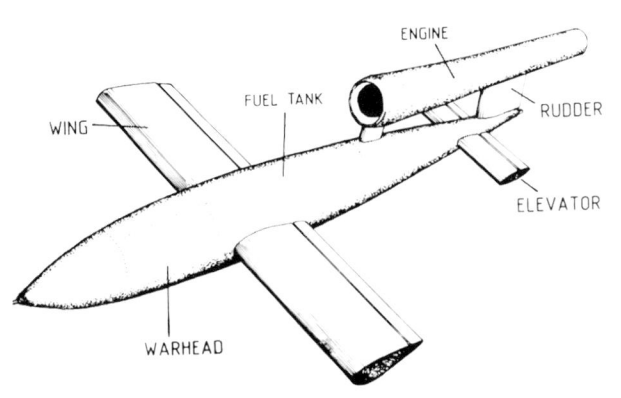

Often these V1s went over at about 100 feet (30m), and on one occasion the anti-aircraft battery at Worth lowered their guns to try to hit them but without success. In fact the only thing they hit was a cottage now called 'Larksfield'. Some shells went through the wall of the house and the WRAC girls who were billeted there had a narrow escape.

The problem with these guided missiles was that a vast number of people heard the air raid sirens but did not see or hear the missiles. They were deliberately aimed in the direction of London in what was termed 'Bomb Alley' with over 3000 of them arriving in a five week period, and with the alert signal and the 'all clear' almost continuous created a great deal of needless unrest. Although London was the worst affected casualties and damage occurred in areas of Sussex and most of Kent.

During the months of June and July, Glouster Meteor F1 jet fighters of No. 616 Squadron arrived at RAF Manston to be employed against V1s. They were armed with four 20mm cannon and had a top speed of 415mph.

On 17 July the War Cabinet met and the defences against flying bombs reviewed. The cabinet decided to redeploy our defences as follows:

Fighter Belt at Sea – Aircraft to operate at a distance of not less than 10,000 yards (9,230m) from the shore line.

Coastal Gun Belt – Anti-aircraft guns will be deployed in a narrow strip 5,000 yards (4,615m) wide – extending along the coast from Beachy Head to St. Margaret's Bay. Guns to fire out to sea up to 100,000 yard (92,300m) limit.

Inland fighter Belt – To operate between coastal gun zone and the balloon barrage – To be assisted at night by searchlights.

Balloon Belt – No change.

It was a major logistical exercise moving and re-siting in four days nearly 400 heavy guns and 600 Bofors, along with 23,000 men and women. This move proved very beneficial and with the help of new radar, predictors and shells armed with new

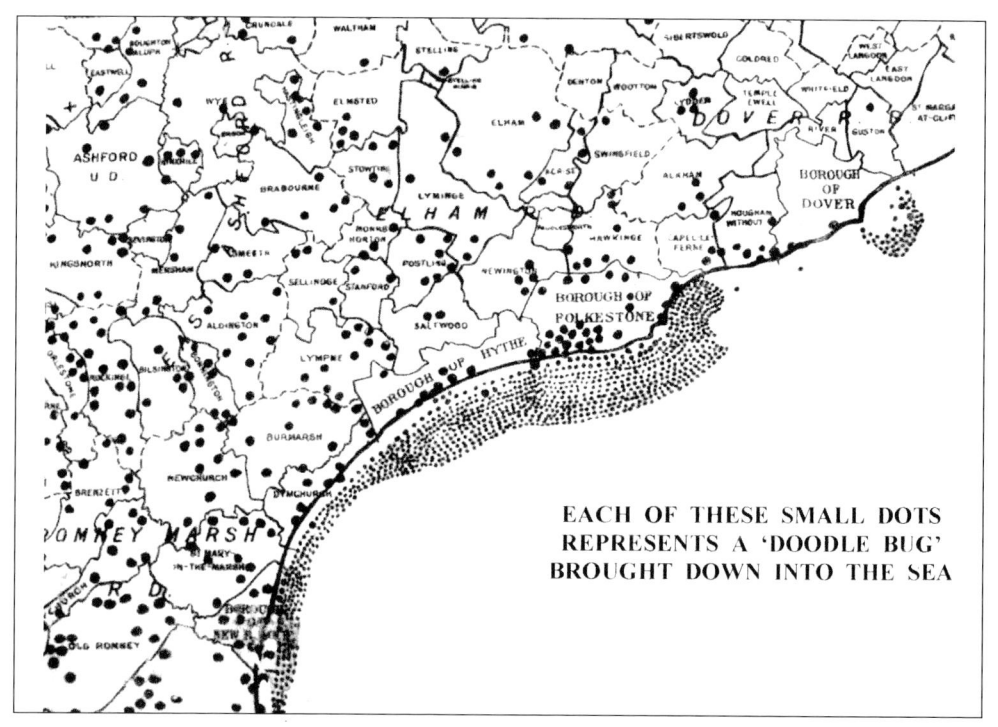

EACH OF THESE SMALL DOTS REPRESENTS A 'DOODLE BUG' BROUGHT DOWN INTO THE SEA

proximity fuses, the gunners by the end of August exceeded all hopes and not more than one in seven 'doodle bugs' got through to the Capital.

A large searchlight was sited at Foxborough Hill, Woodnesborough. It is understood it was fitted to sound locators that automatically aligned it onto the target. Stationed close by was a detachment of RAF Regiment with armoured cars and ground-mounted Hispano 30mm aircraft cannons previously based at Deal.

The Ministry of Health announced on 18 August the separation of Local Ambulance Services from Fire Service control, also suggesting that the Civil Defence Ambulance Service might provide for manning, maintenance and operation of local ambulances.

On the 20 July, two Messerschmitt Bf.109s landed at RAF Manston and both pilots surrendered. The strange thing was that it was revealed later that an attempt had been made on Adolf Hitler's life at Rastenburg the same day. It was never established but raised the possibility that there was a connection?

During the summer months the enemy again stepped up the shelling of the coastal towns. Many landed on the beach at Walmer and in the Kingsdown area on 29 August. However these resulted in little damage and no casualties. On the 1 September, there was a continuous shell warning all afternoon when about ten shells were fired at Deal. It was estimated that over 200 properties were demolished or seriously damaged but reports gave only seven people as being injured. A further 16 landed in the North Deal area on 10 September damaging about 70 properties. Fortunately only three civilians were reported injured.

A Second Terror Weapon followed on 8 September. These were known as the V2 being a long-range rocket weighing 12 to13 tons and having a 1 ton warhead with a capability of travelling over 200 miles (320km). They had a maximum speed of about 4000 mph and the whole flight took 3 to 4 minutes. In all about 1,200 were successfully launched against London in seven months before our armies liberated The Hague where most of the rockets had been sited for launching.

During the early summer the government urged the press to continue warning the general public about lighting bonfires. The following is a typical announcement – 'Fires in Wartime Aid the Enemy. Don't just be **careful** – take extra care – for every fire in wartime is an enemy behind the lines'. Then later in the year when the war was going well for the allies, the Government proposed replacing total blackout with what was termed 'dimout' in some parts of the country. However in some of the coastal towns full blackout remained in place. The area was repeatedly shelled by the long-range German artillery on the other side of the Channel, and subjected to attack by occasional flying bomb or large V2 missiles passing overhead.

Two allied soldiers sit astride one of the huge guns of Todt Battery which they had just captured.

On 6 October the *Kentish Express* announced under the banner headlines:
BATTLE OF THE COAST
> The last of the big guns on the other side of the Channel have been silenced. After four years of tribulation the people in the southeast coast towns once more breathe and move freely. No longer need to take their meals in shelters, no longer spend sleepless nights ever on the alert for the sound of the shells and the crash of masonry.

In Dover the loudspeakers which had previously been used to warn people to take cover, now broadcast the wonderful news, thanking God it's all over. It's only those who underwent the ordeal who can realize what it had been like.

Casualty figures from shelling in coastal towns:

As reported in the County newspapers King George VI and Queen Elizabeth visited the bombed and shell-torn ports of Dover and Folkestone on 18 October. In the afternoon at a sports field in Folkestone large detachments of civil defence workers and members of the National Fire Services were inspected by their Majesties. They also met firefighters from the reinforcing units under the 'Colour Scheme' who had come to Kent eight months earlier to assist the local brigades when there were possibilities of an invasion and increased air raids, and were now about to leave the area.

At the October Quarter Sessions at Wingham a farmer from Guston was fined £60 (a fortune in those days and a severe punishment) for receiving 144 gallons (655 litres) of stolen army petrol. He said in his defence that he had given a Canadian serviceman some eggs and the soldier left the petrol at the farm.

Town	No. Shells	No. Killed	No. Injured
Broadstairs	2	?	?
Deal	120	12	50
Dover	2,225	107	440
Folkestone	219	28	200
Kingsdown	?	12	50
Margate	2	?	?
Ramsgate	42	10	43
St. Margaret's	687	few	few

A circular dated 7 November was addressed to the Sandwich Housing Authority informing them that very high priority should be given to the rebuilding of houses which had been destroyed by enemy bombing, which attracted a cost of works payment under the War Damage Act. For the present this arrangement would be confined to houses which could be rebuilt at a cost not exceeding £1500, and steps must be taken to secure the maximum economy in materials and labour.

Then on 13 November the Minister of Health issued a document permitting evacuees to return to their homes. It stated that those who were residing in distant parts were requested, if possible, to make part or whole of the journey by normal transport links but where necessary special transport might be available. It was emphasized that the resources of the Volunteer Car Pool were limited, and there were restrictions on the use of petrol and mileage payments being paid out of public funds.

Queen Elizabeth visiting Warden's Post Z4 somewhere in Dover.

After the allied Normandy invasion in June and the rapid advance through France, people thought the war might be over by Christmas. In some places the need for a blackout was considered unnecessary and even churches were permitted to allow lights to shine through their stained glass windows. This was the first time for four years. People longed for peace but it was not to be with news of death and destruction from Europe, and with the terror of 30 'doodlebugs' hitting this country on Christmas Eve victory seemed a distant hope.

1945 On 2 March, the Minister of Health sent all Local Authorities a folder giving details of a new educational campaign on venereal diseases. The document stated that large posters had been displayed on hoardings throughout the country with the object of drawing public attention to the seriousness of the problem. This was the first time this subject had been brought to light in this way. It aroused no criticism meeting with the approval of the vast majority of the public. It highlighted root causes which led to this problem being, particularly in wartime, the temptations of promiscuous sexual behaviour and consequently to the spread of these diseases.
The popular magazine *Woman's Own* carried a series of articles promoting marriage and warning young women of transmitted diseases, unwanted pregnancies, and advising women wrestling with various ethical problems.

The Prime Minister, writing to various Ministries in March, proposed that women leaving the Land Army should be given a special allocation of ration coupons and a proportionate grant to take account of the fact that they had surrendered coupons in excess of the special industrial allowance for their uniforms.
In July an announcement was made to all women in the Services or working on munitions they were to be released from duty. The statement said that a half a million would be out of uniform or out of munitions factories within three months.
Another announcement stated that many doctors had already returned to civilian life, and proposed to release a further 1,600 from the Services in October to ensure adequate medical cover for civilians that coming winter.

Although in August 1944 the Secretary of State for War had issued a circular allowing removal of restrictions of entry into areas where they had been imposed earlier in the year, in some areas restrictions remained such as in Sandwich where military activity continued in The Bay. In a letter titled 'Ranges with Coastal Danger Areas' addressed to the Clerk of the Sandwich Corporation from a senior military man who was the District Claims Officer, it continued:
> ...earlier this year Def. Reg. 16 was revoked, the effect of which has been to open to the public the foreshore along the whole coastline in Kent.
> It will be appreciated that it is necessary to safeguard the public in cases where sections of the foreshore form part of the Danger Areas of ranges firing out to sea when firing is in progress.
> This office has accordingly been instructed to issue a Notice under Def. Reg. 52 in respect of all such areas at present in use.
> In pursuance of the provisions of Regulation 52 it authorized the use of the land in the area of sea shore between High and Low water mark within the danger area where the public was prohibited. The land specified may be required for military exercises, the erection of encampments, the construction of military works of a non-permanent character, including the use of live ammunition during the period 1-31 August 1945.

On 8 May, Winston Churchill appeared on the balcony of the Ministry of Health building in Whitehall to be acclaimed by a huge crowd. Many people had waited hours and just before 6 pm. the Prime Minister appeared with the inevitable cigar in his mouth, and accompanied by some of his War Chiefs and Ministers. He spoke in his strong firm voice saying:

*'God bless you all. **This is your victory**. Victory of the cause of freedom in every land. In all our long history we have never seen a greater day than this.*

Everyone has done their bit. Everyone has tried. Neither the long years, nor the dangers, nor the fierce attacks of the enemy have in any way weakened the independent resolve of the British nation. God bless you all'.

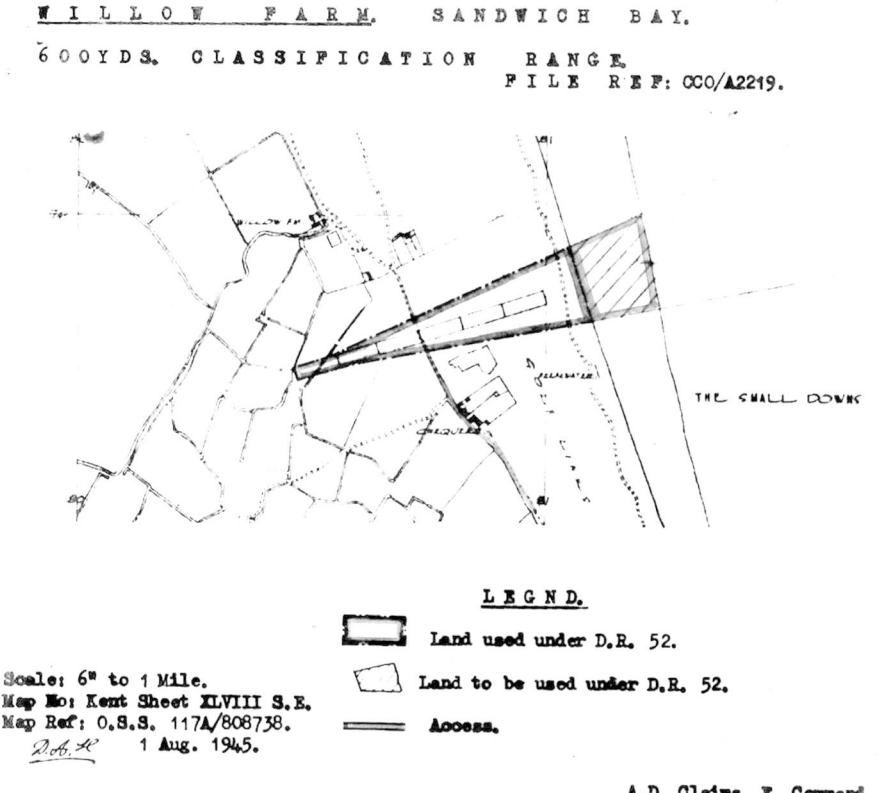

```
W I L L O W     F A R M.     S A N D W I C H     B A Y.
6 0 0 Y D S.   C L A S S I F I C A T I O N     R A N G E.
                                       F I L E   R E F: CCO/A2219.
```

LEGND.

☐ Land used under D.R. 52.
☐ Land to be used under D.R. 52.
═══ Access.

Scale: 6" to 1 Mile.
Map No: Kent Sheet XLVIII S.E.
Map Ref: O.S.S. 117A/808738.
1 Aug. 1945.

A.D. Claims, E. Command.

The *Dover Express* reported that the 'dimout' in coastal areas had been lifted at midnight on 10 May. Later in the year the Ministry of Home Security issued a directive that all street lighting could be reintroduced on 15 July.

On the 30 April the Minister of Health issued a circular sanctioning the Parish Councils to permit reasonable sums of money being spent on celebrating the cessation of hostilities in Europe but not to discourage subscriptions of money from private individuals'.

When the end of the war in Europe, or VE day as it was called, was announced on 8 May there were peace celebrations and countless parties throughout the land and beyond. Due to the nation's war weariness and the shortages of food and money, communities celebrated with very low-key events usually arranged just to give the children a party but nevertheless a time of rejoicing.

An emergency meeting of the Eastry Parish Council was called and a hurried sports programme drawn up to take place in The Gun Park on the 10 May at a total cost of

£11. Another typical event was in the village of River, Dover, where the youngsters assembled at Crabble Athletic Ground for their victory treat and fancy dress parade. The *Dover Express* of 20 July reported, *'races were run and great fun prevailed in ideal weather'*. Each child was given a 'thrupenny piece' (approx. 1p) and a bag of sweets before they returned home. At Guston near Dover an event was organized by the village school mistress. The Parish Council allowed £10 to be expended on tea and games for the children.

The following table gives the reader a rough indication of the extent of civilian casualties, bombs and damage in southeast Kent:

Local Authority	Killed	Seriously Injured	Properties Destroyed	Air Raid Warnings	Air Craft Attacks	HE Bombs	Incendiaries
Broadstairs	7	6	18	3,628	52	278	300
Canterbury	115	140	808	?	?	?	?
Deal	64	55	172	3,676	?	173	118
Dover Borough	199	307	910	3,059	100s	464	1,500
Dover Rural Dist.	5	10	36	?	?	389	2,380
Eastry Rural Dist.	20	32	27	?	?	667	1,700
Folkestone	85	181	290	?	?	378	1,113
Herne Bay	9	21	12	?	?	104	1,090
Margate	35	40	268	3,541	83	584	2,489
Ramsgate	84	89	393	3,655	53	860	283
Sandwich	0	2	7	?	?	52	1,000
Whitstable	10	35	84	?	?	232	700

When war with Japan ended later in the year a more detailed programme of celebrations was arranged with a series of events in Peak Pasture at Eastry on 22 September. Despite the inclement weather over 600 children and adults were entertained to tea and games as well as some 80 entrants taking part in a fancy dress parade. In the evening there was a huge bonfire followed by fireworks, and an open air dance with floodlighting in Church Street.

Victory in Europe Celebrations in the garden of The Bull public house in Eastry.

In October a circular was sent to all local councils entitled the *'Utilisation of Structural Materials'*. It outlined a policy to be adopted in the use of waste materials arising from the demolition of shelters, Civil Defence works, Emergency Water Supplies, etc., and from the clearance of war debris. During the war over £14 million had been spent on construction of public, communal, domestic, school shelters etc., thus resulting in very large quantities of waste materials. In addition, there were 2½ million Anderson shelters and 1¼ million Morrison shelters with a total weight of over a million tons to be disposed of, and millions of tons of debris from war-damaged buildings, military works, road blocks and other obstructions, all to be cleared away. Therefore in the national interest every effort should be made to find uses for these materials.

Families could now venture out on the sandy beaches of Sandwich Bay without detonating a mine.

Early in 1946 the signposts which had been removed when there was a danger of invasion were replaced, and the Anderson shelters removed unless the householders wished to buy them. In some cases they had become a feature in people's gardens often becoming a garden shed or part of a rockery.

As the war in Europe ended some enemy prisoners of war (POWs) were brought back to this country to assist in work, previously undertaken by men called up for military service. Even in 1946 it was estimated that more than 40,000 were still held in Britain. The postwar government deliberately ignored the Geneva Convention by refusing to let the prisoners return home well after the war was over. During 1946 about one in five farm workers were German POWs. Others were employed on road works and building sites.

Immediately after the war this country underwent a tremendous social change. Britain was bankrupt after the war, the wartime Prime Minister Winston Churchill was voted out of office and a new Labour Government elected which nationalized many industries. This country faced a long road to recovery from the cost of this war.

Their job completed, the guns were broken up and East Kent returned to peace again.

Chapter 4

THE HOME GUARD

This section of this book is mainly restricted to a portion of East Kent and the five Coastal Battalions of the Home Guard, covering the coast from Sheppey to Camber. These battalions were initially raised as the Loyal Defence Volunteers (LDV) in the spring of 1940, but by the autumn of that year were renamed the Home Guard, gradually taking on a more offensive role in the defence of this country.

The big question still remains, even in the twenty first century, had Germany invaded would a battle for the Kent and Sussex coastal strip have decided Britain's future? It was thought at the time the enemy would attempt a 'Blitzkrieg' – style of attack with aircraft, armour and infantry such as they had successfully employed in other countries. It would involve rapid thrusts of motorized infantry, spearheaded by tanks and dive bombers. After gaining a firm foothold in the coastal areas of Kent and East Sussex, this would be followed by simultaneous landings along the coast between Worthing and Ramsgate, possibly more concentrated in the Romney Marsh area, before pressing on to capture Dover Harbour from the landwardside, and then advancing towards the Medway towns and London. The coastal Home Guard Battalions and their 'stay behind units' would have played a major part in the bloody battle that would have taken place. Fortunately this invasion was never activated, mainly due to the Luftwaffe not being able to gain complete air superiority, and after the Battle of Britain such an attack became less likely.

1940 On 14 May, Anthony Eden made his first speech as Secretary of State for War, asking for volunteers. He announced that men aged between 17 and 65 years who were not eligible for military service, were to serve in the newly formed Local Defence Volunteers (later known as the Home Guard.) They would form the last line of defence against an expected invasion and were intended primarily to combat enemy paratroopers landing behind our forward positions. They would be part-timers and unpaid but would receive a uniform and be armed. They were told to report to their local police station to sign up. Police stations were inundated with volunteers and it was said that they kept coming through the night. It was estimated that 10,000 enrolled in Kent in the first 24 hours. The following day Brigadier General H.S. Franklin was appointed to organize the Local Defence Volunteers in the county.

At a meeting in Ashford on 16 May, a meeting was arranged by the Kent organizer at which Major General A.L. Forster accepted the appointment as Group Organizer for

East Kent. The two immediately set about selecting from the police lists the names of suitable commanders for Companies which were to be formed in each Group. At the local council offices in Sandwich it was understood that in joining the LDV, members of staff could only undertake duties during their spare time and in their home locality, and enlistment should not interfere with the performance of their official work. The volunteers were given instructions as to how and where to site roadblocks. The most suitable place, for instance, would be a narrow stretch of road making it impossible for an approaching vehicle to be able to turn around, and how to quickly build roadblocks from barbed wire, felled trees, farm vehicles and equipment etc., but not to obstruct normal business or to impede our forces. At first they had little fighting capability, with very few rifles and no ammunition, but busied themselves by harassing innocent civilians for their identity cards, putting up and manning road blocks. There was a slogan used at this time which was meant to rally the troops, **'You can always take one with you'** if the enemy landed. Perhaps it was fortunate that patriotism was not put to the test.

On the 17 May, Brigadier General Franklin was ordered to have 1,500 men armed and ready for patrol by the next morning. How weapons and ammunition were obtained from Chatham and delivered to police stations at such notice is a mystery. After collecting, distributing and cleaning there were more than one thousand armed men on duty in parts of Kent by late evening the following day. A remarkable achievement!

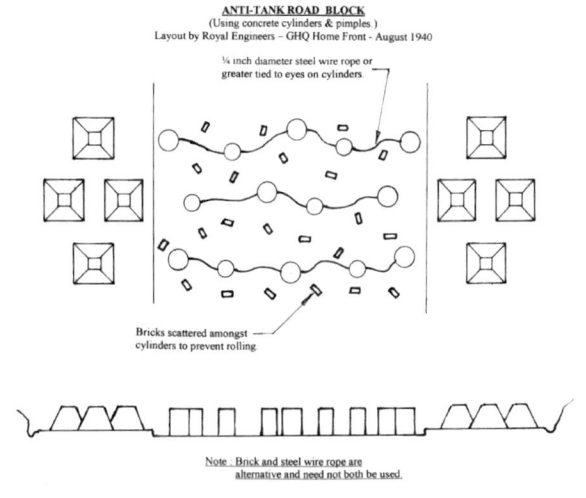

After the quick response shown by the Brigadier there was some delay in local organizations being set up due to the police lists not being arranged into parishes, and much sorting out was required before Company and Platoon Commanders could determine to which sub-units a volunteer should belong. However a supplementary force with over one million men was in place by the summer. They were given military style training although at first they had no uniforms just an armband, and little other equipment. They were told that they would soon be supplied with bombs made from pint size bottles containing a petrol mixture with a simple fuse, to be known as a Molotov cocktail.

Anthony Eden had agreed in Cabinet on 17 June that the supplementary force was to be a 'broomstick army' until supplies of weapons became available. It was pointed out that there were small quantities of the standard army Lee-Enfield rifle available. In Kent some rifles had been in storage since the end of the First World War and were distributed to police stations in Canterbury, Ashford, Maidstone and Tonbridge.

Ernie Friend of Eastry poses for a photograph in his new uniform..

Elderly Tom Pointer of Eastry. He had served in the Boar War (1899-1902), the First World War and now ready to engage a new enemy.

Jimmy Langdon an ex-miner known as Taffy from Tilmanstone on guard.

With the continued prevarication and the shortage of weapons the Margate platoon took the initiative and visited the harbour to find piles of abandoned arms and ammunition left by the returning troops from Dunkirk. The authorities were soon asking for the weapons to be returned but it is understood their request was met with a stony silence from the platoon. However, members of the public were invited/requested to hand in any weapons they might have to their local police station to be used by the Local Defence Volunteer Corps, and within a few months over 20,000 weapons of all shapes and sizes were handed in. Many of these were shotguns and to use these weapons more effectively a single-slug cartridge was developed.

In June 1940, Churchill writing to the Secretary of State for War said *'I hope you like my suggestion of changing the name Local Defence Volunteers, which is associated with Local Government,* **to Home Guard***'*. From about this time they acquired better weapons and became a force to be reckoned with. In late June the Government appears to have been overwhelmed by the number of volunteers wanting to sign up.

Originally the force was organized into Companies, subdivided into Sections. Then on 23 August 1940, the name Local Defence Volunteers was officially replaced with Home Guard, the companies becoming battalions with the same organization as battalions in the regular army. Their leaders were designated Battalion, Company and Platoon Commanders.

Local Home Guard commanders initially received little training guidance except that which had been laid out in a memo from the War Office, and it was left up to them to develop their own tactics. The plan was to organize the men in sections of about twenty four with a leader having the rank of sergeant. Up to four sections would be grouped into a platoon under a leader, and platoons were under the control of a company commander. Up to four companies made up a battalion also under a commander. In fact about 40% of recruits in the first year were First World War veterans offering a great deal of military experience to the ranks. In the autumn in a letter to the Secretary of State for War the Prime Minister wrote:

> 'Due to the lack of equipment and other facilities it might be necessary to limit the numbers wishing to join the Home Guard and create a Home Guard Reserve. Members of the Reserve would pro tem be given an arm-band, and asked to attend courses of instruction in the use of weapons and making 'Molotov cocktails', and also to report for orders in the event of an invasion'.

It was estimated that only half the men in the Home Guard had a weapon at the time. The estimated figures show that they had 850,000 rifles, 47,000 shotguns, and 49,000 automatics which were used as single shot rifles. This lack of offensive weapons was complemented with the War Office issuing 250,000 pikes, that is to say a bayonet welded onto a metal pole.

The following is an early résumé of the Home Guard ethos:
>   Its role was to delay and obstruct the enemy should they gain a foothold.
>   Be able to adapt itself from defence and even be able to attack.
>   To co-operate and augment the military and civil defence services.
>   Protect vulnerable installations such as telephone exchanges, factories, railway bridges etc.,
>   Check for subversive individuals and hostile parties.
>   Help to maintain morale in the civil population.

Under General Ironside, as Commander-in-Chief British Home Forces, a plan for new land fortifications had to be made quickly and in depth following the evacuation of British and Allied forces from France in the summer of 1940. This plan was based on the fear that the German invasion would be similar to that seen in Europe where armoured fighting vehicles roared through country after country which were not properly defended. His strategy had three main elements:
>   To delay the enemy on the beaches and break up the initial attack.
>   Develop lines of anti-tank obstacles well inland.
>   Have a mobile reserve for reinforcement or counterattack.

Main lines of defence would be positioned some distance inland with systematic demolition being an essential factor in the plan. The area would be divided into zones consisting of a series of stop lines. The main stop line which would defend London ran west through Maidstone to Bristol. The zone to the south had three stop lines. The main stop line from London going north to protect the industrial cities in the Midlands included five smaller stop lines covering the flat terrain of East Anglia. The idea behind this system of defence was to STOP or DELAY the enemy's rapid advance which had broken through the forward defences by armoured fighting vehicles (AFVs), thus allowing time for support to arrive from bases further inland. In the event the defences would be manned by local Home Guard. Although this strategy would in theory have worked they would have been outmanned and outgunned and as such could have expected heavy losses.

In the rush to complete 'Stop Lines' the Royal Engineers and the Pioneer Corps who were to provide the labour force, still required a substantial undertaking by civilian contractors. John Mowlem & Co. was the overall managing contractor, with Taylor Woodrow & Co. being one of the main sub-contractors in the south east. As early as May 1940, the War Office stated that Home Defence preparations were to be given priority over ALL other works. They immediately asked for designs of pillboxes conforming to certain requirements, namely:

> To be splinter and bullet proof: have no living accommodation and
> most important a design that could be produced in quantity and quickly.

Designs were submitted and approved in days. Additional criteria was proposed including, where possible, existing buildings to be utilized but any buildings, trees and hedges were to be removed if they were in the line of fire. It was estimated that a standard pillbox would require 2½ tons of concrete with more than 2 tons of steel reinforcement plus sand, aggregate and a large amount of wooden shuttering. Several designs were produced of which the FW3/22 and the FW3/24 were the most popular models.

A pair of multi-directional pillboxes built on the outskirts of Eastry in response to the threat of a German invasion from the Sandwich Bay direction. The lower gun slot was introduced to position a Boys anti-tank rife.

At Eastry, in addition to roadblocks, two pillboxes (as illustrated above) were built in the autumn on the edge of the village at Statenborough, to guard against AFVs and troops coming across country in the event of the enemy landing at Sandwich Bay. Much of the low lying marshy land in this area was planted with mines, and the roads for miles around were plastered with anti-tank traps and other obstacles

During the early summer months thousands of men were employed working long hours, sometimes even at night. The whole of the area around the Channel Ports was heaving with troops employed to dig trenches and erecting barbed wire entanglements to assist the beach defences where these were secured on steel poles with mines attached on the water's edge, together with minefields being laid in the bays and inlets, in an attempt to prevent landing craft from reaching the beach. At Ramsgate, Walmer and Dover a series of pipes were laid just below the low water mark through which a petroleum mixture could be pumped from large storage tanks intended to spread a wall of fire on the sea as the enemy was about to land.

At the harbours of Dover and Folkestone the authorities worked with the Royal Engineers preparing demolition charges in readiness to destroy the installations, rendering them useless to the enemy for landing supplies and reinforcements. The military manned roadblocks and machine gun posts by day and patrolled the cliff tops by night.

The War Office in an attempt to complete this mammoth task abandoned financial controls which prompted some unscrupulous companies to make huge amounts of money, often at the expense of quality work. In some cases pillboxes were in the wrong location and their field of fire in the wrong direction. In the rush to complete the work there were mistakes but as it was never intended to be an impregnable barrier, it did provide a broad line of defence in a remarkably short time.

In addition to pillboxes the workforce produced a large variety of anti-tank obstacles, including concrete pyramids known as pimples - others called dragon's teeth, beach defences, ditches, flame traps and tank traps. As the enemy attempted to move inland they would be faced by a great variety of objects designed to hinder advance, with railway bridges and lengths of track destroyed adding to the mayhem.

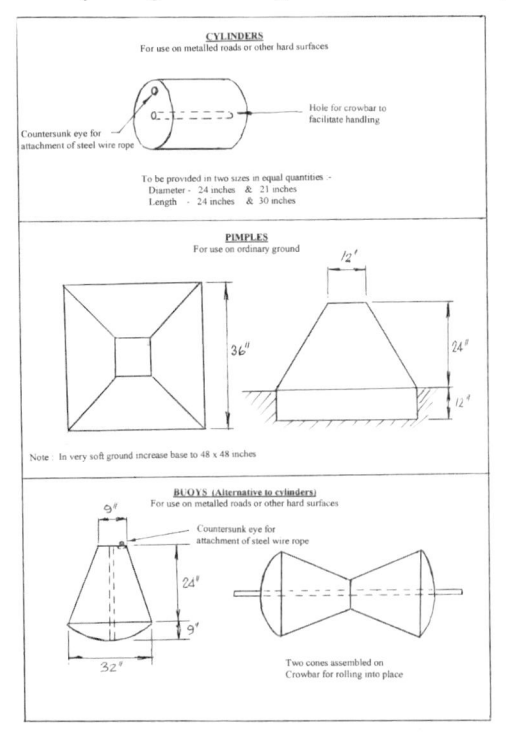

The Boys Mk.1 anti-tank rife. With a calibre of 13.97mm it had an armour penetration of 21mm at 300 metre. The gun had an overall length of 1.6 metres. However it was said that it had a kick like a mule.

Various designs of anti-tank obstacles.

On the home front things were desperate in the summer months of 1940 regarding training and converting the large group of volunteers into a proper defensive army capable of resisting and retaliating against an enemy invasion. So a campaign to turn the Home Guard into a people's army was begun, much to the alarm of the government who had probably conceived a more British solution. The leader of this campaign was Tom Wintringham, Military Correspondent of the *Daily Mirror*, who had gained expertise in guerrilla fighting during the Spanish Civil War in leading a British Battalion against the Fascists. One article, published in the *Picture Post* in June, giving practical instructions for a people's war to resist invasion was bought by the War Office who printed off thousands of copies and distributed them to Home Guard units.

Using various contacts Wintringham set up the first guerrilla warfare school at Osterley Park near London. Hundreds of Home Guard volunteers turned up and trained on how to fight the enemy, the use of explosives, and training in guerrilla tactics. He argued that the conventional system of roadblocks was a passive defence against the tank and a more active defence was needed. Should the enemy successfully land and advance inland the Home Guard must be prepared for warfare even behind enemy lines. His success with the volunteers was nicknamed 'Osterley Reds' and alarmed the government as he had fought for the Communists in Spain, and some believed that he was covertly training an army that one day might be used against the establishment in this country. However, the War Office recognized the value of his techniques gradually taking over his school and replacing it with several training camps, much on the lines promoted by the Osterley Park School. In the spring of 1941 Wintringham was dismissed from his post as Director of the training school.

In mid-July the Secretary of State for War recommended that General Alan Brooke should replace General Ironside in command of Home Forces. On 19 July, the Prime Minister visited Southern Command with General Brooke. Churchill appeared to be reassured with his new commander for not only had he acquitted himself in battle but had shown singular firmness and dexterity in very difficult situations, and was in agreement on the methods of Home Defence. On taking command of the Home Forces in late July General Brooke was not impressed with his predecessor's strategy. He felt that an all-round defence was needed to meet the threats of a seaborne and airborne attack in the form of a large number of mobile groups of mechanized infantry ready for a rapid counter offensive.

As plans were being made to turn the Home Guard into a Fighting Force, questions were being asked about how much all this was going to cost as the situation was changing from a voluntary force to a part-time military occupation on a huge scale. This concern was expressed by General Brooke writing to Anthony Eden in August. He was of the opinion that anyone who had the energy or time to be involved in the new Home Guard should enlist in the army.

>Note: On 3 August the Home Guard in Kent became affiliated to infantry regiments in their particular area, and those in East Kent came under the East Kent Regiment (The Buffs).

Those in: West Kent to Queens Own Royal West Kent Regiment.
A part of the Sheppey Battalion to the Royal Artillery.
The men were also permitted to wear the cap badge of the local regiment.

By November orders were received that battalions were to be numbered throughout the county. At the time there were twenty four general service battalions and four utility ones each numbering about one thousand men. They were lightly armed but consisted of a significant proportion of experienced troops. Above all they were fighting for their families and homes. They might have been desperate but very determined formidable opponents; quite different to the array of comic figures portrayed in the television series 'Dad's Army'. From this point on the Home Guard were fast becoming a resolute armed force.

Towards the end of the summer ships from America brought a vast quantity of P17s and P14s First World War .300 bore rifles, with about 50 rounds apiece of which only 10 were issued, mainly to be used by the Home Guard. It was said that as the ships docked there were special trains at the ports to receive them and to take the cargo to pre-determined destinations. Once the rifles had been distributed the local Home Guard members worked night and day to make them fit for use. This enabled the transfer of thousands of .303 inch British type rifles to the rapidly expanding Regular force.

Then suddenly on the 7 September, Church bells were heard ringing as alarm had spread that the Germans were about to attempt an invasion. Roadblocks were quickly moved into position on many of the Kent and Sussex roads, and it was said that some road bridges were even blown up in the belief that the enemy had landed but it all turned out to be a false alarm.

The Prime Minister addressing the House of Commons on 5 November stated:
'A country where every street and every village bristles with loyal resolute armed men is a country against which the kind of tactics which destroyed Dutch resistance - tactics of parachutists or airborne troops in carriers or gliders, Fifth Column activities – would prove wholly ineffective. A country so defended would not be liable to be overthrown by such tactics.'

General Brooke's new policy included strengthening beach defences and introduced fixed fortified areas or anti-tank islands known as NODAL POINTS. The 'nodal point' idea is based on the fact that in this part of the country the roads are narrow and twisty usually converging on a town or a village, and it was vital to counter Blitzkrieg tactics. From experiences on the continent German tanks preferred to keep to the roads and eventually to enter a built-up area. These 'nodal points' would be based in towns and villages or at major road junctions, and in most cases the Home Guard would be there waiting for them behind heavily defended positions. This idea was developed further to make each nodal point a fortress or castle. The centre of each was to have a heavily defended strong point or keep which would be made tank-proof by roadblocks. Some distance from the strong point an outer ring of defences would be constructed. A good example of this is in the village of Ash where major roadblocks each end of the High Street were constructed along with three machine gun posts. The village was termed a Category 'A' nodal point and being heavily defended was intended to hold up an invading army for two days. It was in place by November 1940, positioned to hold up an enemy advance from the Pegwell/Sandwich Bay direction advancing toward Canterbury. The village High Street had substantial roadbocks at either end, one on the Sandwich side and the other at the Guilton end. Slots were dug in the road surface into which steel girders could be dropped at a minute's notice or removed to allow troop movements. To strengthen each roadblock houses were fortified on each side of the road at grid references: (Sandwich) TR 288585 / TR287586 and (Guilton) TR 289586 / TR281584. Additional to the main defence along all roads and lanes on the approach to the village the enemy would have to contend with a variety of roadblocks, pillboxes etc., making their advance even more difficult and protracted. It would be defended by Ash Platoon 'B' Company of 5th (Wingham) Battalion Home Guard.

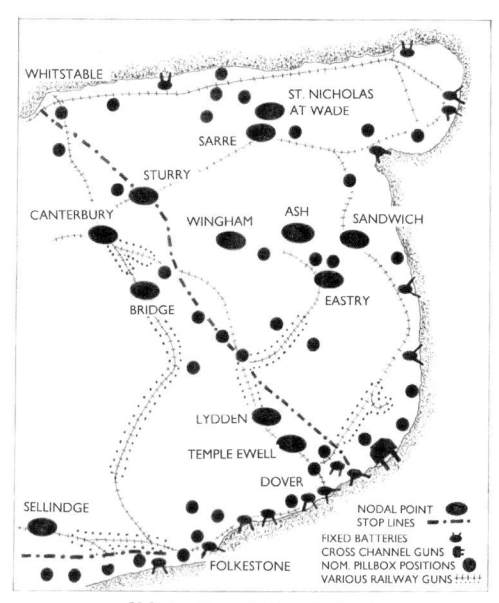

At the village of Eastry on the main Dover/Sandwich Road, another Category 'A' nodal point existed where a different tactic was employed. The village was surrounded by numerous pillboxes and roadblocks reinforced with an anti-tank trap of the conical variety designed to catch in the tracks of enemy tanks. A roadblock existed beneath the railway bridge in Selson Lane (TR30495527). It consisted of a series of removable steel girders. The farmer at Wells Farm remembers having them stored in his barn long after the war had finished.

In the centre of the village there was a fixed position 'Petroleum Flame Fougasse' weapon, positioned where the Woodnesborough Road and the Sandwich Road meet (TR309549). This weapon, if activated against a tank or AFV, would have created a major blockage with burning vehicles in the village's narrow street. In Lower Street there is evidence of a flame trap. This weapon was constructed with lengths of perforated piping along each side of the road into which a mixture of petrol and oil was pumped under pressure. The mixture would be sprayed out along the length of the pipes and ignited remotely, setting alight tanks and vehicles and creating a major roadblock.

At Sandwich the Bay was always considered a possible point where the enemy might attempt a landing. Therefore the whole beach was barricaded off, occupied by the Regular Army and secured with a massive minefield. Further inland a Flame

Fougasse weapon and pump house was built with piping leading to the beach defences. In November an additional Fougasse defence system was constructed in the town's moat. A huge fuel tank was buried and a pump house constructed between the present day bowling green and Knightrider Street.

At the key village of Sarre situated on the Thanet Way, there was another Category 'A' nodal point. The main defence was a ring of fortified buildings which were well defended. There were roadblocks on the approach roads with pillboxes, slit trenches and weapon pits protecting the rear of the village. It was prepared for all-round defence by 1st Canadian Pioneer Battalion in July and August 1940 with the local Home Guard having their headquarters in a disused quarry nearby. During 1941 the 131st Infantry Brigade took over establishing their Brigade headquarters at Sarre Court, and their 'battle' headquarters were in the tunnels dug into the banks of a disused quarry. It appears that the Army took over and enlarged the underground workings, and it is said that gangs of miners from Kent Coalfields worked on this project.

Other strategic and vulnerable areas such as airfields, factories etc., were to be guarded by regular soldiers. Less important sites were to be protected by home defence battalions of the Home Guard with their own specific type of defence arrangement. By now various camouflage techniques had been developed and were being employed to help mask these sites from the air.

With many types of equipment in desperately short supply there was a frantic need to develop new types of weapons quickly. As most of our country's oil came from America it was not in short supply which greatly eased the situation. By July the Government as an anti-invasion precaution, had petrol stations near the coast emptied or their pumps disabled to prevent petrol falling into the hands of the enemy. Their plan was to use it to impede him, and in considering this possibility the Petroleum Warfare Department was created.

This newly formed department quickly undertook some experimental trials at Dumpton Gap between Ramsgate and Broadstairs which quickly led to the development of a static flame trap. This weapon allowed a length of street or lane to be ignited in flame at a minute's notice. By September mobile flame traps had become available and delivered to about 300 Home Guard units as a kit of parts together with a set of DIY instructions. It was light enough to be wheeled along roads and would be used as part of an ambush in conjunction with Molotov cocktails. The design permitted about 66 gallon (300 litre) of petrol mixture to be pumped through a hose giving a flame up to 58 feet (18m) in length. This would have been a formidable addition to our armoury.

As mentioned earlier a flame Fougasse was sited in Eastry High Street. It was most likely to have been a 40 gallon (182 litre) steel drum buried in an earthen bank with one end exposed. At the back of the drum an explosive charge was placed, and when activated would rupture the drum and throw out a flame some 100 feet (30m). It was armed with a petrol mixture and a sticky substance which would adhere to a vehicle or tank and catch fire. A variant of this weapon was devised to be rolled over the cliff edge on to the enemy on the beach below. Other known flame traps where pumped petrol mixture was delivered by perforated pipes on the side of the road were constructed on the Deal/Sandwich Road by Sholden Church, at Dover Road, Upper Walmer (Walmer Brewery) and at Bay Hill, St. Margaret's. An adaptation of the Fougasse was called the Hedge-hopper. In this case barrels of the mixture could be projected over a hedge or wall, landing in the road and igniting. In addition to these weapons the standard flame-throwers were available.

The Petroleum Warfare Department experimented with 'setting the sea on fire' by burning oil on the water's surface but this resulted in a complete failure. From this, however, came a surprising success. It was in the form of an inspired invention of a false rumour that the British could set the sea on fire, and was encouraged by openly talking about it in neutral countries throughout the world. It soon became evident that the enemy had believed it and possibly an invasion attempt thwarted by this lie. The allied rumour machine went into overdrive with the RAF dropping leaflets but the German High Command soon realized this rumour and others were untrue. By then, however, the enemy had fallen for this propaganda believing that they might be asked to attempt a landing in England. On 25 September, Berlin was officially forced to deny the rumours.

Initially Local Defence Volunteers and later the Home Guard were specifically targeted at men, and any thought of women being enlisted was resolutely resisted. This typically Victorian idea was opposed by the Labour MP Edith Summerskill, and by December 1940 the Women's Home Defence was set up. This early plan was only to make use of women in the event of an invasion but not to be armed.

1941 Initially Home Guard Battalions in Kent were in Southern Command, but early in the year this command area was divided up with Kent in South East Command. Within this new command a system of Sub Districts was introduced. The Home Guard battalions covered by this book are now under the direction of Canterbury Sub District and became known as the East Kent Coastal Battalions. Folkestone was later added to Ashford Sub District in August 1944.

    5th (Wingham) Battalion Kent Home Guard
    6th (Thanet) Battalion Kent Home Guard
    8th (Cinque Ports) Battalion Kent Home Guard

With this reorganization came more rigorous training and positive leadership. The Commander-in-Chief of all the forces in the British Isles, General Sir Alan Brooke, in March 1941 stated:

> 'The Germans have developed a strategy of infiltration which results in the battle fields not being confined to front lines of opposing forces. To meet this

> *strategy and its accompanying tactics, there must be a widely dispersed force to take the shock of the enemy's primary attacks. Consequently, the most modern defensive strategy involves just such a force as the Home Guard and its function is just as important to the organization of the defence of a country as the functions of any of the other forces such as the regular army'.*

The new Home Guard tactics were becoming clearer and could be grouped into three categories:

Warning, Delaying and Harassment

Warning: Warnings could be achieved through patrols and outlying observation posts. Due to their numbers and knowledge of the terrain observation could be maintained over a large area of countryside.

Delaying: Parachute troops and airborne landings. The mission of the Home Guard was first to warn the regular forces and secondly attempt to wipe out the enemy or contain. Delay fast moving mechanized detachments. Stop progress and by falling back and manning their prepared defensive positions. These defensive positions were organized strategic areas ie., important road junctions, bridges, tunnels etc., or even within a town. Certain important positions were designated as 'Nodal Points' and the mission of the Home Guard was to hold the position as long as possible. They were expected to die fighting and without surrendering the position to the enemy.

Another group assigned to the Home Guard was the 'Scorched Earth' mission. This entailed destruction and immobilization of vehicles and the destruction of all food and water supplies.

Harassment: The Home Guard were to be taught tactics of guerrilla warfare. Once the enemy was in the country it was the duty of every member of the Home Guard to see that they had no rest at night. Harass them in daytime with sniping, booby traps and mines.

From the tactics above the 'Tom Wintringham' training methods were beginning to be considered, moving away from the role that the War Office preferred to a much more proactive attacking force bordering on outright guerrilla tactics. It had been noticed on the Continent that tanks proved to be all powerful on open land but would be less effective on the narrow roads and lanes of this country, and was to be the weakness the Home Guard could take full advantage of. In his book Wintringham, suggests that in guerrilla warfare you should operate in small groups,

> '…they should use their imagination and turn every possible means
> they come across to the disadvantage of the enemy…..Therefore be audacious;
> but at the same time always give yourself some way out of trouble ….
> A live guerrilla is much more use to your friends than a dead hero.'

Late in November 1941 the Prime Minister writing to the Secretary of State for War, considered that if the German invasion plan was to go ahead next spring it would be necessary to have a selected proportion of the Home Guard ready for use as military formations. This special section would be made up of men now in reserved occupations who were not eligible to join the Army but had volunteered for the Home Guard. This section would attend additional drills and be paid for attendance. They would not come out full-time until the ALERT was given (estimated as being a fortnight before zero day). They would be armed with rifles, machine guns and equipped with Bren gun carriers. They would not alter their characteristic civilian status until the ALERT had been given.

East Kent Coastal Battalions

5th (Wingham) Battalion Kent Home Guard

The Wingham Battalion was made up from the communities residing in the towns, villages and hamlets in what was then the Eastry Rural District Council, and included parts of Deal & Sandwich Borough Council districts. Owing to the position of this battalion in the heart of the Kent coalfields, some companies had many miners. In others farmers and agricultural workers swelled their ranks.

In April 1941 the Ash Platoon featured in an illustrated magazine designed to show the Home Guards high level of morale and preparedness to their readers.

The following list illustrates the mix of communities in this battalion.
Ash, Ashly, Aylesham, Barfrestone, Betteshanger, Deal, Deal Castle, Eastry, Elvington, Eythorne, Finglesham, Great Mongeham, Nonington, Northbourne, Preston, Ripple, Sandown Castle, Sandwich, Sandwich Bay, Sholden, Snowdown, Staple, Stourmouth, Sutton, Tilmanstone, Waldershare, Westmarsh, Wingham, Woodnesborough, Woolage and Worth.

The list above was divided into Companies and Platoons – as follows:
    'A' Company had No.1, 2, 3 & 4 Platoons
    'B' Company had No.1, 2, 3 & 4 Platoons also
            338th (Sandwich Bay) Battery Coastal Artillery
    'C' Company had No.1, 2a, 2b, 3a, 3b, 3c, 4a & 4b Platoons
    'D' Company had No.1, 2 & 3 Platoons
    'E' Company had No.1, 2, 3 & 4 Platoons also
            296th (Deal Castle) Battery Coastal Artillery

The Eastry Platoon: For the first six weeks of its existence, the Loyal Defence Volunteers had little or no administration, and on the local level much of the work of organizing the sub-units depended on local and often self-appointed individuals. Many of the men had served in the First World War just over twenty years earlier and with their military discipline and knowledge of the use of arms, took the initiative. The Parish Council Minute book refers to LDV being set up with Mr. Tordiffe in command. An old granary at Cross Farm in Mill Lane, where the present day fire station now stands, was converted into a Guard Room. His brief was to guard the telephone exchange in the High Street, maintain observation, and be prepared to block the main roads should the enemy land. Shortly afterwards a lady in the village placed her three cottages in Church Street at the disposal of the authorities. She furnished No.1 as a First Aid Post; No.2 became the headquarters of the Home Guard (Eastry Platoon) and No.3 the ARP Wardens Post. These had to be manned every night and also during the day when air raids took place. Often with bloodshot eyes after sleepless nights, members of the platoon would have gone to work next morning as if little or nothing had happened the night before. These men were truly on Britain's front line.

Members of the Eastry Home Guard on parade.

A member of the Home Guard (Eastry Platoon) remembers having to patrol without rifles through the darkened streets of the village, and being in more danger from our own regular troops than from the enemy. On another occasion a woman had the fright of her life as she was hanging out her washing when a German airman parachuted into the road beside the house. To her relief the airman was promptly arrested by her husband!

The old church hall in Church Street was taken over by the military and the Council Room opposite was used for village societies and lectures on air raid precautions. The village newsagent, Mr. Woodruff, acted as Transport Officer for the Platoon, and contributed a map of the local footpaths which would be useful in the event of an invasion.

The battalion being so close to the perceived invasion coast was amongst the first units to receive arms. In fact within hours of the battalion being formed, six Lee-Enfield rifles were issued to each platoon with six rounds of ammunition allocated to each rifle. (Initially they were kept under lock and key only to be issued in an emergency until additional weapons and ammunition became available).

At Hammill Brick Company brick-works in the parish of Woodnesborough the brick drying tunnels were adapted for the local 5th (Wingham) Home Guard for

A publicity photograph showing the Ash Home Guard ready to hurl Molotov cocktails at any approaching enemy tanks heading down the village High Street.

Front Row—Left to Right—Lieut. R. D. Rees, Capt. F. S. Solley, Capt. F. G. Garlinge, Capt. E. F. J. Mugliston (Quartermaster), Major I. B. McCrae (Bn. M.O.). Major C. W. Ashwell, M.B.E., Major L. Howard Smith, Lieut.-Colonel F. D. C. Newport, O.B.E. (Commanding), Major D. T. Jenkins, Major F. D. Edge, Capt. R. McI. Stobart (Adjutant), Capt. B. W. Whitaker, Capt. W. L. S. Adams, Capt. J. J. Head, Lieut. R. White.
Second Row—Left to Right—Lieut. S. F. Grant, Lieut. C. J. Stentiford, 2/Lieut. N. G. Sedgewick, Lieut. P. T. Judge, Lieut. J. Knott, Lieut. N. G. Gardner, Lieut. T. E. Austen, Lieut. C. A. Woodruff, Lieut. C. E. Clark, Lieut. E. Passmore, Lieut. G. E. Hyde, Lieut. T. W. Thomas, Lieut. L. D. Downing, Lieut. C. F. Burch.
Third Row—Left to Right—2/Lieut. H. S. Hill, Lieut. H. Williams, Lieut. R. Woodruff, Lieut. J. Dudley, 2/Lieut. D. J. Collins, 2/Lieut. J. McMahon, Lieut. G. E. Lewis, 2/Lieut. W. V. Green, 2/Lieut. R. F. Hopper, 2/Lieut. F. L. Chidwick, 2/Lieut. K. W. Thomas, Lieut. J. D. S. Solley, 2/Lieut. A. Dona'dson, D.C.M., 2/Lieut. J. Wadbrook.
Back Row—Left to Right—2/Lieut. J. Mathers, 2/Lieut. R. Dunn, 2/Lieut. K. Lloyd, 2/Lieut. J. W. Harper, 2/Lieut. G. Davidson, 2/Lieut. F. A. Hollyer, 2/Lieut. J. E. Graves. 2/Lieut. A. G. Watts, Lieut. R. V. A. Johnson, 2/Lieut. A. Castley Smith

Officers of the 5th (Wingham) Battalion Kent Home Guard.

Members of the Ash Home Guard platoon. on parade

Members of the Sandwich Home Guard platoon.

149

rifle practice. The facility had become available due to the demand for bricks having declined, therefore providing a suitable place for the local volunteers to practice out of sight of the general public. Gradually they became a semi-mobilized force, sometimes deployed on patrols on bicycles or horses, in addition to various improvised vehicles built around a standard car chassis.

Eric Marshall, a former Eastry Parish Councillor, was too young to be called up for military service so he joined the Home Guard at Ash. He remembers proudly cycling around the village wearing a tin hat and carrying a rifle and ammunition balanced precariously on the handlebars. No one batted an eyelid! He was given instructions that in the event of an invasion he was to hurl Molotov cocktails at the approaching enemy tanks heading down Ash High Street! These experiences made him determined NOT to join the Army when the time came.

By the end of 1942 Sandwich platoon took over the 338th Civil Defence Battery Royal Artillery guns at Sandwich Bay.

In May 1943 some of the local Home Guard platoons were allocated guard duties on the Coastal Defence guns in the District. This permitted some regular troops to be released for other duties. The Ripple and Great Mongeham platoons were detailed guard duties on the twin 6 inch Royal Artillery weapons installed at Deal Castle.

Events during 1944: On 7 May, the 5th (Wingham) Battalion was awarded the Kent Home Guard efficiency cup by the Zone Commander Major General E. G. Miles CB, DSO, MC. at a big parade in Aylesham. It is understood that 80% of the battalion were presented with Home Guard proficiency certificates. They were also engaged in a large-scale exercise at the Sandwich Bay Battle School with the Wiltshire Regiment. The exercise was watched by General Bernard Montgomery and officers and NCOs from the XII Army Corps. The exercise was made realistic with the use of live ammunition throughout as the men advanced along a three and a half mile course, supported by 25 pounder guns, machine guns and mortars.

6th (Thanet) Battalion Kent Home Guard
The Battalion was made up of five companies consisting of over 2000 officers and men – Margate, Broadstairs, Birchington, 'C' (Minster) Company and 'D' (Ramsgate) Company.

Shortly after being formed the Loyal Defence Volunteer battalions organized nightly armed patrols operating from Richborough to Birchington. Many of the men were armed with makeshift weapons such as clubs, knives, together with a few shotguns.
In June 1940, an enemy bomber crashed into the sea off Margate one night killing one of the crew. The rest of the crew attempted to escape in a rubber dinghy but a

patrol of the Margate LDV, waded into the sea and took them all prisoner. So the LDV proved they were very much on the alert.

Shortly after being renamed and having a few weapons, a message was received on 16 September that the Germans were on the move and landing barges were being made ready for a possible invasion along the southeast coastal area. Locally it was thought that the enemy would attempt commando style raids along this part of the coast and they had to be ready to combat this type of attack. Some of the Ramsgate platoons took up positions around Pegwell Bay providing crossfire, with other gun positions around the exposed and vulnerable stretch of water. One platoon was armed with 6 x .300 Browning heavy machine guns. The Bay was also patrolled by men on foot and a mobile patrol on bicycles. The main position was at 'Pegwell Lodge', with a concrete gun position constructed over a cave complex which was probably an old smugglers' cave on the beach. Two other pillboxes manned by the Home Guard were near The Sportsman public house at Cliffsend and at the old train ferry dock at Richborough Port.

Miners who lived in the area and worked at Chislet Colliery formed their own platoon and manned a 6 inch naval gun close to the bandstand on East Cliff at Ramsgate.

8th (Cinque Ports) Battalion Kent Home Guard
This Battalion came into being in July 1940 made up of the Loyal Defence Volunteer detachments from Deal, Walmer, Dover and Folkestone formed earlier in May.
On 14 May 1940 volunteers had flocked to Deal Police Station and were formed into 'D' Company. They had no uniforms but were identified with an LDV armband.
Deal Gas Works platoon was 'A' Company. This platoon was made up of Deal Gas Company staff who were responsible for guarding the gasworks at night as well as keeping a fire watch in the event of incendiary bombs being dropped. The collieries in the area all formed their own LDV platoons. The miners in Mill Hill, Deal, raised their own LDV platoon based at the Territorial Army Drill Hall but were later absorbed into other units.

The Folkestone Company consisted mainly of local government employees and members of the public in reserve occupations who had remained in the town

Dover Company's first patrol went out on 26 May 1940. Due to extensive damage from shelling the Company spent a great deal of time on anti-looting patrols and protecting people's property in the town.

It has to be noted that the battalion lost many members as a result of enemy shelling and bombing.

East Kent Home Guard Transport Column
In 1942-3, Home Guard Transport Companies with headquarters in Canterbury were formed to provide mobility so that they could react quickly when required.
    2113 (Kent) HG Motor Transport Company (Dover).
This company was formed from employees of East Kent Bus Company in Dover. In 1942 during their off duty periods they received basic training in map reading and the use of small arms weapons. One member of the company was local bus driver,

Joe Harman, who in his book 'My Dover', recalls being in the Home Guard and being able to read a map probably saved his life. In March he and some workmates joined up with the Royal Army Service Corps (RASC) at Aylesford Priory for an exercise in which he was detailed to drive a TCL 'troop carrying lorry'. After completing this exercise successfully he returned to his billet to find the day's newspaper which gave an account of heavy bombing of a south coast town the previous day during which a bus garage had been hit. Later that day news of this raid came to light, detailing that his manager and ten members of staff had been killed at Dover's Russell Street Garage. He recalled that had he been doing his normal shift it was likely he would have been killed too. On another occasion Joe mentions an exercise in Thanet when a convoy of various trucks and mobile anti-aircraft guns were attacked by allied aircraft on a training exercise dropping bags of flour. He does not admit to having been hit!

Other companies in our area:
    2090 (Kent) HG Motor Transport Company (Folkestone)
    2096 (Kent) HG Motor Transport Company (Canterbury)
    2114 (Kent) HG Motor Transport Company (Deal).

1942 As already mentioned Home Guard battalions were formed on an area basis normally covering towns or districts, and originally all members were volunteers but in 1942 the National Service Act made it possible for compulsory enrolment to be applied in areas where units were below strength.

As a means of regulating homeland security a circular arrived at the Town Clerk's Office in Sandwich in early February. This document related only to men who were already in the Home Guard and not to men subsequently enlisted. The document stated that the Home Guard would be divided into two classes:
    1. Members will, on mustering in an emergency, be required to join immediately for full-time service.
    2. Members will report within 48 hours, and will then be directed either to join for full-time service or to remain until further orders at their civilian work.

On the 14 February a question was addressed to the Minister of Home Security in the House of Commons, on the subject of closer co-operation between the Civil Defence Services and the Home Guard. The scheme would enable some members of the Civil Defence Services to receive training enabling them to take an active part in resisting an invasion. An element of caution is seen in an order from Southern Command Headquarters to their Battalion Commanders, warning them of their key responsibilities and not to become like partisan units:

> The word **'guerrilla'** will not be used in future, as it is often misunderstood and if guerrilla activity is generally regarded as a possible secondary role for the Home Guard there is a great risk that the obligation to fight to the last in defended localities will not be met.

In some defence services this proposal seems to have had complications because by 10 March the Minister of Labour stated that the plan would reduce the number of persons available to perform fire prevention duties if they had to do Home Guard duties in addition.

From a statement on 24 March, *The Daily Telegraph* reported that for the first time for some months enemy aircraft had attacked the coastal towns the previous night. Being a bright moonlit night many people observed the attack in which an enemy plane was shot down in flames. The aircraft appeared to dive from about 5000 ft. (1540 metres) and was met by a blaze of gunfire from our ground defences where a Home Guard platoon was being trained. The paper stated that the platoon turned their weapons on the raider and saw it dive to the ground. Describing the incident later, a Home Guard officer said: *'It was just the opportunity our lads had been waiting for.'*
Note: It was during this attack a number of employees of the East Kent Bus Co. who were sheltering in their garage in Dover were killed.

The expected invasion never materialized. Instead the main role of the Home Guard was redefined to capturing enemy airmen whose planes had been shot down, and guarding munitions dumps, factories and aerodromes together with checking people's identity cards. But should the invasion materialize the Home Guard would be empowered to requisition certain petrol stations in order to ensure petrol supplies for their transport.

1944 With the build up ready for D-Day all southern England had become a vast military camp. The Home Guard had waited patiently for a worthwhile job and now it was here. Not only were they detailed to man sections of anti-aircraft and coast defences, they took over many routine and security duties thus releasing other soldiers eager to come to grips with the Germans across the Channel.

The Prime Minister, writing from Marrakesh on 7 June 1944 to the Secretary of State for War, concerning the duties of the Home Guard, wrote that:
> *'... their work is the most exhausting than of any other part of Civil Defence, and thought that attending parades could be removed from their commitment to complete 48 hours duty a month. He felt it unfair as the anti-aircraft Home Guard are credited with 12 hours for each night's duty whether there is an 'Alert' or not, but the ordinary Home Guard had to attend parades in the evenings and every week-end.*
> *He stressed that many of these men have had little free time for more than three years, and with compulsory parades, resulting with fines or imprisonment if they do not attend can cause unrest'.*

The Prime Minister said at this stage the Home Guard's hours should be reduced and not left to the discretion of the unit commander. Guards and exercises should be cut to a minimum.

Stand Down parade 26th November 1944. No. 3 Platoon "A" Company passes Saluting Base.

As the autumn approached the battalions stood down from active duty. Parades, training and other activities occurred on a voluntary basis. The *Kentish Express* wrote on 6 October, that during the year the Ash Platoon 'B' Company 5th Wingham raised £271 for charities by social events in the village.

On Sunday 15 October, some 3,000 officers and men of the Kent Home Guard marched through Canterbury to the Cathedral passing cheering crowds for a service of Recognition, representing the 60,000 of the county's total strength. The band of the East Kent Regiment (The Buffs) entertained the congregation before the service started.

The 5th (Wingham) Battalion held a Drumhead Service and the Stand Down Parade at Gobery Hill (Camping Ground) on the south side of Wingham Sunday 26th November. This was followed by the battalion marching to the High Street where the Salute was taken by the Commander of the Kent Home Guard, Brig. General H.S. Franklin, CMG, CBE, DSO. The band of H.M. Royal Marines provided the music.
Then finally, along with other battalions, they became an inactive reserve unit and finally disbanded on 31 December 1945.

The Prime Minister in his Victory speech, said:
> 'Growing to two million men at the peak, although working all day, were formed into the Home Guard. They were armed at least with rifles and armed also with the spirit CONQUER OR DIE'

Note: The Home Guard was reformed in 1952 during a period of international tension in the same role as had been developed before but the battalion sizes were be smaller. Their responsibilities were to be on the lookout and to capture enemy parachutists, to relieve territorial units and regular troops from anti-aircraft and coastal artillery duties should we be attacked.
In March, 1956 the Kent Home Guard was once again stood down from its active role to reserve status. This meant carrying on in a reduced capacity until it was finally disbanded in August 1957 when the Lord Lieutenant of Kent sent a letter to all serving Home Guard members thanking them for their service and their patriotism.

In the years when our Country was in mortal danger

NORMAN GEORGE SEDGEWICK

who served 22 July 1940 to 31 Dec 1944 gave generously of his time and powers to make himself ready for her defence by force of arms and with his life if need be.

George R.I.

THE HOME GUARD

Chapter 5

THE BRITISH RESISTANCE ORGANISATION

Whilst researching the local Home Guard, I was asked by a friend if I had heard of Tom Miller who had farmed close by in Eastry and had been involved with the 5th Wingham Battalion in the 1940s. I made contact with his daughter who explained that she knew very little, but had some documents that she was willing to lend me plus an abridged copy of the 'Secret Army' which had been shown on Meridian TV a few years previously. Armed with this information I began to find out little 'snippets' of this clandestine organization called the 'stay behind resistance movement', of which I had had no knowledge previously.

Between the wars a Lieut. Colonel J. Holland formulated a strategy to counter and embrace 'Irregular Warfare'. In 1938, Lieut. Colonel Holland and Colonel Colin Gubbins were instructed to form a unit called Military Intelligence (Research) to explore different possibilities. From this unit various sections evolved such as the Auxiliary Units, Commandos, Special Weapons, Special Operations Executive (SOE) and others. With the increasing threat of Nazi Germany's militancy, the idea was conceived of organizing some form of resistance by civilians in the event of an invasion. Britain was the only European nation during the war that was able to mobilize a 'stay behind resistance movement' in advance of such an event.

Colonel Gubbins was a regular British Army soldier who had gained considerable experience and expertise in guerrilla warfare, and had just returned from Norway where he headed the Independent Companies, the predecessors of the Commandos.

The GHQ Auxiliary Units or Stay Behind Resistance Movement
'One of the best kept secrets of the war'

As identified in an earlier chapter, after the Tom Wintringham debacle the government had some plans for a counter offensive. The enthusiasm shown by the Home Guard to Wintringham's ideas seemed to make the authorities at Whitehall sit up and think, and to plan a new strategy.

A new resistance organisation had the blessing of Winston Churchill following the fall of France in May 1940, and later in his book 'Their Finest Hour' on the war Churchill wrote, *'Active measures were prepared to harass the enemy from behind: to interfere with his communications; and to destroy material'*. He also makes reference to a very high-class battalion of the 'Gubbins' type ready to strike at any landing.

Colonel Gubbins and a few other senior like-minded officers formalized plans setting up what was to be called the Auxiliary Units. These men, who would be answerable to GHQ Home Forces, were to be organized as if they were part of the local Home Guard. Gubbins commanded the Auxiliary Units from its inception in June 1940 until his transfer to Special Operations Executive in November 1940 from its Headquarters at Coleshill House, Highworth (about 10 miles from Swindon).

The men chosen to be in the Auxiliary Units were provided with Home Guard uniforms as a cover, but without any distinguishing letters or battalion numbers of the local battalion as they were not actually in a Home Guard unit. They were to be attached to battalions which had no official recognition. This meant they were not covered by the Geneva Convention and would be shot as spies if caught by the enemy. Later, when off duty, members sometimes sported a small lapel badge bearing the distinctive 'GHQ Special Reserve Battalion' numbers 201- 203.

Colonel Gubbins had set up a network of Auxiliary Units to cover regions from south Wales to Scotland. Each unit was usually contained within county boundaries with priority being given to Kent and Sussex, the counties most at risk from an enemy invasion. This was undertaken by a team of selected regular officers whose task was to recruit very fit men with leadership skills usually from their local Home Guard who knew their areas intimately, such as farmers, gamekeepers etc.,

Whilst Colonel Gubbins was setting up the nationwide Auxiliary Units, a similar group called the XII Corps Observation Unit had already been formed earlier in the Kent and Sussex coastal area that General Thorne's XII Corps were defending. This small unit was commanded by Captain Peter Fleming (brother of Ian the novelist), a Guards officer with considerable experience in intelligence work, and Captain Mike Calvert. This unit appears to have been made up of regular soldiers, and stationed at The Garth, Bilting (between Ashford and Canterbury). Their job was to go to ground and, had the Germans landed, cause as much havoc as they could by mining bridges and access roads: very similar to the plans set out by Colonel Gubbins for the Auxiliary Units. It is understood that Captain Calvert had another plan which was to sabotage each road between the coast and the North Downs behind the advancing Germans cutting their main lines of supply and communication. It would have been undertaken by groups of civilians, who would have placed explosives in position, pressed a time fuse and then disappeared.

Winston Churchill in a letter to the Secretary of State for War on the 25 August 1940 wrote:
> *'I have been following with much interest the growth and development of the new guerrilla formations of the Home Guard known as Auxiliary Units. From what I hear these units are being organized with thoroughness and imagination, and should in the event of invasion prove a useful addition to the regular forces. Perhaps you will keep me informed of progress'.*

The National Auxiliary Unit Headquarters and training centre was set up at Coleshill House, Highworth, with large parklands and woods very suitable for guerrilla training. Every Thursday evening numbers of patrol members would arrive at the village of Highworth's Post Office where the postmistress, Mrs. Stranks, would ask for a password and arrange for their transport to Coleshill House. The recruits were accommodated in the large stable block, spending the following two days receiving instruction in the use of modern explosives and weapons and unarmed combat. The training was intensive including instruction on silent killing. Whilst at night they were transported several miles into the surrounding countryside and required to find their way back in the dark.

On returning to their local areas the patrols continued their training several nights a week. Each patrol was a self-contained cell, expected to be self-sufficient and operationally autonomous in case of invasion. In some cases it was noticed that these men were not taking part in normal Home Guard exercises and, being sworn to secrecy, were unable to explain their absence at night. They came under suspicion of being engaged in some devious acts, and in some cases were sent 'white feathers' in the belief they were skipping duties and not being patriotic.

About 3,500 men were trained at Coleshill and, with a number trained locally, nearly 5,000 well-trained and armed men awaited a possible German invasion. As stated the mission of these units was to carry out attacks and acts of sabotage against invading forces from behind their lines, targeting enemy occupied airfields, fuel and ammunition dumps, railway lines, convoys etc., whilst conventional forces fell back to the so-called 'GHQ Line' just south of London. Members anticipated being shot if they were captured, and were expected to shoot themselves or take poison rather than be taken alive. Those who survived this period would revert to their civilian occupations in the hope and anticipation of a successful Allied Forces counterattack.

Auxiliary Units hideouts or operational bases (OBs) were supposed to be merely the places to which Resistance men could withdraw to eat, sleep and lie low, and usually sited at least one mile from the shore because it was thought that mustard gas would be used on the beaches. By the end of 1941 over 500 OBs were in use nationally.

At first they were little more than foxholes, so badly ventilated that due to the lack of oxygen, men who slept in them awoke with headaches. Eventually OBs were fitted out with bunk beds, cooking stoves and Tilley lamps, and each stocked with food and water enough to sustain a patrol for a couple of weeks. Each OB was constructed by the military or outside private contractors, and was so well concealed that anyone walking over them would not notice anything. Most had trapdoors which could either be lifted out or were hinged.

Initially personnel learnt the tricks of the trade by word of mouth, but by July 1942, each patrol was issued with a comprehensive manual of destruction: This booklet resembled an agricultural catalogue and was issued to all Auxiliary Unit volunteers. Its innocent title however disguised a handbook on explosives and timing devices suitable for sabotaging targets.

> THE COUNTRYMAN'S DIARY - - - 1939
>
> **HIGHWORTH'S FERTILISERS**
>
> DO THEIR STUFF UNSEEN UNTIL YOU SEE
>
> RESULTS!
>
> With the Compliments of
> HIGHWORTH & CO.
>
> YOU WILL FIND THE NAME HIGHWORTH WHEREVER QUICK RESULTS ARE REQUIRED

As this is potentially a dangerous document in the wrong hands only a few details are included-

> The index contains chapters on fuses, detonators, high explosives, grenades, incendiaries, booby-traps and improvised mines.
>
> In a section on selected targets details of methods on how to blow up ammunition and fuel dumps, trucks, aeroplanes, armoured cars, semi-tracked vehicles and tanks are given.
>
> In the concluding chapter on blowing up tanks, the advice was 'Best of all, attack the repair lorries ...... and let the field army do the 'tank bursting'.

Another booklet: **Calendar 1937**, resembling a calendar, appears to have been issued to a patrol with a pack of incendiaries or explosives, with instructions on how to prepare and use:

> Paraffin and Magnesium Incendiaries, detonators and the use of pencil timer fuses and the storing and use of Liquid Phosphorus Bottles.
>
> The booklet gives 'Golden Rules' in handling High Explosives –
>
> Blasting Gelatine and Plastic Explosive. Noting some packs contained both types and were easily distinguishable by their colour, the Plastic Explosive (Yellow or Black) handles like plasticine and is twice as powerful as Gelatine (Brown).

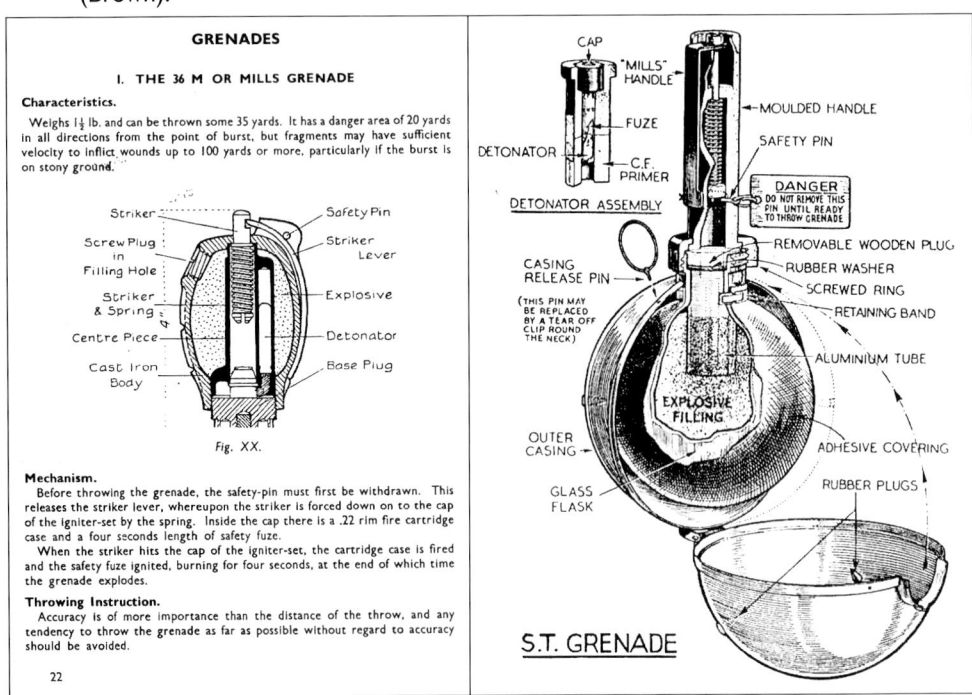

GRENADES

1. THE 36 M OR MILLS GRENADE

Characteristics.
Weighs 1¼ lb. and can be thrown some 35 yards. It has a danger area of 20 yards in all directions from the point of burst, but fragments may have sufficient velocity to inflict wounds up to 100 yards or more, particularly if the burst is on stony ground.

Fig. XX.

Mechanism.
Before throwing the grenade, the safety-pin must first be withdrawn. This releases the striker lever, whereupon the striker is forced down on to the cap of the igniter-set by the spring. Inside the cap there is a .22 rim fire cartridge case and a four seconds length of safety fuze.
When the striker hits the cap of the igniter-set, the cartridge case is fired and the safety fuze ignited, burning for four seconds, at the end of which time the grenade explodes.

Throwing Instruction.
Accuracy is of more importance than the distance of the throw, and any tendency to throw the grenade as far as possible without regard to accuracy should be avoided.

S.T. GRENADE

High-Explosive Grenades which weigh 1½ lbs. (0.67kg.) can be thrown some 35 yards (32m).

S.T. Grenade or Sticky Bombs which were extremely sticky and primarily intended to be used against small enemy tanks and armoured cars having plating under 1 inch (25mm) in thickness.

Note: During June 1940, Churchill was requesting the development of Sticky Bombs as an effective weapon against tanks but trials undertaken by the Auxiliary Units proved that they would not effectively stick to vehicles that had a coating of mud or were covered in dust, so they abandoned the idea of using them. In any case as the invasion did not take place they were never used in this country.

Operational Instructions issued in August 1941 by HQ Auxiliary Units.
If the enemy should ever be successful in obtaining a bridgehead of any size in this country, or if a part of the country should be completely overrun, it is clear that no fighting patrol behind the enemy's lines would be certain of being able to use any standing building as an operational base. Some form of 'hide' or concealed base was therefore essential if the patrol is to function at all.

Patrols Operational Base (OB): The ground to be worked on must be prepared beforehand. If the site is not near any existing track either use some approach which can easily be camouflaged afterwards or make an artificial track leading PAST the base. This effect can be achieved by entering the base one way and leaving along the continuation of the track. Disposal of spoil from the dig must either be contained in sand bags to be laid over the galvanized corrugated iron roofing or disposed of away from the base. The finished OB must have adequate drainage, ventilation (2 vent holes) and a supply of water (150 gallon (682 litre) tank or milk churns suitable for 5 men for 20 days), sterilisation tablets and an Elsan chemical toilet.

The entrance and camouflage is a problem and calls for a local solution but in all cases a second entrance should be devised, even if only by means of a crawling tunnel.

Communication with the observer and some means of transmitting warnings of enemy approach should be devised, be it a field telephone or a string or wire would serve the purpose.

The minimum space to accommodate a patrol of 5 or 6 men comfortably is as follows:
12 ft. (3.7m) x 9 ft. (2.8m) with 7ft. (2.1m) headroom, a 2 ft. (0.6m) square entrance. The depth of excavation should be 9 ft. (2.8m) allowing for a 2 ft. (0.6m) layer of sandbags and earth and with a wooden floor or duck-boards.

Dumps: The space in an operational base is likely to be congested, and it is NOT advisable to fill up the space with stores and ammunition, etc. It is recommended that a 'dump' be constructed some 40-60 yards (37-55m) from the base to keep all stores NOT wanted for immediate use.

Equipping an Operational Base and Dump varied but the following provides an approximate idea:
Ammunition:
>200 rounds per Browning, 60 rounds per rifle and 24 rounds per revolver, also 3 boxes of grenades.

Food:
>A packing case per man, which was considered as iron rations, containing – tea, sugar, condensed milk, cheese, jam, tins of pilchards, cooked bacon and service biscuits.
>As the patrol must live off the land, every endeavour should be made to obtain fresh vegetables, eggs, butter, apples, chickens, game and rabbits etc.

Cooking:
>Silent Primus or methylated stove with paraffin or spirit and matches, cooking utensils, tin plates, mugs and cutlery etc.,

Tools:
>2 each of shovels and buckets, pick axe, hand axe, saw, hammer and nails etc., torches with spare bulbs and batteries, ball of string, candles and hurricane lamp

Personal Equipment:
>To consist of a groundsheet, bedding, washing items, toilet paper, some spare clothing, 2 pairs of rubber-soled shoes, jack knife, hunting knife, maps, compass, paper and pencils: also a Balaclava helmet, close mesh black veil. Black, brown and green camouflage colours to apply to the hands and face.

General Stores:
>10 gallon (45.5litre) of paraffin, rope, 2 tins of Renadine (a deterrent for use against enemy dogs), bucket for latrine purposes, a Periscope (provided by Headquarters).
>
>First aid kits which included morphine for use as a pain killer or, in a larger dose, for suicide.

It is necessary to provide a 'hide' to enable the observer to go to ground if the enemy was nearby, and so save the opening up of the Patrol's OB, which might jeopardize the lives of the whole Patrol. It is intended that the Observer's OB is NOT intended to be his Observation Post.

For security reasons a password should precede the conversation and the bell should be muffled, and the call up made on the buzzer only.

As Scout Patrols would be acting in enemy territory the task in hand must be worth the risk of their lives, and constitute a justifiable mission. The patrol would either have to infiltrate through the enemy lines or work from a hide-out in his territory.

Observation at Night: After the men's eyes had got used to the dark they would be able to see quite well in the dim light. The eye has the power of becoming 10,000 times more sensitive in dim light. This process is called 'dark adaptation' and occurs very slowly. In the first seven minutes the sensitivity is increased by 100 times but the maximum is not reached for an hour. Instructions were to:

>Keep downwind of farms and houses where DOGS might give the alert by barking. Avoid spinneys where pigeons are KNOWN to roost.
>
>The Hun has a habit of giving bursts of machine gun fire without having seen or heard anything. Don't therefore let it worry you. Be ready to FREEZE when meeting enemy unexpectedly as the Boche use patrols freely.

The patrol should not have unnecessary kit, the essentials are:

>Tommy or Sten gun may be required to cover withdrawal. Rubber soled boots should be worn. Avoid carrying letters or documents. Steel helmets will not be worn on night patrols. A water bottle and reserve of rations should the patrol be out longer than one night.
>
>Loaded Revolver (12 rounds of ammunition), Mills bomb & Fighting Knife.
>
>First aid field dressing.

Each man to have special weapons enabling him to be a complete demolition unit in himself.

>Your task is either to destroy by incendiaries, demolition or ambush enemy stores, aeroplanes and vehicles or to overpower isolated sentries.

The following is an example of stalking a sentry:

The Boche invariably wears his helmet with the chin strap (with no stretch or 'give' at all) around the neck. Stalk him quietly from the rear, then place your left hand round his waist and at the same time seize the front of his helmet with your right hand and pull it vigorously upward and backward. He will be unable to utter a sound (in fact too severe a pull might easily dislocate his neck) as the back of his helmet cuts down at the base of his skull, whilst the strap throttles him.

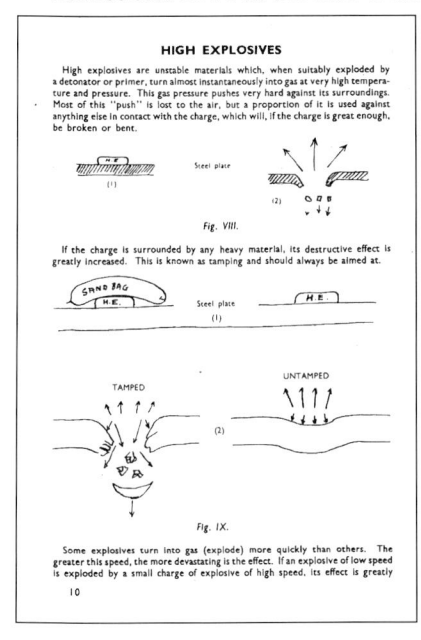

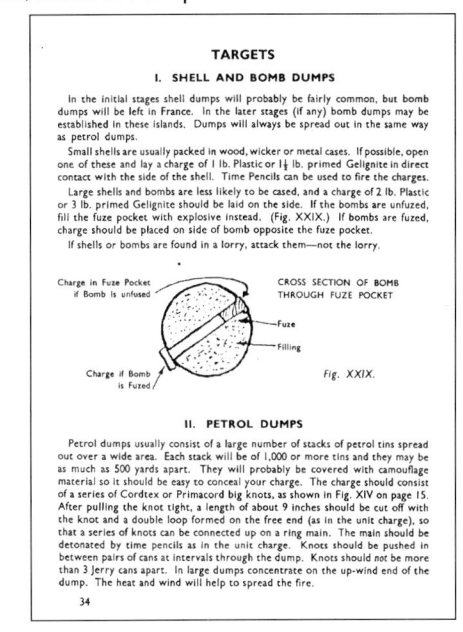

HIGH EXPLOSIVES

High explosives are unstable materials which, when suitably exploded by a detonator or primer, turn almost instantaneously into gas at very high temperature and pressure. This gas pressure pushes very hard against its surroundings. Most of this "push" is lost to the air, but a proportion of it is used against anything else in contact with the charge, which will, if the charge is great enough, be broken or bent.

Fig. VIII.

If the charge is surrounded by any heavy material, its destructive effect is greatly increased. This is known as tamping and should always be aimed at.

Fig. IX.

Some explosives turn into gas (explode) more quickly than others. The greater this speed, the more devastating is the effect. If an explosive of low speed is exploded by a small charge of explosive of high speed, its effect is greatly

10

TARGETS

I. SHELL AND BOMB DUMPS

In the initial stages shell dumps will probably be fairly common, but bomb dumps will be left in France. In the later stages (if any) bomb dumps may be established in these islands. Dumps will always be spread out in the same way as petrol dumps.

Small shells are usually packed in wood, wicker or metal cases. If possible, open one of these and lay a charge of 1 lb. Plastic or 1½ lb. primed Gelignite in direct contact with the side of the shell. Time Pencils can be used to fire the charges.

Large shells and bombs are less likely to be cased, and a charge of 2 lb. Plastic or 3 lb. primed Gelignite should be laid on the side. If the bombs are unfuzed, fill the fuze pocket with explosive instead. (Fig. XXIX.) If bombs are fuzed, charge should be placed on side of bomb opposite the fuze pocket.

If shells or bombs are found in a lorry, attack them—not the lorry.

Fig. XXIX.

II. PETROL DUMPS

Petrol dumps usually consist of a large number of stacks of petrol tins spread out over a wide area. Each stack will be of 1,000 or more tins and they may be as much as 500 yards apart. They will probably be covered with camouflage material so it should be easy to conceal your charge. The charge should consist of a series of Cordtex or Primacord big knots, as shown in Fig. XIV on page 15. After pulling the knot tight, a length of about 9 inches should be cut off with the knot and a double loop formed on the free end (as in the unit charge), so that a series of knots can be connected up on a ring main. The main should be detonated by time pencils as in the unit charge. Knots should be pushed in between pairs of cans at intervals through the dump. Knots should not be more than 3 Jerry cans apart. In large dumps concentrate on the up-wind end of the dump. The heat and wind will help to spread the fire.

34

The weapons you are given are for self-protection, for destruction of stores, etc., by burning and demolition, and for overpowering INDIVIDUAL men. Each member of the patrol must clearly know the task in hand and his own particular role before he leaves the Operational Base.

> NEVER leave a wounded comrade who should be taken to a friend's house and NEVER to the OB.
>
> Only strike when you are positive of success. Therefore you must avoid a free fight. It is the undefended stores/lorries you want to destroy. Allow for covering fire in case of opposition, a Tommy gun should be in position to cover withdrawal. NEVER try to ambush twice in the same place.

The Kent Section

By June 1940 the XII Corps Observation Unit at The Garth had amalgamated with the GHQ Auxiliary Units (British Resistance Organisation) set up by Colonel Colin Gubbins with their national Headquarters at Coleshill House.

The Garth became a Training Centre (Headquarters) for Kent in the village of Bilting near Wye. The staffing at the headquarters consisted of a captain and a sergeant who were explosive experts, a sergeant and a private in charge of clerical duties, drivers, two batmen and a couple of RAF radio operators. At weekends some 50 to 80 men gradually became proficient in the use of weapons and plastic explosives.

Close by an airship hole constructed during the 1914-18 war became a secret hide-out (TR0500 5000). It was intended to be a collecting point for Auxiliaries on the run having accommodation for about 100 people. Captain Fleming regarded it as the most spectacular hide-out in the county, and reasoned that the last place the enemy would look for a hide-out would be beneath an existing one. From a path well away from the edge of hole, Fleming had his men dig a 10 foot (3m) vertical shaft and a connecting tunnel about 45 feet (13.7m) long into the hide-out. The trapdoor entrance was a large tree trunk weighing about half a ton, counterbalanced so that it would swing aside at the touch of a finger.

There were 30 separate units each with about 20 men, divided up into patrols with a leader and six or seven members. Each Patrol Leader selected men from his community and their activities would only be known to their patrol. By June the selection and training of the patrol members had begun in earnest. Each unit to be comprised of two parts, the Operational Patrols and the Special Duty Sections.

These covert units were one of the most intriguing aspects of the home front. Those chosen were often farmers or landowners, many in reserved occupations, with a good knowledge of their local area, and physically capable of living rough and living off the land; fighting and harassing enemy forces, and creating as much havoc as possible. Everything about them was to be kept highly secret. Nobody was to know of the men's dual role and their hide-out – not even their wives and family.

Each patrol had an operational base (OB) initially designed and sited by Capt. Fleming's team. Among the pre-invasion preparations carried out by the Auxiliary Units were the pre-primed charges attached to bridges and buildings considered to be of value to the enemy which could be detonated in a few minutes if the need arose.

The other part of the Auxiliary Units was the Special Duty Sections which were entirely separate from but supported the operational units. A system of spies trained to gather intelligence and to leave reports in dead letter drops. This information of enemy activity would then be collected by runners and passed on for relaying to the radio stations which, in turn, transmitted the information to the area HQs attached to conventional forces. Here in the southern counties the network would be activated by the Commanding Officer of XII Corps to attack the enemy when the time came.

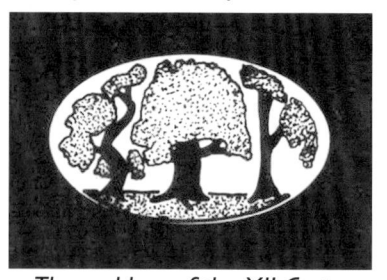

The emblem of the XII Corps, worn as a sleeve badge. It shows the oak, the ash and the thorn. The sign was selected to link the corps commander General Thorne with the trees mentioned in Rudyard Kipling's book Puck of Pook's Hill.

In November 1940 Captain Fleming was succeeded by Captain Norman Field and then by Captain G. McNicholl as Kent Intelligence Officer or Area Organizer.

Kent's Coastal – GHQ Special Reserve Battalion 203 Auxiliaries Units

The coastal area from Sheppey to Camber was covered by five Home Guard battalions and, in turn, had an Auxiliary Unit:

5th (Wingham) 6th (Thanet) 7th (Lyminge) 8th (Cinque Ports) 30th (Sheppey).
This book includes some details on three, the Wingham, Thanet and Cinque Ports Auxiliary Units. Of the three the 5th Wingham covered the Eastry Rural District area including Sandwich and parts of the Deal area, embracing many small hamlets, villages and mining communities, and is the one which this book concentrates on in some detail.

The following lists do not purport to be complete as they have been researched from different sources and by word of mouth. Note : Some documents show names marked # no reason given.

The 5th Wingham
J. C. Robertson – Wingham. A.K. Henderson – Wingham. Arthur W. Marchant – Guilton.
T. Foat – Cop Street, Ash. H. G. Philpott – Ash. Arthur W. Benbow – Ash.
J. P. Ash – Ash. Guy P. Steed – Finglesham. L. N. Hogben – Tickenhurst, Eastry.
N. E. Fuller – Sutton, Dover. S. W. Stiles – Sutton, Dover. C. (Tom) Miller – Selson, Eastry.
F. W. Stone – Eythorne, Dover. J.W. Bullridge - East Sutton. J. H. Hirst – Wingham.
Robert S. Chandler – Goldstone. Ash. J. A. Hunt – Selson, Eastry. H.L. Swingford – Ash.
    # J. S. Dunn – Lower Goldstone. #G.W. Densham – Ashley, Dover.
    W.P. Spanton – Eythorne. # L. G. Hyde – Northbourne, Deal.

It is understood that Tom Miller of Eastry, came to hear of the Auxiliary Units for the first time when one of his friends, Guy Steed, together with a military officer came to visit him at his fruit farm. During the conversation he was asked whether he was willing to be part of a sabotage unit should the Germans invade. He obviously convinced them of his integrity because the officer said 'he was the right sort of chap for the job' and asked Tom to sign the Secrets Act informing him that they would be in touch shortly.

Toms naval fitness and training naturally suited the job description required to be a member of the secret army.
The photograph shows him as a young cadet who was stationed at Greenhithe on board the training vessel HMS Worcester. On joining the cadets Tom Would automatically become a cadet of he Royal Naval Reserve. On completing his training he entered either the Royal Navy or British Merchant Navy.

From an interview with BBC Radio Kent, Tom indicates that the 5th Wingham had more than one patrol (each having an obscure cover name eg. Ash Patrol was Marrow in Grape area) and their own operational base. His patrol had theirs cleverly constructed by the Royal Engineers in Betteshanger Woods in an old chalk pit. The patrol also had a one man observation base beside the main Dover-Sandwich road close by. The following are stories told to the author during his research of this operational base.

(a) A couple of men out checking their rabbit snares in a wood near Tilmanstone during the hours of darkness suddenly became aware that they had walked into what was an Auxiliary Units or Home Guard night training exercise, and quickly beat a quiet retreat.

(b) Years after the war, two old men were overheard talking about their experiences in a local Auxiliary Unit whilst having a drink in a pub in Eastry. During this conversation one recalled sending a coded message on a radio to another group in the area. The other person with a look of surprise said, *'Blimey that must have been me on the other end'.*

Operational Bases (OBs) connected to 5th Wingham.

The following diagram shows a patrol OB near Northbourne at NGR. TR 319512 and is likely to be the one that Tom Miller mentions above. This OB was spotted as it was being constructed by a group of small boys looking for bird nests in a wood. They noticed that the Army had been digging trenches and dugouts in the woods, and knowing that they would be in trouble if caught made a quick exit. It was only after the war that the significance of this casual observation became apparent when one of those boys was wandering in the woods and discovered the abandoned OB. The following account is based on his recollection some 40 years before.

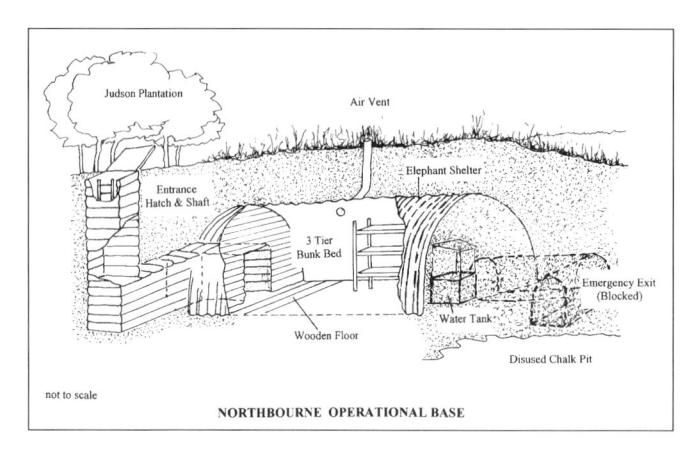

It was located on sloping down land, adjacent to a wood known as Judson Plantation and built into the side of a disused chalk pit. Entry was by means of a trap door, down a vertical shaft some 3 feet (0.91m) square and about 7 feet (2.1m) deep and lined with wooden shuttering. The shaft led to a passage which made a right angled turn before entering the main chamber. This chamber was constructed of arched corrugated iron sheets with a wooden floor. A two or three tier bunk bed was positioned in the east corner. On the opposite side there was a large galvanized water tank set in a recess above the wooden floor. Leading from the main chamber was a chalk-cut escape tunnel. This small tunnel made a right-angled turn before stopping in a dead end. This last undug portion covered by chalk rubble could rapidly be removed in the event of an emergency.

The site was revisited in December 1984, but found to be destroyed, and the only indication of its presence was an elongated depression. It may be significant that the hide-out was within easy reach of at least two of the Kent Collieries, Betteshanger and Tilmanstone. These would almost certainly have been prime targets for attack following a successful German invasion.

ASH UNDERGROUND – DOUBLE LEVEL HIDEOUT
(Possibly used as a collection point for Resistance Fighters on the run)

Tree Cover
Entrance Hatch & Shaft
Bushes
Elephant Shelter
Concrete Pipe Air Vent
3 Tier Bunk Beds (possibly 3 on each side)
This is likely to have been a blocked Emergency Exit (Now exposed)
not to scale

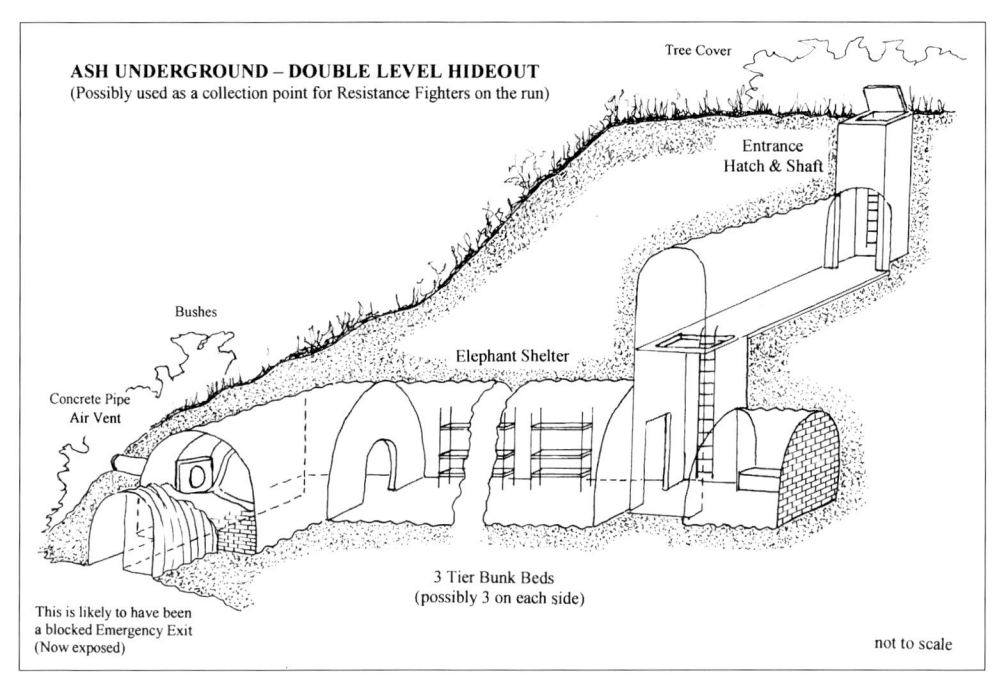

The upper level.

View of the lower level showing the remains of the bunks.

Young explorers descending to the lower level.

A ladder to the upper level.

Ash (near Ringleton Manor): The situation at Ash is confusing as the only physical evidence of a possible OB is a large underground double level hide-out. It has been suggested that it was intended to be a collecting point for stray resistance men on the run and NOT as a normal OB for a single patrol (as The Garth). It would have contained food, water, chemical toilets and sleeping accommodation for about 20 to 30 people. The building quality of this hide-out was good and until quite recently been in a fair condition. More recent photographs reveal that it has begun to collapse and should be filled in as it is highly dangerous.

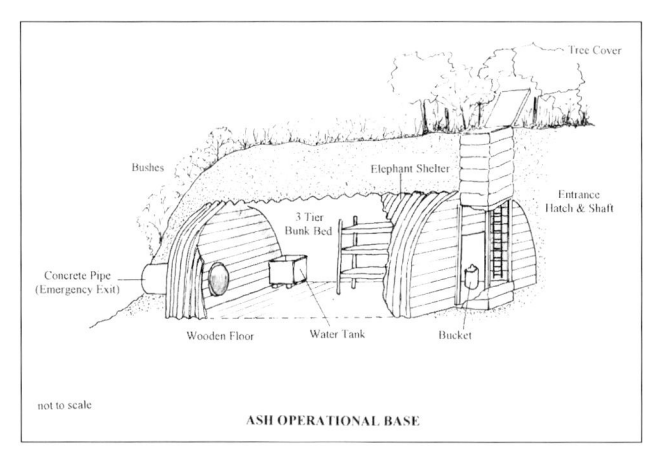

ASH OPERATIONAL BASE

Information is difficult to discover as to its use as the only surviving member of the 5th Wingham (Ash patrol) Auxiliary Unit, is Mr. Robert Chandler. When shown photographs and interviewed by Mr. John Guy in June 2011, Mr. Chandler said -

' It was not their bunker and he did not recognize any of it. After they had to abandon the first OB they dug a large hole, put an elephant shelter in the bottom, created an entrance shaft and an emergency exit, made from concrete pipe and then filled it in again. He said they did not have any bricks and there are too many rooms in the photos.'

According to Mr. Chandler their patrol had their fair share of problems with their OB. The first one constructed in a sandpit at Coombe by Captain Fleming's team collapsed. A second one which was described by Mr. Chandler (from which the above plan was drawn), and used by the patrol has now been swallowed up in the undergrowth and cannot be found. A radar station which was moved from Sandwich in the 1960s which has been decommissioned possibly resulting in the OB disappearing.

Note: Often the OBs were so well hidden and disguised even the Royal Engineers, with the view to destroying them, failed to find them all after the war. When they were in operation it was general policy that should an OB be discovered or thought to have been compromised it would be abandoned and another constructed.

The 6th Thanet

The Thanet Units operated round the coast from Richborough to Birchington, and were made up of the five companies based at :

Ramsgate, Margate, Birchington, Broadstairs and Minster.

W(Billy) G. Gardner – Birchington.   R.F. Linington – Birchington.   G.M. Fuller – Birchington.
R. Willett – Birchington.   B.H. Stephens – Minster.   F. Pettman – Birchington.

Norman H. Steed – Acot.   N.C. Austen – Manston.   G.J. Stennett – Broadstairs.
J.A. Montgomery – Ramsgate.   R.M. Montgomery – Ramsgate.   R. Steed – Margate.
W.R. Tyrrel – Margate.   T.M. Willett – Monkton.   #T.E. Spanton – Minster.

One of the Thanet OBs had been built by the Army in a disused chalk pit near Margate. The unit decided later that they wanted their base elsewhere, so they constructed one in an old cellar of a burned down farm house at Nash Court (TR3580 6880).

The 8th Cinque Ports
The Cinque Ports Battalion were made up of detachments from:
Walmer, Dover and Folkestone.

H.G. Burrows – Swingfield, Dover.   W.S. Roberts – Lydden.   C.R. Godden – Acrise.
S.M. Martin – Acrise.   F. Tuson – Guston, Dover.   G.W. Mitchell – St. Margaret's Bay.
H.W. Curling – Swingate, Guston.   G.H. Pickard – Walmer.   #F. Harris – Whitfield, Dover.
R.L. Norris – Guston, Dover.   #F.E. Thurley – Guston, Dover.
F.W. Castle – Hawkinge, Folkestone.   # K.V. Dewar – Hawkinge, Folkestone.

One of the Cinque Ports OBs was constructed at (TR236 415) in the Alkham Valley on the B2060 at a place called Drellingore. A story was told to the author about the wife of a member of the local Auxiliary Unit who took the family dog out for an evening walk. The dog ran off into the woods and picked up her husband's scent. The husband managed to distract the dog away from the unit's OB and met up with his wife in another part of the wood. The husband reported this incident to his local commander whose recommendation was not to do anything but keep to it to themselves but should an invasion take place, his wife would certainly have been taken care of which sounded extremely sinister!

Another OB was built at Winterage Farm (TR189 410) on the A260 near Hawkinge airfield.

Further Information
Due to the secrecy of the Auxiliary Units and the lack of hard evidence, little pieces of information have gradually come to light during this research:

Another story told by an ex Auxiliary Unit member possibly attached to 7th Lyminge Home Guard and published in a book 'East Kent – Within Living Memory' recalled that his unit was at Huntstreet and trained at The Garth at Bilting. This gentleman said that his OB was in a deep hole in Capon Wood which had been fitted out with bunks and equipped with a water tank and rations for ten days. Explosives were hidden in a dump some distance away. They practised overnight training, sometimes with a unit of the Lovat Scouts who were considered one of the most experienced regiments in this type of warfare. His wife thought he was doing general Home Guard duties, and did not find out the truth until long after the war. He recalled how long after the war his sons searched for the hide-out but never discovered it until years later when the roof rotted and it fell in.

An operational base for the Barham Auxiliary Unit was constructed at Wootton (TR220 480) close to the A2. Records exist of a further one at Blean (TR130 600) on the A290 Canterbury to Whitstable Road.

Stand Down Orders

The Auxiliary Units were maintained long after any immediate enemy invasion threat had passed. They underwent additional training and inter-unit efficiency competitions at the national headquarters at Coleshill House training site until 1943. Some of the younger members of the Auxiliaries later joined the Special Air Service (SAS), and saw action in the campaign in France in late 1944.

When in November 1944 the War Office decided to disband the Operational Branch of the Auxiliary Units, members received a couple of formal letters thanking them for their services. As they did not officially exist they would not receive any publicity or public recognition.

GHQ Home Forces.
18th November 1944

In view of the improved war situation, it has been decided by the War Office that the Operational Branch of Auxiliary Units shall stand down, and the time has now come to put an end to an organisation which would have been of inestimable value to this country in the event of invasion.

All ranks under your command are aware of the secret nature of their duties. For that reason it has not been possible for them to receive publicity, nor will it be possible even now. So far from considering this to be a misfortune, I should like all members of Auxiliary Units to regard it as a matter of special pride.

I have been much impressed by the devotion to duty and high standard of training shown by all ranks. The careful preparations, the hard work undertaken in their own time, and their readiness to face the inevitable dangers of their role, are all matters which reflect the greatest credit on the body of picked men who form the Auxiliary Units.

I should be glad, therefore, if my congratulations and best wishes could be conveyed to all ranks.

General H.E. Franklyn
Commander-in-Chief.

C /O G.P.O. Highworth,
Nr. Swindon (Wilts).
30th November 1944

To:- The Members of Auxiliary Units – Operational Branch.

The War Office has ordered that the Operational side of Auxiliary Units shall stand down! This is due to the greatly improved War situation and the strategic requirements of the moment.

I realize what joining Auxiliary Units has meant to you; so do the officers under my command. You were invited to do a job which would require more skill and coolness, more hard work and greater danger, than was demanded of any other voluntary organization. In the event of 'Action Stations' being ordered you knew well the kind of life you were in for. But that was in order; you were picked men; and others, including myself, knew that you would continue to fight whatever the conditions, with, or if necessary without, orders.

It now falls to me to tell you that your work has been appreciated and well carried out, and that your contract, for the moment, is at an end. I am grateful to you for the way you have trained in the last four years. So is the Regular Army. It was due to you that more divisions left this country to fight the battle of France; and it was due to your reputation for skill and determination that extra risk was taken – successfully as it turned out – in the defence arrangements of this country during that vital period.

I congratulate you on this reputation and thank you for this voluntary effort.
In view of the fact that your lives depended on secrecy no public recognition will be possible. But those in the most responsible positions at General Headquarters, Home Forces, know what was done; and what would have been done had you been called upon. They know it well, as is emphasized in the attached letter from the Commander-in-Chief. It will not be forgotten.

Colonel F. W. R. Douglas
Commander, Auxiliary Units.

In researching this section of this book I quickly came to realize that when Tom Miller's daughter said she did not know much about her father's wartime activities this was indeed correct. I immediately discovered that Tom and his fellow members of the Auxiliary Unit had to sign a secrecy document that prevented them from disclosing information for a period of 50 years. Therefore more than seventy years later there is very little personal information available for researchers other than in this case a few documents found at the back of a drawer.

Fortunately the Auxiliary Units training was never put to the test and when peace was declared their clandestine activities of 'the stay behind army' were quickly erased as the men returned to their everyday life in the community. Although their services were not required we still owe these very brave men a vote of gratitude by remembering that they were willing to give their lives, if required, to the defence of this island, its democracy and its people. So thank you Tom and all your comrades.

5th (Wingham) Battalion
KENT HOME GUARD

Stand Down Parade
Sunday, 26th November, 1944
at Gobery Hill · Wingham

Ash · Sandwich · Woodnesborough · Worth · Sandown Castle
Ashley · Waldershare · Elvington · Eythorne · Tilmanstone · Sholden · Deal Castle
Sandwich Bay · Eastry · Bettesbanger · Northbourne · Tingleham · Gt. Mongeham · Ripple
Sutton · Deal · Barfrestone · Woollage · Snowdown · Aylesham
Staple · Wingham · Nonington · Preston · Stourmouth · Westmarsh

Chapter 6

DIG FOR VICTORY

Although growing vegetables in gardens and on allotments was encouraged in towns and communities during the First World War it was generally considered a Second World War phenomenon. Photographic evidence usually showed young people, particularly school children, tending small vegetable patches called 'war gardens' in built-up areas. In another case photographs of King George V appeared in newspapers inspecting a vegetable garden on Clapham Common in the final months of the war when food was short and rationing began to take effect.

Between the two wars 'Demonstrationa Allotments' were promoted by the Agricultural Sub-Committee of the Kent Education Committee, and proved to have been of value to allotment holders and cottage gardeners alike. Where these allotments existed, an experienced local person would be supplied with seeds and fetilizers etc., This person would be required to cultivate the allotment and have the results evaluated at a meeting of experts and the general public.

There was a revival of the idea at the start of the Second World War, when the War Agricultural Executive Committee (War Ags) set out examples of 'DIY Food Production'.

Prior to the start of the Second World War Britain imported 75% of the country's food requirement by ship. By September 1939, however, shipping was increasingly being attacked and sunk by enemy submarines. The British Government considered these tactics were to be part of the enemy's strategy to isolate and starve us into submission. Therefore 'DIG FOR VICTORY' was in response to wartime problems of the food supply to this country. To encourage people to get involved the Dig for Victory slogan and poster campaign were introduced. At the same time, on the lighter side, several music hall songs were written, one such ditty ending in 'Dig, Dig, Dig to Victory'.

With considerable foresight the Women's Land Army had been set up in June and sprang into action under the banner headline **Help the Farmer Scheme**. Volunteer women mostly from towns and cities, enlisted with little knowledge of the task they had signed up to. After passing a medical they were posted to various farms or in some cases to hostels anywhere in the country. Generally the girls thought hostel life was great fun. Rules were strict and they had to be in by 10pm otherwise they were in trouble, so life was disciplined.

Some of the volunteers found their new occupation extremely hard, particularly working long hours outdoors in all kinds of weather. Work varied from one farm to another with girls digging ditches or mucking out one day and the next picking frozen sprouts with frozen fingers. The best season enjoyed by the 'Land Girls' was the summer and helping at harvest time.

In October 1939, Rt. Hon. Robert Hudson, Minister of Agriculture, announced: 'We want not only the big man with the plough but the little man with the spade to get busy this autumn. Let 'Dig for Victory' be the motto of everyone with a garden.'

As in many towns and villages throughout the country, Town and Parish Councils appealed to their residents to use part of their gardens for growing vegetables, and to take up community allotments. It proved fortunate that one village in the area had an Allotment Association which had been formed some years earlier, and allotment holders were well set up to produce an abundance of extra crops for the community. It is ironic that shortly after the conclusion of hostilities an inspector from the Ministry of Agriculture discovered that 'eel worm' was present, and instructed that no potatoes should be grown on the allotments for at least 10 years!

1940 On the 8 June *The Kent Messenger* reported that 'Voluntary Land Clubs' were being formed in different parts of the county to assist farmers. Several clubs were ready to go out and help on farms in the evenings for a couple of hours daily, all Saturday afternoons and on Sundays, if required.

In some areas where people had been evacuated abandoned gardens and allotments were left. *The Thanet Advertiser* on 23 July reported that local residents had contacted the paper about vegetables being left to rot on allotments. The reporter thought it was a great shame to allow this produce to go to waste and wondered how it could be utilized. Undoubtedly local people soon rallied to the challenge.

Song of Potato Pete

Potatoes new, potatoes old
Potato (in a salad) cold
Potatoes baked or mashed or fried
Potatoes whole, potato pied
Enjoy them all, including chips
Remembering spuds don't come in ships!

The idea of self-sufficiency became more attractive to many people and competitions to encourage a competitive spirit existed. The Ministry of Food even created comic characters for their nutrition campaign. Potato Pete and Dr. Carrot were two of the most popular images. The promotion of carrots carried slogans like 'carrots keep you healthy and allow you to see in the blackout'. There was a Radio Doctor who gave regular talks on health. He often exhorted his radio listeners to eat carrots, and in the weeks leading up to Christmas recommended that these should be added to the ingredients of cakes, puddings and mincemeat to give sweetness and colour.

In some towns and villages competition resulted in communities forming pig or rabbit clubs. These, in turn, utilized kitchen waste, and rabbits were not only excellent to eat but their skins could be used for glove making. In many communities Women's Institutes were at the forefront of the action and, with the help and encouragement of the Ministry of Agriculture & Fisheries, produced thousands of pounds of home-made jam and preserves.

The government was keen to encourage jam making and with an abundance of fruit being available, the Ministry of Food announced that in August a special additional allowance of 2 lbs.(0.91kg) of sugar was to be allocated to each household for jam making and the bottling of fruit.

Further promotion of this important war effort was made by Churchill in one of his rousing speeches in November 1940 saying:

> 'Every endeavour must be made to grow the greatest volume of food of which this fertile island is capable.'

1941 Not everything went according to plan when on 25 February the Food Minister, Lord Woolton announced to the House of Commons that, *'We have hundreds of thousands of tons of potatoes. The need is for people to eat more and for caterers to use more of this first class food. There shall be no shortage of seed potatoes for the spring.'*

This statement caused the Prime Minister to write to Mr. Hudson enquiring what was to be done with the tons of Northern Ireland potatoes that were destined for feeding pigs? This large surplus had occurred due to a radical reduction in the number of pigs due to the fear of shortage of feeding stuffs. Churchill said there must be some way of utilising the potatoes as we could not afford in these days to throw away hundreds of thousands of tons of edible material. In another letter Winston Churchill proposed that more sugar beet should be grown the following year in order to save on shipping space. He appears to have had an uphill battle with farmers because for financial reasons they preferred to grow potatoes.

Replying to a question in the House of Commons on 23 May, Mr. Hudson stated that 5 million copies of the Dig for Victory leaflet 'Vegetable Production in Private Gardens' had been distributed during the past two months. Over 600,000 copies of the Ministry's free coloured cropping chart and more than a million copies of the various free advisory leaflets had also been distributed. Every effort had been put into the promotion.

On the 13 June, the Ministry issued guidelines on unwelcome garden visitors as many

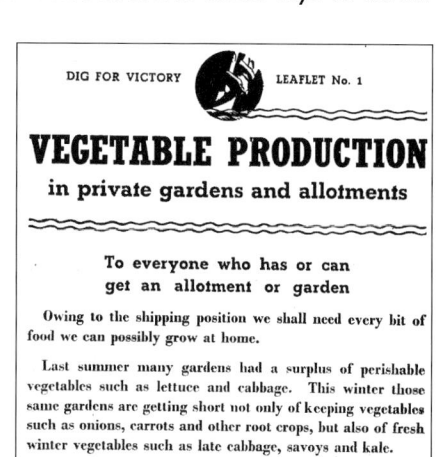

> DIG FOR VICTORY   LEAFLET No. 1
>
> **VEGETABLE PRODUCTION**
> in private gardens and allotments
>
> To everyone who has or can get an allotment or garden
>
> Owing to the shipping position we shall need every bit of food we can possibly grow at home.
>
> Last summer many gardens had a surplus of perishable vegetables such as lettuce and cabbage. This winter those same gardens are getting short not only of keeping vegetables such as onions, carrots and other root crops, but also of fresh winter vegetables such as late cabbage, savoys and kale.
>
> We must try to prevent that happening this year. Next winter is going to be a critical period.
>
> This leaflet tells you how to crop your ground to the best advantage so as to get vegetables all the year round.
>
> Please study it carefully and carry out the advice it contains.
>
> MINISTER OF AGRICULTURE & FISHERIES.

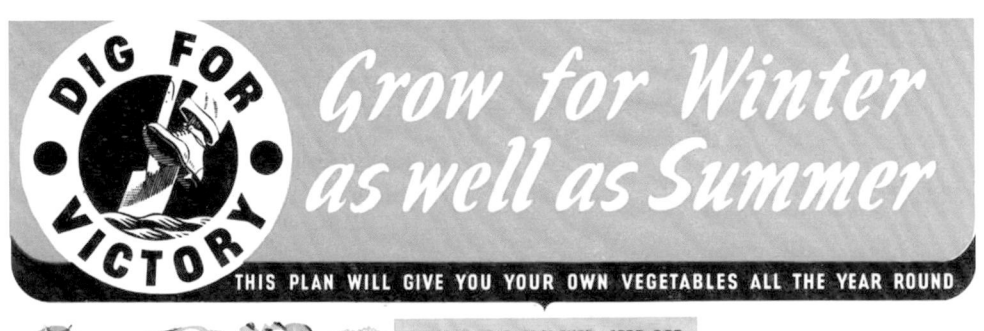

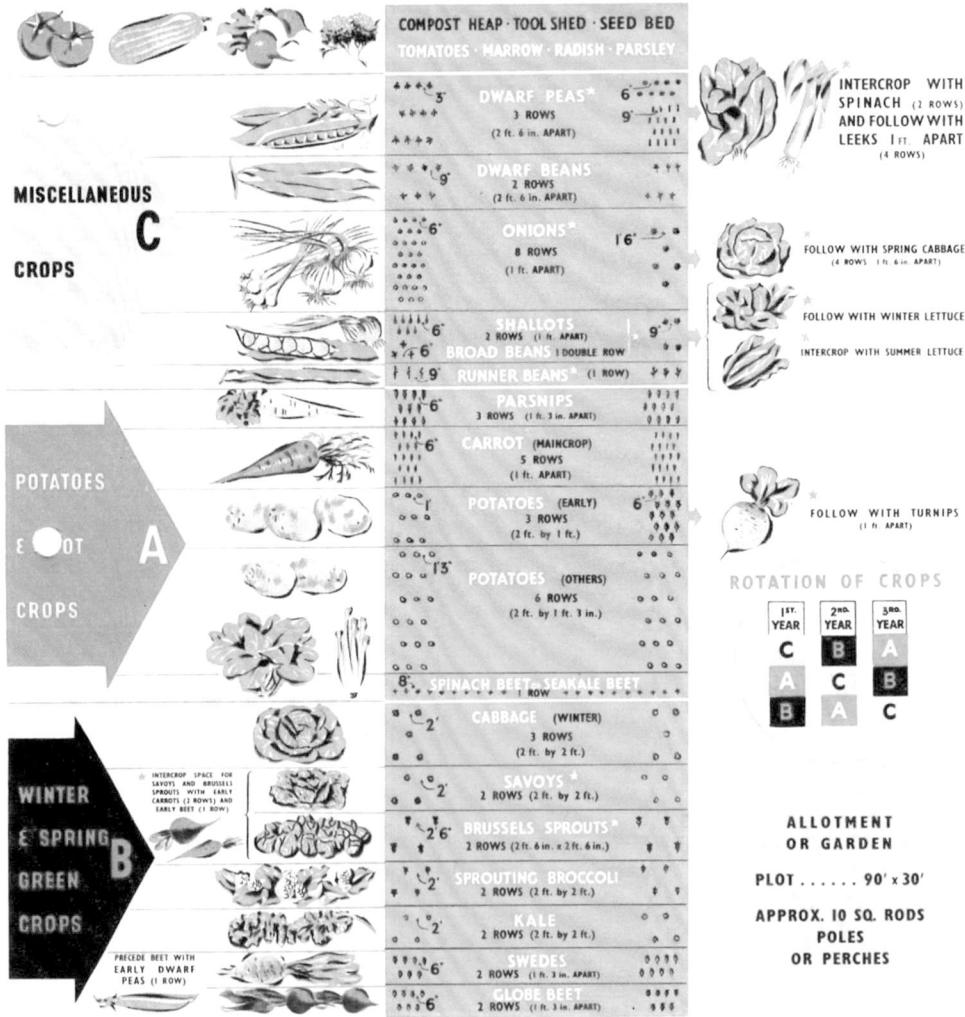

complaints had been received from allotment owners in recent months about the damage caused by dogs. The thousands of allotments up and down the country were producing valuable supplies of essential foodstuffs. These must be protected against thoughtless people who allowed their dogs to run wild and damage the crops. Accordingly a new Defence Regulation 1937.62AA was made, the effect of which was that the owners of a dog, and any person in charge of it, who allowed an animal to stray on any allotment, was liable on summary conviction to a fine not exceeding £5.

The Town Clerk in Sandwich received a letter in late June from the Ministry entitled:
Technical Advice for Farmers
'As part of a scheme to make the best technical advice more readily available to farmers, the Minister has decided to set up a bookstall at Sandwich Market on 8 July for the purpose of distributing free advisory leaflets and selling publications'.

During July, the Ministry of Agriculture & Fisheries issued a circular announcing that farmers would be looking for workers to replace the men who had been called up for military service. In many cases there was to be a requirement to engage boys who were willing to work on a farm. This work would be a form of National Service in helping to produce food, freeing up the food ships to carry munitions.

During the training period, boys of 14 and 15 will receive a personal allowance of 5/- (25p) a week and will be given free board and lodging by the farmers. It is considered that boys of 16 to 19 years of age should be able from the start to be of some value on the farm, and the farmers will pay the appropriate statutory wage for the training period. The boys will pay for their own board and lodging.

The buzz phrase in farming communities in the county was Maximizing Productivity. It is understood that all farms in Kent were inspected and graded by the Kent War Agricultural Executive Committee (War Ags) into three groups A, B and C:

Group A - The most efficient farms which were left alone.
Group B - This group had to conform to instructions laid down by War Ag. and were inspected to see if they were up to scratch.
Group C - These represented the least productive and were taken over by War Ag.

In an effort to maximise home food production, a series of posters were produced. The 'Plough Now' campaign even suggested that farmers should plough 'by day and night'.

Field Officers offered advice, issued cultivation directions, allocated fertilizers, feedstuffs and where necessary specialized machinery. They also had the power to evict farmers in Group C who refused to comply. Most farmers were willing to give up some independence in return for the economic benefits which ensued. In some cases the Women's Land Army provided the necessary labour force to up-grade the less productive farms under the supervision of a War Ag. representative.

In order to maintain maximum productivity, the Ministry of Agriculture issued an order to farmers that unless military action made it impossible for them to farm, they should continue to work as though no invasion was imminent.

The Ministry was also forced at that time to issue a directive to all concerned that stirrup pumps were intended for fire fighting, and should not be used for horticultural spraying which had suddenly become a habit!

In August the Ministry of Food announced that the prices of wild and cultivated blackberries were to be controlled. Wild blackberries, which were plentiful this year, are priced at 5½ d per lb (2½ p per 0.45 kg) retail and 4d (1½ p) wholesale. Pickers will be paid £28 a ton. Cultivated, all of which will be sent to preservers and bottlers, will fetch a maximum price for the grower of £60 a ton. The Minister added that schoolchildren are to be encouraged to gather the wild fruit, and housewives will be asked to make the fullest use of it.

Reservations with retailers for the season's supply of onions limited to 2 lb (0.91 kg) a head were to be made during the first week in September. Those failing to register would not get any. The reservation could be made by using the counterfoil SC4 of the general ration book and taken to the retailer. During the month a 'Potato Pete' campaign was started to encourage people to eat more vegetables, even to eat mashed potato sandwiches, and the retail price of the potato was fixed at a penny a pound for a period of 12 months.

Also in September the Board of Education was asked by the Minister of Agriculture to permit harvest camps to remain open for an additional week or two wherever circumstances made it desirable. The Minister considered that because of the late season there was a danger of part of the corn crop being lost unless measures were taken. Government action came just in time to prevent the boys returning home. Farmers undoubtedly appreciated the way schools and scholars responded to the national need and were performing a grand job in the war effort.

On 3 October, the Minister of Agriculture launched the third Dig for Victory campaign stating:
> 'We must have vegetables and we must grow them ourselves and where
> land is needed for vegetables, flowers must go'.

The Government announced in the press that food production must have precedence over flowers, and advised commercial flower growers that no transportation of flowers on the railways would be permitted after 1 October that year. During the same month the Ministry issued a pamphlet stressing the need for more food production:
> We are fighting the Germans on the farms and allotments and in private gardens
> of Britain, as surely as we are fighting them in the Libyan Desert, on the oceans
> and in the air. Food is as potent a weapon as the tank or the plane, and the
> Germans know that.

On 12 November, the Ministry of Supply issued a Control of Paper Order, under which it was possible to secure the maximum economy in the use of paper. They had the foresight not to ban seed catalogues which would otherwise have interfered with the very successful 'Dig for Victory' campaign.

1942 In May, the Ministry announced that Rabbit Clubs had continued to grow in popularity and 1000 new clubs had been formed last month with prospects of a new record being set this month. This contributed greatly with over 2000 tons of unrationed meat being produced nationally.

In the Dig for Victory Newsletter published on 5 June, by the Ministry of Agriculture it highlighted the need to have a concerted effort to kill house sparrows. The article stated:
> 'The damage that house sparrows do to our crops is far greater than most people realize. Gardens and allotments suffer considerably from the ravages of this pest. The damage can be reduced by systematically destroying nests wherever they can be found.'

Ironically today the house sparrow population is in decline!

In late July, the 'Waste not Want not' slogan was being used. The Ministry was recommending that gardeners should offer surplus plants to anybody who could use them or to set up a surplus plant exchange at their place of work.

In a circular on 4 December, the Minister of Agriculture advised the public to start planning to grow vegetables, especially to maintain health for the winter of 1943-44, as reductions in the supply of rationed foodstuffs would be inevitable. The Minister stressed that farmers were concentrating on maintaining milk supplies and on increasing their acreages of essential crops such as wheat and potatoes, and could not be expected to meet all the Nation's requirements of fresh vegetables. Furthermore the burden on rail and road traffic would make it increasingly difficult to transport perishable crops in winter.

In a national newspaper at the time a throwaway statement was printed:
> **Self help has become a religion that we ought all to be practising.**

1943 The Ministry of Agriculture announced on 5 February, that people of this country were going to face a food shortage. You have been warned that you are going to have less meat and the basis of your food must be vegetables:
> 'Few people realize what the shipping position is, but nobody wants meat if it means less munitions for the Middle East. You must not expect the farmer to provide in addition all the vegetables you require.
> Nor must you rely on the Merchant Navy to bring you plentiful supplies of other food. Every single bit of space that can be spared must be used to carry troops, guns and planes. You will have to make up by eating more vegetables'.

On 26 March, the Ministry issued new advice to gardeners and allotment holders:
> Potatoes – eat more, but don't grow more. There can be no doubt about its virtues – and we must never forget that it is the nation's iron ration against all eventualities.

The problem that the authorities were now facing was that many allotments were producing too many main crop potatoes at the expense of other vegetables, in particular greens.

THIS PLAN WILL GIVE YOU YOUR OWN VEGETABLES ALL THE YEAR ROUND

A

SEED BED TOMATOES | COMPOST HEAP MARROW

BROAD BEANS
1 DOUBLE ROW

PEAS
2 ROWS

ONIONS OR SHALLOTS
4 ROWS

POTATOES (EARLY)
2 ROWS

RUNNER BEANS
1 ROW

SPINACH BEET
1 ROW

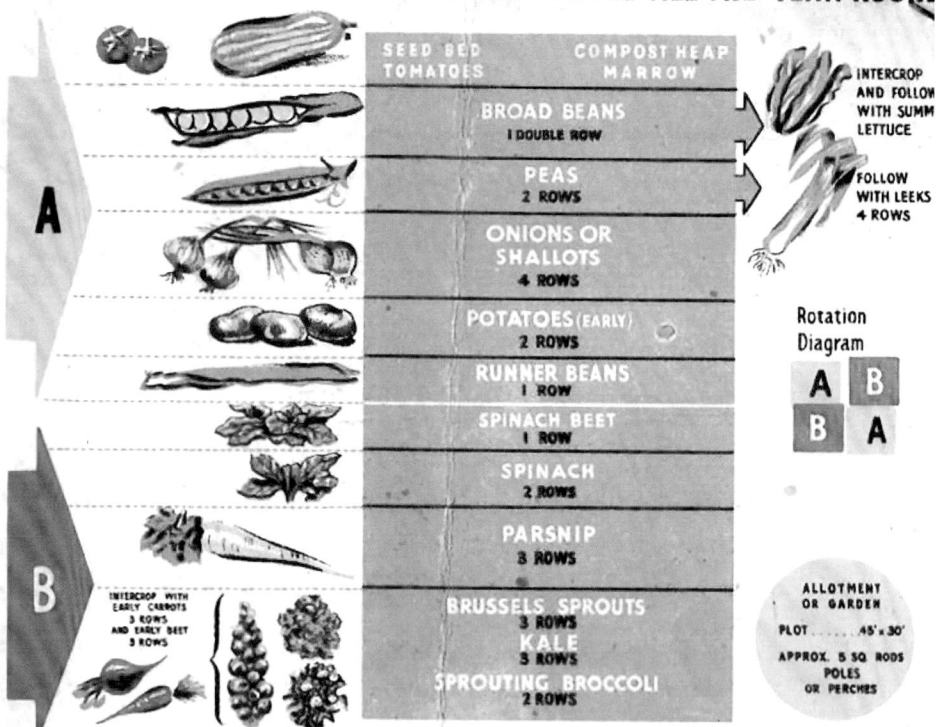

SPINACH
2 ROWS

PARSNIP
3 ROWS

B — INTERCROP WITH EARLY CARROTS 3 ROWS AND EARLY BEET 3 ROWS

BRUSSELS SPROUTS
3 ROWS
KALE
3 ROWS
SPROUTING BROCCOLI
2 ROWS

INTERCROP AND FOLLOW WITH SUMMER LETTUCE

FOLLOW WITH LEEKS
4 ROWS

Rotation Diagram

A	B
B	A

ALLOTMENT OR GARDEN
PLOT .... 45' x 30'
APPROX. 5 SQ RODS POLES OR PERCHES

TABLE OF PLANTING AND PERIOD OF USE
WINTER SUPPLIES PRINTED IN GREEN

CROP	TIME OF SOWING	DISTANCE APART Rows	DISTANCE APART Plants	PERIOD OF USE
BEANS (Broad)	Feb.-March	1 double row	6 in. by 9 in.	July
BEANS (Runner)	Mid-May		9 in.	July-Oct.
BEET	April	15 in.	6 in. (thin)	July-April
BROCCOLI (Sprouting)	Mid-May Plant Mid-July	2 ft.	2 ft.	April-May
BRUSSELS SPROUTS	March Plant May-June	2½ ft.	2½ ft.	Nov.-Mar.
CARROTS (Early)	April	1 ft.	6 in. (thin)	June-Sept.
KALE	May Plant Mid.-July	2 ft.	2 ft.	Jan.-April
LEEKS	March Plant July	1 ft.	6 in. 9 in.	Mar.-May
LETTUCE	March and every 14 days	Between other crops	9 in.	May-Oct.
MARROW	May		3-4 ft.	July-Feb.
ONIONS	Mid.-Feb.	1 ft.	6 in. (thin)	July-June
PARSNIPS	Mid.-Feb.-Mid.-March	15 in.	6 in. (thin)	Nov.-Mar.
PEAS	March and April	2½ ft.	3 in.	June-July
POTATOES (Early)	March	2 ft.	1 ft.	July-Aug.
SHALLOTS	February	1 ft.	6 in.	Jan.-Dec.
SPINACH (Winter)	Sept.	1 ft.	6 in. (thin)	Spring
SPINACH BEET	April	3 in.	3 in. groups	July Jan.
TOMATOES	Plant end May		15 in.	Aug.-Oct.

Printed for H.M. Stationery Office by T. G. Porter (Printers) Ltd., Leeds. 51-3308

On the same day the Town Clerk at Sandwich received a letter 'Making the most of a small plot'. The letter said:
> Not everyone has time, strength or available land to cultivate the standard allotment of 90 x 30 feet (27.7 x 9.2m). Therefore the ministry has published a special leaflet to enable smaller gardens and busier people to do their useful bit in food production. It has been designed for a space roughly 45 x 30 feet (13.8 x 9.2m), and will help you to get through a lean winter and keep you fit.

On the 9 April, the Joint Parliamentary Secretary to the Minister of Agriculture stated in the House of Commons:
> *'It is my firm opinion that we ought to take a pessimistic rather than an optimistic view of the situation. As some people may think that the Ministry has cried WOLF unnecessarily in urging people to grow their own winter vegetables or go short. But if there is to be any change in the food situation it is NOT likely to be for the better.'*

In an attempt to recover the situation after the Joint Parliamentary Secretary's remarks, the Ministry went on the offensive a fortnight later in the Dig for Victory newsletter with the following statements under the headline 'You against Hitler':
> The battle of the brussel, the broccoli, the cabbage and the cauliflower is as important as any that has been fought. No allotment holder must think that his efforts to bring about victory are too small and insignificant to have any effect. Don't think of this war in terms of millions. Think of it personally, remembering that in Germany there is bound to be your counterpart doing the same job as yourself, and say to yourself – I can beat that person.

In defence of the nation's bee-keepers, the Prime Minister wrote to the Ministers of Food and Agriculture on the 19 April in regard to the discontinuation of the small sugar ration that had been allowed to bee-keepers. Winston stressed that 'it was needed in the spring months and what is the saving in starving the bees?'

On 28 May, the Minister of Agriculture announced that due to the increasing number of persons trespassing on allotment land for the purpose of stealing vegetables:
> *'It is now an offence to trespass on allotments without reasonable excuse, even though no warning notices are displayed there. Any person found guilty is liable, on summary conviction, to a fine not exceeding £50'.*

A Sunday newspaper on 4 June carried a light-hearted article reading:
> There are no deck chairs in sight – and, in any event few lawns to put them on. Instead, we find bean-sticks and rows of lettuce, spadesmen looking into the seeds of time, and possibly a chicken-run covering the old dahlia bed. Digging for Victory has ceased to be a hazardous experiment most plots are superbly vegetarian, and the deck-chair pressed into cellar service during the blitz - remains in hiding.

The Ministry of Food announced in the press –
New Potatoes at pre-war prices
Thanks to fair weather, farmers' foresight and the subsidy, we have a record potato crop. This is WAR NEWS of the greatest importance.

Potatoes are the great energy food.
They give strength to the men and women who make munitions.
They are home-grown. They are ship-saver No.1. They are cheap, they are delicious (especially now), they are easy to cook in new ways for every meal.
More potato and less bread – better for you, better for the Nation!

On the 25 June, the Minister of Agriculture announced that our prisoners of war in 67 camps in Europe had benefited from the 456 parcels of vegetable and 196 parcels of flower seeds sent through the Royal Horticultural Society. This effort from the RHS must have been a real morale booster for those prisoners and a welcome diversion from their plight.

1944 On the 14 January, a circular arrived in Sandwich giving the Local Authority their 'battle orders' for the year ahead on the 'Dig for Victory' front. The Minister told them that the need for maximum production of vegetables by the public was as great now as at any previous period of the war. He impressed upon them how essential it was that they should maintain and even intensify their efforts that year. In short, 'Don't let up' and 'Every plot a better Plot'.

In an attempt to encourage the thousands of gardeners and allotment owners in the land to continue their sterling work, the Minister wrote in a Dig for Victory newsletter on 28 January:

Growing food on our allotments or gardens is a kind of second front and a vital one. In these days we have but scanty leisure and all of us find it increasingly difficult to carry on our gardening operations.
Digging for Victory is a form of self-preservation.

On the 4 February, the Ministry reiterated that growing vegetables was still our top priority and it's NOT the 'time for the Pretty Garden'. Yet disturbing reports were reaching the Ministry that some amateur gardeners were already turning their minds from crops to flowers. It would be deplorable if people were to go back to growing flowers now in preference to vegetables.

1945 Requesting a reply, the Prime Minister wrote to the Minister of Agriculture on 22 January regarding a shortage of potatoes!

'I am much concerned at the potato shortage because we had been taught to rely so much upon this form of food. I need to know why this shortage has come about, and what measures are being taken to remedy it'.

This statement is indicative of just how important home production was and taken very seriously at the highest possible level.

DIG FOR VICTORY — LEAFLET No. 17

POTATO BLIGHT

BLIGHT attacks potatoes when the weather is warm, wet and muggy, and may kill the tops as early as the end of July or the beginning of August. If this happens, not only is the yield reduced, but the tubers may become infected and rot in the ground, or in storage.

Spraying will protect the tops from blight, if it is properly done, and care at lifting time will protect the tubers from infection. In time of war, when maximum production is essential, every allotment holder and gardener (except those in smoky industrial districts) should consider spraying his maincrop potatoes as an insurance against blight. And all growers, without exception, should take precautions to avoid infection of

DIG FOR VICTORY — LEAFLET No. 16

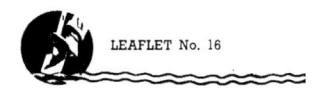

'Dig for Victory' GARDEN PESTS AND HOW TO DEAL WITH THEM

AT any time, the loss of crops through pest attack is a great disappointment to the vegetable grower. In war time, when every ounce of home-grown food is needed, such loss is a serious waste. This waste is largely avoidable, and in this leaflet, methods are outlined for dealing with the more common pests.

No elaborate apparatus is required for spraying or dusting. The simplest types will suffice if used with care and intelligence. The plants treated must be thoroughly wetted or dusted. Careless work is merely waste of insecticide.

Notes on four of the most important materials for pest control, namely, Derris, Pyrethrum, Nicotine and Metaldehyde are given at the end of this leaflet.

Dealing With Wireworms

Wireworms are most frequent where grass or waste land has been cultivated. Some gardeners believe that the risk of wireworm attack is reduced by removing the turf and stacking it separately for a year or two instead of burying it. This is only true if the turf is removed at a time when the wireworms are working in the top two or three inches. But wireworms move up and down in the soil in accordance with weather conditions, and there is grave risk that many will be left in the lower parts of the soil when the turf is removed. These are likely to be specially harmful, since in the absence of buried grass they are forced to concentrate their attentions on the crop.

It is generally better to bury the turf. This not only adds fertility to the soil, but will probably attract some of the pests away from the crop during the first year.

When wireworms are present, there is no quick way of getting rid of them, but the following measures will help to deal with them :

What to do

(1) Spit damaged potatoes or carrots on short sticks and bury about 4 in. deep, with the stick projecting from the soil. Pull up these potato or carrot traps every three or four days and destroy any wireworms on them. Persistent trapping can practically rid a garden of the pest.

(2) Grow crops less subject to attack, such as broad beans, peas, kale and leeks. French beans and Runners are also useful. Brassica crops (cabbages, Brussels sprouts, etc.) may escape the worst of the attack when planted out in early summer, while potatoes on wireworm-infested

In March Mr. Churchill in a letter to the Minister of Food, stated how pleased he was to see there was a proposal to increase the production of both pigs and eggs, particularly since wheat was now more plentiful. Winston Churchill was keen to see this as an incentive and campaigned personally on behalf of the domestic poultry keeper, particularly when there was a surplus of grain. In a letter to Clement Attlee, the Prime Minister said:

> 'I hope you will manage to help …. It costs no labour, and the extra eggs are not an undue reward for the enterprise and initiative of the owner. The present miserably small allowance of grain does not allow enough hens to be kept to justify putting up a poultry run. If it were increased many more people would produce their own eggs thus save shipping and labour'.

In a letter earlier in the war Churchill was very concerned about rationing poultry. He wrote to the Minister of Food saying, 'The hen has been part and parcel of the country cottager's life since history began. What is the need for this tremendous reduction to one hen per person'. In a further letter he urges various ministries 'not, I pray you, to give up the egg scheme and the chicks necessary for full-scale production'.

In a personal plea from the Minister of Agriculture in the press on 18 May, he said:

> 'Now that the war in Europe is over, I wish to convey my deep thanks and high appreciation to all who have worked so hard in our food production campaign. You have played an excellent part in achieving victory, and you have every right to be proud of that part.
> I can, however, offer you NO prospect of relaxation. Food here and in the world at large is desperately short. I must call on you all to carry on in the same unselfish and patriotic spirit you have already shown'.

This message from the Minister endorses an article in a popular gardening magazine a month earlier which painted a horrific picture of what was round the corner. The correspondent wrote:

> 'There is every probability that the risk of shortages of food will be as great and grave within the next twelve months as it has been at any period since the outbreak of war in 1939'.

Land Army insignia

Land Army release certificate

In June the same year questions were being asked of the Government. 'Now that Germany is beaten, can I stop Digging for Victory?' A spokesman said we should be producing more food not less because the general food situation was now much worse than during the war as rationing systems had collapsed. Only 30% of seed sowing had been completed and there was an intense dislocation of transport.

On the 28 July 1945, approximately two thousand Kent Land Girls filled Canterbury Cathedral in the presence of the Duchess of Kent for their official stand down service. During its time the Women's Land Army nationally had provided approximately 90,000 women to work on the land, and helped keep this country in food for the duration of the war. Although we had rationing no-one starved – a testament to the work done by our women!

The desperate shortage of food in this country, not only during the war but also in subsequent years, prompted the arrival of generous gifts of food from various member countries of the Commonwealth for distribution. South Africa sent dried fruit and tins of different fruit varieties whilst Australia joined in with gifts of parcels of food, all sent in appreciation of this country's war effort. In villages and towns throughout the land local authorities decided the fairest method of distribution was to hand out items as they arrived amongst the old people and the less well off.

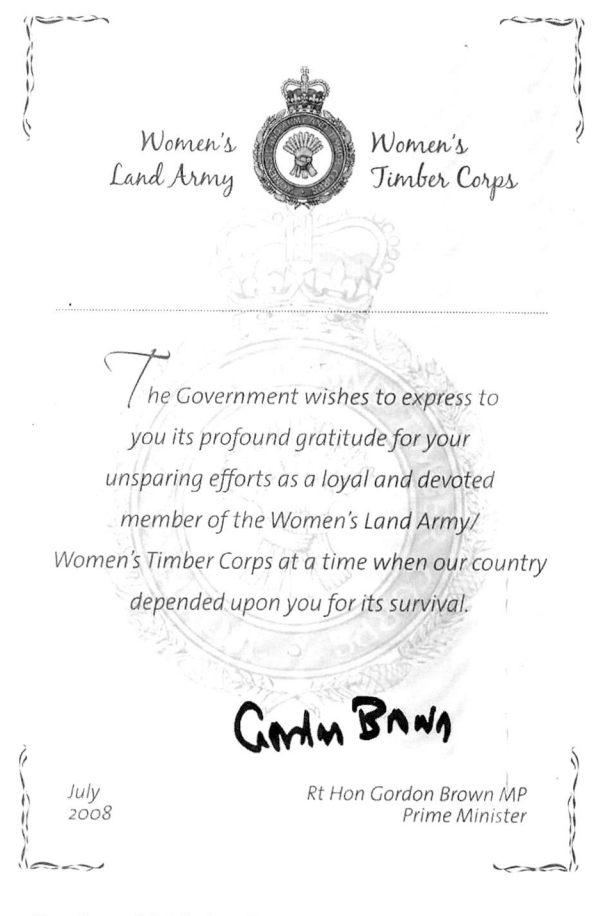

Women's Land Army *Women's Timber Corps*

The Government wishes to express to you its profound gratitude for your unsparing efforts as a loyal and devoted member of the Women's Land Army/ Women's Timber Corps at a time when our country depended upon you for its survival.

Gordon Brown

July 2008

Rt Hon Gordon Brown MP
Prime Minister

Finally in 2008 the Government acknowledged the valuable service the Women's Land Army and Timber Corps rendered to the nation during the Second World War.

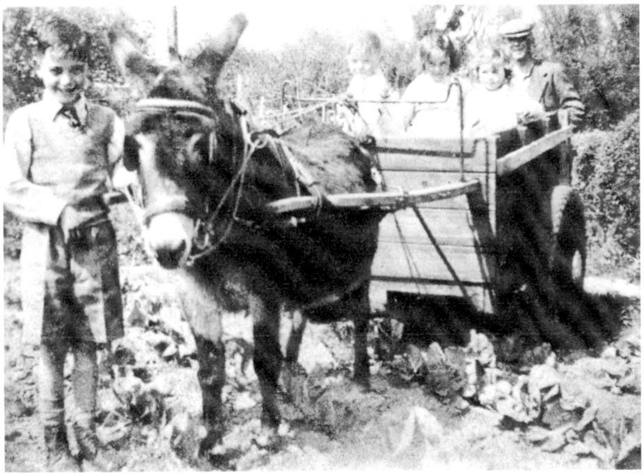

BIBLIOGRAPHY

Acknowledgment is made of the following printed sources of information:

A Glint in the Sky	Martin Easdown with Thomas Genth	2004
A History of Deal	Gertrude Nunns	2006
An Historical Atlas of Kent	T. Lawson & D. Killingray	2004
Ash-An East Kent Village	David Downes	2000
Conflict across the Strait	Col. B.E. Arnold	1982
Battle of Britain Diary	David Collyer	1980
Deal and District at War	David Collyer	1995
Dover & Folkestone during the Great War	Michael & Christine George	2008
Dover's Forgotten Fortress	Janice Welby	1983
East Kent at War	David Collyer	1994
East Kent – Within Living Memory	E.K. Federation of WIs	1993
Handbook of Kent's Defences	D.H. Bennett	1977
Keep Smiling Through 1939-1945	Susan Briggs	1975
Kent – A Chronicle of the Century vol 1925-1949	Bob Ogley	1997
Kent and Sussex 1940 – Britain's Frontline	Stuart Hylton	2004
Kent Home Guard	K.R. Gulvin	1980
Kent's War 1939-1945	The Kent Messenger Group	2005
My Dover – Joe Harman	Derek Leach	2001
Our Village and the Great War – re. Shepherdswell	Richard Higgs	1920
RAF Manston	RAF Manston History Club	1993
Reflections of River the Kentish Village	Douglas Welby	1997
Royal Marines at Deal	Andrew Lane	2000
Sandwich Haven & Richborough Port	Robert Butler	1996
Soldiers of the Castle – Dover Castle Garrisoned	G.M. Atherton	2003
The Blitz – The British under Attack	Juliet Gardiner	2010
The Kentish Village of Eastry 1800-2000	Douglas Welby	2007
The Making of Modern Britain	Andrew Marr	2009
The Second World War – Vol. 1-6	Winston Churchill	1948-54
The Volunteer Movement in Kent 1914-18	S.V. Hurst-Bygone Kent	1996
To Fire Committed – Fire-Fighting in Kent	Harry Klopper	1984
Wartime Kent 1939-40	Oonagh Hyndman	1990
When airships flew from Capel	David Collyer – Bygone Kent	1984

Unpublished material:

Deal, Walmer & Sandwich Mercury	Various issues	
Dover Express	Various issues	
Eastry Village News	Various issues	
Godmersham Airship Hole	Folkestone Library	
Invasion 1940	Brian Boreham – Folkestone Library	1995
Kentish Express	Various issues	1944
Northbourne – Tip & Run Raids 1942	Andrew Parkinson	2011
Quex at War – VAD Hospital 1914-19	Hazel Basford – Powell-Cotton Museum	2003

The Battle of Britain -August-October 1940.......................... An Air Ministry Account   1941
The Daily Telegraph .... Various issues
The Engineer   1919
The Kentish Gazette .... Various issues
The Illustrated London News .... Various issues 1939-41

Photographs and various documents :
The author would like to thank the following for permission to reproduce photographs and documents in their possession.

The Sandwich Town Archive – Hon. Archivist – Ray Harlow and his staff whose help has assisted greatly to this publication.

The Staff of Sandwich Library - Help in ordering books.

Jack Bones – Information on local people who were involved with Auxiliary Units and the Home Guard.

Margaret Harlow – Sandwich Photographs

Bob & Kath Hollingsbee – Photographs and information.

David Gregory – Photographs and loan of books.

Ray Sedgewick – Home Guard information and photographs.

Sheila Smith – Information on Eastry Home Guard.

Edna Dray – Information documents on Coldred and Shepherdswell.

John Hollyer – Wartime photographs

Eric Marshall – Ash Home Guard

Ben Found – Auxiliary Unit Information

Mr. & Mrs. J. Bradley – Information on the local Auxiliary Unit and photographs.

John Guy – Help and guidance on Auxiliary Units/ Home Guard also providing photographs.

Keith Parfitt – Information on Northbourne Auxiliary Unit OB.

Mrs. D. Deverson – Wartime photographs.

Special Notes: I am especially indebted to my wife Doreen for patience, making valuable suggestions and carefully reading the proofs.

Although every effort has been made to trace the present copyright holders, the author apologizes for any unintentional omission or neglect and will be glad to insert the appropriate acknowledgements to sources.

Index

Adisham 11, 77
Admiralty Pier 15
Air Defence Research Committee 40
Aircraft Production 47
Aircraft Week 47
Air Ministry Experimental Stations 100
Air raid precautions 31-3, 36-7, 48
Air raid protection tunnels 35, 36
Air raid siren 27, 29
Air Raid Wardens 48, 50, 83, 85, 93, 125
Air Sea Rescue 84
Airships 14, 16, 19, 162
Air Transport Auxiliary 39, 50
Alien Companies 35
Aliens 45, 102
Alkham Valley 167
Allied Supreme Commander 124
Allotment Associations 172
Ambulance trains 41
American Forces 16
Anderson shelters 48, 61, 123, 133
Anderson Sir John 35
'anti-tank islands' 142
'anti-war propaganda' 90
Antwerp Harbour 83
Appeal Tribunals 22-3
Archbishop of Canterbury 31
Archcliffe Fort 26, 56
'armed insurrection' 81
Army Cyclist Corps 15
Ash 12-3, 52, 77, 89, 114, 142, 165-6
Ashford 136, 156
Ash Platoon Home Guard 143, 147-50, 154, 163
Ashley 147
Asquith Herbert PM 8, 22
Attlee Clement PM 181
Austerity 109
Austrian refugees 33
Aux. Fire Service 37, 44, 54, 61, 83, 85, 89
Aux. Military Pioneering Corps 35
Aux. Territorial Service 96-7, 107
Auxiliary Units 155-7, 159, 162-4, 167-9
Aylesham Cemetery 47

Baden-Powell Lord 56
Balloon Barrage 38, 41, 46, 68, 73-5, 99
Balloon Squadrons 40
Barfrestone 12, 147
Barham 167
Battle of Britain 66, 135
Bayonet practice 23
Beaverbrook Lord 47
Beckets Caves 36, 50
'bee-keepers' 179
'beetles' 123
Bekesbourne 27
Belfast 53
Belgian refugees 8
Belgian soldiers 23, 24

Belgium 8, 9, 52-3, 61, 63
Berlin 145
Betteshanger 12, 147, 163
Betteshanger Colliery 114, 164
Betteshanger Park 33
Bevan Hospital 24
Bevin Boys 120
Bevin Ernest 91, 120
Bilting 156, 161, 167
Birchington 24, 150, 166
Blackout 10, 36, 40, 43, 46, 48, 50, 83, 85, 88, 128-9
'black shirts' 82
'black smoke' 60
Blasting Gelatine 158
Blean 167
Blister Gas 95
'Blitzkrieg' 135
Blockhouses 60, 80
Board of Education 92, 102, 176
Board of Trade 109, 118
'bomb alley' 126
'bomber's moon' 85
'booby-traps' 158
Boulogne 40, 55, 82, 120
Boy Scouts 46, 56
Brandenburg Regiment 56
Bristol 138
British Aircraft Industry 38
British Expeditionary Force 55
British Legion (Women's Section) 39
British Resistance Organisation 155, 161
British Restaurants 100
Brittany 35
Broadstairs 15, 60, 76, 132, 144, 150, 166
Brooke General Alan 83, 141-2, 145
'broomstick army' 136
Buckland (Dover) 35, 67, 69, 72
Buckland Hospital 55
Buffs (The) 26, 52, 141, 154

Calais 55, 77-8, 82
Calvert Captain Mike 156
Camber 135, 162
Canada 34
Canadian Army Corps 80
Canadian Pioneer Battalion 144
Canterbury 13, 94, 97, 100, 114, 132, 136, 143, 152
Canterbury Cathedral 154, 182
Capel Airship Station 27
Capel Battery 110
Capel le Ferne 16, 19, 69
Central Hospital Supply Service 45
Chamberlain Neville PM 41, 43-4
Charlton (Dover) 35
Chatham 29, 77, 136
Chillenden 11
Chislet Colliery 151
'church bells' 29, 81, 142
Church of England 121

Index

Churchill Winston 43, 50, 52, 55, 57, 60, 63, 67, 71, 73, 76-7, 82, 88, 90, 96, 99, 102, 109, 115, 118-9, 122, 124, 130, 134, 137, 141, 155-6, 159, 173, 181
Cigarette cards 37
8th (Cinque Ports) Bat. Home Guard 145, 151, 163, 167
Citadel Battery 7, 16, 78, 80
Civil Defence 33, 44-5, 48, 59, 61, 65, 89-90, 98, 100, 102, 107-8, 111, 113, 116-7, 152-3
Civil Defence Ambulance Service 127
Civilian evacuation 11-13
Cliffsend 76
Cliftonville 78
Clyde 53
Coal Production 102
Coastal Artillery 147, 150
Coastal Command 100
Coldred 12
Commander in Chief BHF 138, 141
Communist Party 90
Connaught Barracks 71, 78
Conscientious Objectors 54, 96, 102
XII Corps 52, 150, 156, 161-2
Coventry 116
Cranbrook 12
'Cromwell' 57, 78, 81
Cuffley (Essex) 29
Czechoslovakian refugees 33

Dad's Army 142
Dalton Hugh 119
'Dam Buster Raid' 119
D-Day 58, 121, 123-4, 153
Deal 8, 15, 20, 22, 29, 31, 54, 60, 66, 71, 73, 76-9, 88, 109, 116, 119, 122, 127, 132, 147, 151-2, 167
Deal Castle 75, 147, 150
Deal Fire Service 61
Deal Gas Works Home Guard Platoon 151
Deal Police Station 151
Deal Pier 51, 55
Deal Railway Station 74, 115
'decoy operations' 85, 120
Defence Regulations 85
Demonstration Allotment 171
Denmark 52
Denton 11
Derby Lord 22
Detling 29
'Dig for Victory' 171, 173-4, 176-7 179-80, 182
'dim out' 131
'doctor carrot' 172
'doodle bugs-flying bombs' 110, 125-7
Douglas Colonel F.W.R 169
Dover 7, 13, 15 25, 27-32, 35-6, 40-1, 56, 58, 60, 71, 73, 76-9, 88, 104-5, 110, 117, 128, 132, 139-40, 151-3, 167
Dover Anti-Aircraft Corps 25
Dover Garrison 118
Dover Castle 25-6, 57, 76, 78

Dover's caves 23, 28
Dover Gas Works 72, 99, 115
Dover Harbour 7, 15, 24, 56, 67-70, 72-5, 83-4, 123, 125, 135
Dover Harbour Batteries 15, 56, 79
Dover Home Guard 151
Dover Patrol 16
Dover's Race Course 8
Dover Strait 40
Drop Redoubt 25
Drumhead Service 154
'dug outs' 23
Duke of York's School 67
Dumpton Gap 144
'dummy airfield' 52
Dungeness 56, 78, 120, 125
'Dunkirk Spirit' 55
Dymchurch Redoubt 60

East Anglia 138
East Church 28
East Kent Bus Company 151, 153
East Kent Hunt 15
East Kent Light Railway 89
East Kent Mounted Scouts 15
East Kent Regiment 141, 154
Eastry 10, 12, 15, 20-1, 30, 32, 38, 41-2, 50, 55, 61, 64, 71, 75, 77, 79, 89, 94, 114-5, 118-9, 131-3, 137, 139, 143, 155, 163-4
Eastry Children's Home 23
Eastry Cottage Hospital 24
Eastry Home Guard Platoon 147-8
Eastry Rural District 32, 37, 41, 53-4, 89, 91-2, 95, 97, 124, 132, 147, 163
Eastry Workhouse 22
Eden Anthony 52, 135-6, 141
Eisenhower General Dwight 124
Elham 59
Elmstone 12
Elvington 71, 74, 147
Emergency mortuary 47
Emergency Powers Act 55
Essential Work Order 90, 104
Etchingham 12
Evacuees 43
Eythorne 12, 89, 147

Fan Bay 7, 76
Fascists 141
Field Captain Norman 162
'fifth column' 81, 111, 142
Fighter Command 51, 69
Finglesham 147
Fire brigades 31-2, 37, 83-4
Fire Services (Emergency Provisions) Bill 104
Fire Wardens 32
'fire on the sea' 140, 145
Fire Watchers Order 86
First Aid Posts 44, 48-50, 86, 89, 148

Index

First Aid Workers 36
Flame Weapons 59, 143-5
Flax 63
Fleming Captain Peter 156, 162, 166
Flying boats 16
Fog Intensive Dispersal Operations 117
Folkestone 8, 15-6, 22, 24, 27-8, 40, 78, 128, 123, 140, 151-2, 167
Folkestone Harbour 60, 73, 123
Folkestone Home Guard Platoon 151
Food & Drugs Act 102
Food rationing 25, 45
Forster Major General A.L 135
Fort Burgogne 57
France 10, 16, 35, 53, 61, 66, 129, 155
Franklin Brigadier General H.S 135-6, 154
Franklyn General H.E 168
Free French pilots 105
French military wounded 24

Gap Gris Nez 71
Garrison Artillery 15, 20, 26
Gas attack (protection) 33, 36, 44, 48-9, 95-6
Gas Rattles 49-50
Gaulle General de 105
Geneva Convention 133, 156
German Batteries 77, 82-3
German High Command 56, 65, 69, 71, 145
'Germany calling' 58
German radio stations 35
GHQ Home Forces 155
GHQ Line 157
GHQ Special Reserve Battalions 156, 162
Gillingham 41, 54
Godmersham Park 16
Goebbels Joseph 58
Goldstone Marshes 52
Goodnestone 11, 74
Goodwin Sands 67
Gordon-Canning Robert 82
Government Defence Area 123
Great Yarmouth 57
Green Howards 65
Great Mongeham 147, 150
Gubbins Colonel Colin 155-6, 161
'guerrilla warfare' 141, 146, 153, 155-6
Guilton 27, 143
Guston 31, 76, 78, 128, 132

Habeas corpus 88
Haig Camp 17, 34
Ham 12
Hamburg 58
Hammill 47, 72, 75, 148
Hand bells & hooters 43-4, 50
Harris Lord 15
Hawkinge Airfield 66-68, 70, 114, 167
Henderson Arthur 22
Herne Bay 55, 75, 132

Highworth 155-7, 161, 168
'hit and run' 80, 114
Hitler Adolf 54, 57, 80, 83, 105, 108, 127, 179
Holland 52-53
Holland Lieut. Colonel 155
Home Defence Battalions 51
Home Guard 45, 50, 52, 63, 81, 111-3, 124, 135, 137-8, 140-6, 148-57
Home Guard Reserve 138
Home Land Security 54
Home Guard Transport Companies 151-2
Hop-growers 64
Hornchurch 51
Horsmonden 73
Hospital Library Service 44
Hougham 67
'house sparrows' 177
Hudson Rt. Hon. Robert 172-3
Hythe 15, 57

Ickham 11
Identity cards 7, 63
Immobilize vehicles 63, 113
Incendiary bombs 37, 48, 63, 72, 86, 93, 115, 117, 151
Incendiary leaves 93
Income Tax 45, 52
Invasion Committee 111-3
Invasion Threat 57-8, 61-2, 80-1, 99, 105, 110-14, 118-9, 135, 138-40, 143, 146, 148, 151, 156-7, 159, 162-4, 168
'irregular warfare' 155
Ismay General 90
Ironside General 138, 141

Japan 132
Jewish refugees 33-34
Johnson Amy 50
Joint War Organization 44
Joyce William 58

Kearsney 30, 72-3, 76
Kent Agricultural Wages Committee 64
Kent Coalfields 144, 147
Kent Cyclist Battalion 15, 26
Kent Volunteer Fencibles 15
Kent Volunteer Regiment 26
King George V 18, 25, 171
King George VI 43, 50, 89, 101, 128
Kingsdown 22, 66, 78, 127
Kingsdown Holiday Camp 116
Kingsgate Battery 60, 72
Kitchener Camp 34
Kitchener Lord 9
Kitcheners 9
Knowlton 9, 11, 77, 119

Langdon Battery 67, 70-1, 74, 77-8, 80, 114, 117, 125

Index

Learn to shoot movement 61
Lend-Lease Act 98, 103
Littlebourne 72
Local Defence Volunteers 52, 54, 135-7, 145, 147, 150-1
London 43, 53, 77-8, 126, 128, 135, 138
London Control 123
'looting' 87-8, 151
Lovat Scouts 167
Luftwaffe 58, 66, 69, 71, 80, 98, 104, 117, 135
Lydden 89
Lydden Spout 67-68
Lyminge 163, 167
Lympne Airfield 70-1

Maidstone 136, 138
Manston 28, 31, 75
Margate 15, 29, 54-5, 60, 70-1, 119, 132, 137, 150, 166-7
Margate Lifeboat 74
Marine Station 68
Martello Towers 60
'martial law' 81, 111
McNicholl Captain G. 162
Mechanized Transport Corps 39
Mechanized infantry 141, 146
Medway Towns 38, 41, 135
Merchant Navy 107, 163, 177
Mersey 53
Metropole Hotel 24
'Mickey Mouse' 48, 96
Military Intelligence (Research) Unit 155
Military Service Act 22, 25
'mine fields' 59, 73, 86, 124, 139, 143
Ministry of Agriculture & Fisheries 64, 172-3, 175-7, 179-81
Ministry of Food 51, 64, 88, 91, 99, 103, 106, 109, 112, 116, 121, 173, 176, 179, 181
Ministry of Health 53, 70, 89, 101, 109, 116 127, 129-31
Ministry of Home Security 49, 60, 74, 86, 89-90, 98, 102, 108, 110, 115-6, 131, 152
Ministry of Information 32, 63, 88, 116
Ministry of Labour 90, 106, 120
Ministry of Supply 46, 63, 65, 86-7, 103, 107, 176
Ministry of Transport 39
Ministry of Works & Buildings 96, 99, 118, 122
Minster 51, 77, 150, 166
Moir Sir Ernest 19
'Molotov Cocktail' 136, 138, 144, 148, 150
Mongeham 12, 71, 114
Monkton Marshes 52
Montgomery General Bernard 150
Morrison Herbert 60, 95, 104, 108, 110, 125
'Morrison shelters' 92-3, 133
Mosley Sir Oswald 82, 88
Mowlem John & Co. 139
'Mr. Chad' 87
Mulberry Harbours 123-5

National Auxiliary Units HQ 156
National Fire Service 104, 109, 111, 113-4, 120, 128
National Health Insurance 35, 92
National Motor Volunteers 15
National Registration 21, 45, 96
National Savings 46-7, 98, 108
National Service 40, 50, 89, 96, 104, 106, 112, 121, 152, 175
National War Bonds 97
'National wheat meal' 51, 101-2
Naval Shore Establishment 118
Nazi 33, 82, 155
Nethercourt VAD Hospital 24
Neutrality Act 98
Nodal Points 142-4, 146
'no-go areas' 86
Nonington 12, 55, 71, 91, 114, 147
Normandy 123-5, 129
Northbourne 12, 15, 78, 147, 164
Northbourne Lord 10, 24
Northdown 73, 78
North Lord 73
Norway 52, 123, 155

Observation balloons 19
Observation Post 80, 86, 159-60
Official Secrets Act 163, 169
'Operation Bodyguard' 123
'Operation Dynamo' 40, 55
'Operation Fortitude' 123
'Operation Harlequin' 119
'Operation Overlord' 123-4
'Operation Pied Piper' 41
'Operation Starkey' 120
Operational Bases 157, 159-67
Ostend 27
Osterley Park School 141

Palestine 34
'partisan units' 152
Pas de Calais 120, 123
Pasteurised milk 102
Peace celebrations 29, 131
Peace Treaty 29
Pegwell Bay 143, 151
'penny a week fund' 47
Petroleum Fougasse 143-5
Petroleum Warfare Dept. 144-5
Petrol Rationing 46
Pevensey 57
'Phoenix' 124
'phoney war' 44
Pigeons 45, 54
'pikes' 138
Pillboxes 19, 60, 80, 139-40, 143-4
Pioneer Corps 54, 139
Plastic explosives 158, 161
Poland 54

Index

Political Warfare Executive 103
Police 12-3, 45, 83, 85, 89, 113-4, 125, 135-6
Polish Airmen & Servicemen 54, 74
Port Winston 125
Post Office 101
'Potato Pete' 172, 176
Powell-Cotton 24
'prefabricated houses' 122
Preston 12, 147
Prisoners of war 44, 70, 88, 133-4, 180
Prondzynski Lieut Von 13
Public Order Act 82
Public shelters 92

Queen Elizabeth 128-9
Queen's Own Royal West Kent Regt. 142
Quex House 24

Rabbit Clubs 177
Radar plotting 107, 115
Radio Doctor 172
RAF Manston 51, 66-7, 70-3, 78, 94, 105, 116-8, 124, 126
RAF Regiment 127
RAF Volunteer Reserve 40
'rag hats' 86
Railway mounted guns 89
Ramsay Vice Admiral Bertram 40
Ramsgate 15, 28, 55, 60, 73, 75, 77, 94, 135, 139, 144 150-1, 166
Ramsgate Airfield 67, 72
Ramsgate caves 36-37
Ramsgate Gas Works 72
Ramsgate Harbour 84, 123
Ramsgate Town Station 24
Ration books 47, 51, 91, 176
Recruiting 21
Red Cross 24, 44-6, 64, 106
Red Cross Hospital 24
Refuge room 32, 40
Refugees 33, 53
Regional Commissioners 111-2
RE Searchlight Company 69
Reserve Occupations 107
Richborough Camp 33, 54, 61, 114, 118
Richborough Castle 121
Richborough Port 19-20, 30, 123-5, 150-1, 166
Rifle Clubs 13
Ringwould 28
Ripple 147, 150
River (Dover) 7, 30, 33, 35-6, 44, 60, 69, 72, 75, 95, 117, 132
River Medway 16
River Thames 50
RM Boom Defence Scaffolding Unit 116
'roadblocks' 63, 136, 140-4
Romney Marsh 60, 135
Roosevelt Franklin D 98, 109
Royal Air Force 83, 120

Royal Army Service Corps 152
Royal Artillery 78, 115, 142, 150
Royal Canadian Navy 98, 120
Royal Corp of Signals 94
Royal Engineers 26, 56, 125, 138, 140, 163, 166
Royal Flying Corp 26-27, 29
Royal Horticultural Society 180
Royal Marines 19, 28, 109, 118, 121, 154
Royal Marine Corps -Commandos 109, 155
Royal Marine Emergency Force 22
Royal Marine Police 40
Royal Marine Siege Regiment 72
Royal Navy 98, 120, 163
Royal Naval Air Service 16, 26, 28-9
Royal Naval Reserve 163
Royal Naval Wireless Reserve 40
Royal Observer Corps 40, 107, 125
'rubber shortage' 103, 121
Russian Aid Fund 106

Sabotage units 156-7, 163
Sandgate 24, 40
Sandown Castle 22, 147
Sandwich 10, 15, 19, 28, 33, 35, 41, 136, 144, 147, 152, 163, 179
Sandwich Bay 139, 143, 147, 150
Sandwich Home Guard Platoon 149
Sandwich Radar Station 39, 121, 166
Sarre 144
Schools evacuated 35, 38, 41
'scorched earth' 146
Seaplanes 16, 28
Searchlights 25-6, 38
Shelters 23, 35, 41-2
Shepherdswell 12, 29-30
Sheppey 135, 162-3
Sholden 12, 28, 145, 147
Shorncliffe Camp 40
Shorncliffe Military Hospital 24
'silent killing' 157
Soup kitchens 25
Southeast Command 145, 152
Southern Railway 40-1
Spanish Civil War 141
Special Air Service 168
Special Constables 9-10, 12-3
Special Weapons 155
Staple 147
'stay behind resistance unit' 135, 155, 169
'sticky bombs' 158-9
Stirrup pump 37
St. John Ambulance 33
St. Margaret's 29
St. Margaret's Bay 145
Stodmarsh 11
Stonar 19
Stone Street 12
'stop lines' 138-9
'storm troopers' 118

Index

Stourmouth 12, 147
Stour Valley 12
Street Wardens 32, 36
'suicide mission' 121
Summerskill Edith MP 145
'Summer Time' introduced 25
Supermarine 'Spitfire' 38
Sutton 147
Swingate Downs 8, 11

Tait Wing Commander 119
Taylor Woodrow & Co. 139
Temple Ewell 33, 72
Territorials 9, 51, 151
Territorial Army Reserve 56
'terror weapons' 125, 128
'The Garth' 156, 161, 166-7
Thanet 57, 79
Thanet Way 85, 144
6th (Thanet) Bat. Home Guard 145, 150, 163, 166
Thorne General 156, 162
Tilmanstone 12, 74, 78, 117, 137, 147, 164
Tilmanstone Colliery 89, 164
Tonbridge 136
Trade Unions 91, 105
Train ferry 18-19
Transit camp 19, 22
Treason 58
Treaty of London 8
Trespassing on Allotments 179
Tuberculosis 12
Tuck-Stanford Wing Commander Robert 73
Tunbridge Wells 12

U-Boats 16
Uckfield 12
'unarmed combat' 156
United States Army Air Force 120
United States of America 34, 58, 103, 108-9, 142
Utility clothing & furniture 100-1 109, 116

V for victory campaign 103
'V2' rockets 128
'VE Day' 131
'Victory Treats' 30
Voluntary Food Officers 105
Voluntary Land Clubs 172
Volunteer Aid Detachments 23-4, 44
Volunteer Aid Detachment Hospitals 23-4
Volunteer Training Corps 13
Vulnerable beaches 59

Waldershare 12, 55, 78, 147
Wales 59, 156
Walmer 27-8, 67, 127, 139, 145, 151, 167
Wanstone Battery 115
War Ag. Executive Committee 171, 175
War Cabinet 55
War Damage Act 118, 129

'war gardens' 171
War Loan 52
'Warship Week' 47, 97
War Reserve Constabulary 65
'War Weapons Week' 97
War Zone Courts 111
'waste not want not' 177
'water tanks' 92, 109
Weapons & Tactical Training 116
Westcliffe 122
Westenhanger 26
Western Front 19, 25
Western Heights 57, 76, 80
West Hougham 7
West Langdon 78
Westmarsh 147
'whale' 123-125
'white feathers' 157
Whitfield 75, 98
Whitstable 70, 132
Wickhambreaux 11
Wiltshire Regiment 59, 150
'Winget' system 17
Wingham 11-13, 128, 147, 154
5th (Wingham) Bat. Home Guard 143, 145, 147, 149-50, 154-5, 163, 166
'Wings for Victory' 97
Wintringham Tom 141, 146, 155
Wood Sir Kingsley 38
Woolton Lord 91, 102
Womenswold 12
Women's Army Aux. Corps 24
Women's Aux. Air Force 39
Women's Aux. Police Corps 39
Women's Home Defence 145
Women's Institute 46, 173
Women's Land Army 25, 130, 171, 175, 182-3
Women's Royal Army Corps 126
Women's Timber Corps 183
Women's Voluntary Service 39, 108, 111, 116
Wood Sir H. Kingsley 52
Woodnesborough 12, 47, 67, 77, 114, 127, 147-8
Woolage 147
Woolton Lord 173
Wootton 11, 167
Worth 12, 23, 76, 114, 126, 147
Worthing 135
Wye 161

Zeppelin airships 26-28